Media Beyond Socialism

International Communication and Popular Culture

Series Editor   John A. Lent, Temple University

---

*Media Beyond Socialism: Theory and Practice
in East-Central Europe,* Slavko Splichal

FORTHCOMING

*The Orchestration of the Media: The Politics of Mass Communications
in Communist Poland and the Aftermath,* Tomasz Goban-Klas

*Human Rights and the Media: International Reporting
as a Global Watchdog,* Frederic Moritz

Asian Popular Culture, edited by John A. Lent

Media Beyond Socialism

Theory and Practice in East-Central Europe

Slavko Splichal

Westview Press
Boulder • San Francisco • Oxford

International Communication and Popular Culture

Copyright © 1994 by Westview Press, Inc.

Published in 1994 in the United States of America by Westview Press, Inc., 5500 Central Avenue, Boulder, Colorado 80301-2877, and in the United Kingdom by Westview Press, 36 Lonsdale Road, Summertown, Oxford OX2 7EW

A CIP catalog record for this book is available from the Library of Congress.
ISBN 0-8133-1819-X
ISBN 0-8133-1818-1 (if published as a paperback)

Printed and bound in the United States of America

The paper used in this publication meets the requirements
of the American National Standard for Permanence of Paper
for Printed Library Materials Z39.48-1984.

10   9   8   7   6   5   4   3   2   1

Contents

Tables

Preface

This book offers a critical view of some basic issues that arose in the former socialist countries of East-Central Europe after the overthrow of the former governments and the fall of the Communist Party as the "avant-garde of the proletariat." This book focuses on the changing relationship among media, state, economy, and civil society in the period of transition from a socialist state system to a Western type of democracy. The notion of civil society and its importance to democracy is central for an understanding of the paradoxes appearing in the transitional period and, accordingly, is central to this book. Although considerable differences exist in the use of the concept of civil society, the dialectic—rather than the dichotomy—between the state and civil society is highly relevant for contemporary social and political transformations and for de- and reconstruction of media systems in East-Central Europe and elsewhere.

It is clear that, in most cases, East European societies are being peacefully altered by fundamental political and economic changes. In contrast to developed superindustrial societies, these changes are not paralleled by technological developments. Whereas information and telecommunications technologies mark revolutionary changes in West Europe, North America, Japan, and some newly industrialized countries—the "four tigers" in Asia, for example—East-Central Europe largely remains a typical peripheral zone in terms of technology. This makes any endeavor to catch up with the "First World" an extremely difficult task in many respects. These societies are peripheral in other ways as well. First, technological obsolescence is directly reflected by economic underdevelopment, which leaves the newly emerging democratic state and its economy at a disadvantage in the international marketplace. Second, the lack of any genuine democratic tradition makes political changes and democratization of society even more difficult. Not only do these obstacles reduce the probability of finding commonly shared objectives and make changes toward a democratic system more difficult; they can also potentially transform emerging democracies into a new form of authoritarian system.

These difficulties and conflicts are clearly reflected in the range of economic, political, and legal issues embraced by widespread discussions about media reform in East-Central Europe. This book offers some theoretical insight and empirical examination of present changes to help understand media controversies arising from recent political and economic developments.

Chapter I introduces several concepts and aspects of central theoretical significance in the social sciences. It discusses the relevance of communications, particularly of the mass media, to democratization debates. Among other topical issues, it addresses from different perspectives—capitalist and socialist—the problems of civil society, the peculiar role of the economy, and the changing role of the state. The chapter also treats the dialectic of integration and differentiation in social systems, some critical issues for the "information age," the merger of the principles of power and profit maximization in the communication sphere, and the role the media have played in the "velvet revolutions" in East-Central Europe.

Chapter 2 looks from a comparative perspective at recent quantitative and qualitative changes in the East-Central European print and broadcast media in terms of ownership, political control, the role of the media, and journalism practice. The chapter combines a theoretical consideration of the media, based on the historical development of democratic practices, with an analysis of actual developments in East-Central Europe. It examines the fallacies in attempts to construe the developments in East European media as radical changes or departures from previous activities and provides a number of concrete examples. Theoretical discussions in the next chapters of the principal components of East-Central European media systems in transition proceed mainly from the cases presented in this chapter.

Chapters 3 and 4 examine paradoxes stemming from the economic and political restructuring of the former socialist societies. They explore the main issues underlying media policy debates in East-Central Europe and the different interests of the major social actors involved. In particular, these chapters are concerned with the power, freedom, and (in)equality of different actors in the media sphere. They challenge the notion that the burial of authoritarian practices in socialist countries coincides with the rise of democratic systems of communication. Instead, Chapters 3 and 4 argue that the postsocialist societies are largely caught up in imitation and duplication of either West European practices (such as the rise of communication systems under private capitalism, which results in loss of control by citizens), the former authoritarian models, or both. Commercialism, paternalism, and nationalism, which tend to dominate in the postsocialist media as a result of deregulation and reregulation pressures from the top to the bottom, are discussed as major constraints to the processes of democratization.

Chapter 5 assesses some of the possible future developments in the postsocialist societies from the perspective of groups that would like to participate in democratic media and be empowered by them. This concluding chapter looks at whether the societies that issue from the process will be democratic and, if so, what the nature of that democracy will be. In this, the mass media systems are certainly of vital importance. The chapter is aimed not at forecasting the future but rather at interpreting the present in terms of its possible implications for the future.

No doubt, this book cannot cover all the important issues emerging now in East-Central Europe or in discussions about it. Even the topic of media restructuring is too broad to be fully elaborated in a single book. My own intention is to give a broad overview of some major, and often controversial, issues and to raise some basic questions for further debate.

The writing of this book was significantly stimulated by discussions at the Slovenia-based International Colloquia on Communication and Culture, which are intended to build intellectual bridges between East and West communication research. At the third colloquium in Piran (1989), which was devoted to an East-West dialogue on democratization and the media, a group of European and North American communication researchers initiated an international comparative project on media systems in transition. The colloquium came at a critical juncture for both West European and East-Central European countries when a breathtaking pace of change dictated a reexamination of the role of major actors in, and barriers to, the realization of democratic communication, but one could not conceive (at that time) the thought of the dramatic (r)evolutions that took place a few months later in the socialist countries. Even though our initial idea was to focus on the prospects for democratic communication processes in both socialist and capitalist societies, our task became in a way simpler and less complex after the East European velvet (r)evolutions and the decay of socialism. But our task also became more complex and difficult, as well as more ambiguous, because the "research subject" in the postsocialist countries is changing with inordinate speed.

Although this book is the result of my transient but intensive research into the "history of the future," earlier versions of some parts of the book have been published elsewhere: "Are the State and Civil Society Merging?" and "Media and State-supported Nationalism in Eastern Europe," *Media Development* 38, 3 (1991) and 39, 3 (1992); "Media Privatization and Democratization in East-Central Europe," *Gazette* 45, 1–2 (1992); "The 'Civil Society Paradox' and the Media in Central and Eastern Europe," pp. 85–109, in *Research on Democracy and Society,* Vol. 1, edited by Frederick D. Weil; and "Reregulacija radiotelevizije v Vzhodni-Srednji Evropi," *Teorija in praksa* 29, 5–6 (1992).

Many ideas presented in this book were subjected to impassioned and critical discussions at scientific meetings, particularly at the Communication and Culture Colloquia in Piran, Slovenia. Without these debates and the information provided by my colleagues from the former socialist countries, this book might not have been completed. I want to thank all my colleagues who participated in the colloquia from 1989 to 1991. Particularly, I express my thanks to France Vreg (University of Ljubljana), Colin Sparks (Westminster University–London), Hanno Hardt (University of Iowa–Iowa City), and Andrew Calabrese (University of Colorado–Boulder) for their intellectual support. Michael Traber, the editor of *Media Development;* Wim Noomen, the editor of *Gazette;* and Frederick D. Weil, the editor of *Democratization in Eastern and Western Europe,* encouraged my work by their initiatives and critical reading. This book would not have been completed without the confidence and support of the publisher. At

Westview Press, I am grateful to Jan Kristiansson, Connie Oehring, and Gordon Massman. Last but not least, I want to acknowledge the Ministry of Science and Technology of Slovenia, whose material assistance helped me finalize this project, and the Faculty of Social Sciences, University of Ljubljana, where I found stimulating conditions for my work.

Slavko Splichal

1 Civil Society, the Information Revolution, and Communication Rights and Freedoms

Contemporary discussions on the democratization of society are particularly focused on communications because, as recently hypothesized by Michael Traber (1993, p. 30), "all genuine revolutions are fundamentally communication revolutions, or they are none at all. . . . When communication is suppressed or if it requires self-censorship, the revolution as an *extension of human rights* has ended. That is the real counterrevolution" (italics added). As Norberto Bobbio (1987, p. 25) maintains, even a "minimal definition" of democracy requires the realization of "the so-called basic rights: freedom of opinion, of expression, of speech, of assembly, of association etc." as the necessary precondition for a democratic system. Similarly, Robert Dahl (1991, p. 10) lists among fundamental characteristics of contemporary democracies (or "polyarchies"—to emphasize the restrictions in contrast to an "ideal democracy") the protection of freedom of expression and access to alternative sources of information that are not controlled by the state or otherwise monopolized.

These complex questions of the relationship between communication and democracy do not apply only to mass communication. Nevertheless, their significance in regard to the mass media more than to other forms of communication becomes quite clear when contemporary society and its communication networks are compared with ancient and medieval societies and when the political and economic significance of the modern mass media is compared with that of other forms of communication. Democracy is believed to ensure to the people (all members of a collectivity) a certain degree of political equality and the fullest possible involvement in procedures for arriving at collective decisions about public affairs. Beyond doubt, both the understanding of "the people" and the scope of "public affairs" to be discussed by the people has varied considerably over time, as has the significance of "public," nonpersonal (or impersonal) communication. Classical Greek democracy was marked by the participation of all citizens in the common life of the city-state, which was based on the free and unrestricted discourse guaranteed by *isegoria,* an equal right to speak in the sovereign assembly (Held 1989, p. 18). Materialization of this right enabled citizens to develop and realize their capacities and skills. For ancient democracy, freedom of opinion and expression was universal in terms of disposable communication technologies (or media), though not in political terms (women and slaves were not citizens and therefore did not have access to the rights of citizenship though they were able to communicate). Citizens' participation in the process of government was restricted only by their "natural skill" in speaking and was acquired by merely belonging to the community. The more communication technologies or means developed toward contemporary, complex, high-tech mass media, the more they not only broadened temporal (past-future) and spatial (geographical) horizons, and reduced the temporal and spatial distance between those communicating, but also required more and more specific communication capacities and skills and finally even the ownership of communication means to use them. Thus, modern communications often represent primarily "a new method of government or a new opportunity for trade. All the new means of communication have been abused, for political control (as in propaganda) or for commercial profit (as in advertising)" (Williams 1976, p. 10).

The growing complexity of communications has generated a totally new communication system in comparison to that typical for classical Greek democracy. The *freedom of expression* guaranteed by contemporary democracies does not have the same meaning and scope it had in ancient societies. When related to the most complex form of communication—mass communication—this freedom clearly represents only one dimension of a far more complex *freedom (and right) to communicate,* which goes beyond normative principles adopted by the international community. Two decades ago Jean D'Arcy wrote a seminal article putting forward the concept of the right to communicate, which he later defined as "the rights to hear and be heard, to inform and to be informed, [which] together may be regarded as the essential components of a 'right to communicate.' . . . The realization of a 'right to communicate' is a desirable objective for a democratic society, so that each individual may know he is entitled to be informed and to be heard, regardless of where he may live or work or travel in his own country" (cited in Fisher 1982, p. 15).

To make the classical concept of freedom of expression functionally equivalent in modern complex societies—that is, in terms of the participation of all citizens in the common life of society—it should be extended together with other specific rights, such as the right to be informed, the right to inform, and the right to privacy. Two clusters of rights may be listed as constituent elements of the right to communicate in addition to those related to the *right to be given information:*

- Those related to the *right to impart information and opinion* and *to have free access to the media*
- Those enabling citizens to *participate in decisions made by authorities* and *in the management of the media*

Clearly, the extension of classical rights is particularly related to mass communication because it is considered the form of communication that is in principle passively or actively accessible to all people. Thus, it is rather understandable—though not always legitimate—that precisely this form of communication is mainly discussed when questions of democracy are at stake.

Democratization Controversies and the Media

Throughout history, the struggle for communication rights and freedoms has been an important part of political struggle for general freedom and democracy. From ancient Greece onward, the general conception of democracy has presupposed an open information and communication system to ensure informed decisions in public affairs. This conception implies that citizens are well informed, interested (as a consequence of socialization processes) in general politics, and have an equal right to speak and participate in decisionmaking and that all decisions are submitted to public discussions. Furthermore, actual democratization implies that the number of active participants in the communication processes *and* the social basis of communication expand.

There are certainly many different ways of achieving a higher level of citizen participation in terms of both quantity and quality. In addition to different political and social actions that may make the ideal of democracy more feasible, new information and communication technologies may play a significant role. However, the question of democratization ultimately rests with a *material base* that does (or does not) provide for the realization of the political and social rights declared in a society.

Democratization should dismantle "the major sources of distorted communications," which include "class privilege, gender preference, racial discrimination, age grade exclusion, and a division of labour which awards authority to a relatively few and mandates compliance to a large majority" (Young 1982, p. 2). Accordingly, a process of societal *democratization* implies a transition from a "political democracy" in the strict sense to a "social democracy" infiltrating various spheres of civil society outside politics in the strict sense. In the case of East Europe this suggests that democratization indicates (or should mean) much more than the overthrow of a nondemocratically elected government and the (re)turn to a market economy. If (civil) society is at stake, "what should concern us is the management and control of information *within and between* groups" (Webster and Robins 1989, p. 326; italics added). Thus, the "revolutionary extension of human rights" discussed by Traber is not a simple process enabling formerly marginalized and deprivileged groups and individuals to participate in social (and particularly "mass") communication; rather, the complex relations among media, state, and civil society have to be normatively reconceptualized and practically restructured.

No historical period has witnessed the full materialization of the fundamental assumptions of democratic communication (Williams 1976, p. 133). The participation of citizens has always been restricted by uneven distribution of communicative competence, informal (privatized) communication channels, and, especially, uneven access to (institutional) communication channels penetrated by authoritative institutions. In socialist countries, for example, a parallel system to that of mass communication was developed to supply state and party functionaries with important and unbiased information about what was going on in the world and the country. Apart from special bulletins that relied mainly on news from Western news agencies, even some newspapers existed, such as *World Economy* in Hungary, whose circulation was restricted to high party and state officials. These information services were not accessible to the general public, except in those countries reached directly by foreign broadcasts. Such obstacles severely reduced citizens' opportunities to obtain relevant information and to make information available to others.

With the ideology of mass consumption as a commercially viable answer to Bolshevism and class thinking, democracy emerged as a necessary product of the capitalist system. Although commercialization of the communication sphere implemented the assumption that all people have the right to speak and receive information freely, this soon gave way to another more important principle—to speak profitably. "With the development of an apparatus for the stimulation and creation of mass consumption, business assumed an expansionist and manipulative approach to the problem of popular consciousness," Stuart Ewen (1977, p. 81) declared. "The control of the masses required that people, like the world they inhabited, assume the character of machinery—predictable and without any aspirations toward self-determination." Based on the liberal conception of negative freedom (freedom *from* political authorities and state censorship), freedom of the press increasingly became a freedom wielded by owners of communication means rather than by citizens. The most important information became that which was profitable. It was increasingly privatized and adapted to suit the interests and needs of those in power rather than the public.

Meanwhile, the media in socialist countries were organized as a state or party monopoly to protect and maintain a socialist system based on the power of authoritative institutions. The media were developed as the "collective propagandist, agitator and organizer," to use Georgy Plekhanov's and Vladimir Lenin's wording, without any critical (*watchdog*) function. They were considered by party leaders as an instrument of propaganda and thus aimed to control public opinion rather than express it. The public was politicized and reduced to a set of social institutions (including the mass media) subject to a strong authoritative pressure and control that prevented any autonomy of social actors. The idea of *glasnost* and, particularly, recent political upheavals in East-Central Europe have buried this authoritarian legacy, but it is another question whether these changes really amount to a genuine democratization of communications and the public sphere.

Traditionally, state- or party-controlled media in socialist countries were used as tools of propaganda against external and internal "class enemies." Opposition press was banned to prevent alternative voices from spreading. Western observers often saw as paradoxical the fact that authorities and journalists in socialist countries were mainly concerned with problems of maximizing power (as they had been earlier with strategies for seizing power from the czars in Russia) and sustaining a permanent political revolution, while in the West journalists were concerned with the revolution brought about by microelectronics and satellites. Despite democratic changes in East-Central Europe in the late 1980s, this paradox continues to exist. While in the West political and academic controversies concentrate on the questions of free speech in an "electronic age" and "technologies of freedom" (Pool 1983), in East-Central Europe such controversies are still (or again) preoccupied with the question of seizing power—from the former socialist authorities.

However, the question of working out a democratic system is no less relevant for capitalist society. Apart from all significant differences between the capitalist and socialist systems, there is at least one important feature both systems had in common. Both systems were successful in rendering the citizenry passive and uninformed as a consequence of the fact that "public information is subordinated to the interests of producers rather than consumers, owners rather than citizens, the interest of capital accumulation rather than the interests of a democratic public" (Simonds 1989, pp. 204–205). Or, as Raymond Williams (1976, p. 10) would put it, in both systems "the means of communication have been abused, for political control (as in propaganda) or for commercial profit (as in advertising)." In other words, information technology mediated by the structure of class or party power tends to reproduce that power regardless of its specific nature. Information is not only power, it is also a *multiplier of power* (cf. Deutsch 1963).

The principle of maximization of power (the state) and the principle of maximization of profit (capital, including state capital) merge in the communication sphere—to the detriment of that structural part of global society that is not governed by these principles. Mass communication processes are subordinated to these two principles through different forms of (indirect) censorship exercised by the state or by private corporations, advertising, and "political marketing." Consequently, the rights of individuals in the communication sphere have been by and large shifted to "legal entities" (corporations, political parties, and the state), which dominate the mass media either directly (as their owners) or indirectly (as the most influential sources of information and opinions). Although revealing the (often indirect) influence of corporate politics in editorial decisions in the mass media is extremely difficult, such influence has been confirmed in a number of cases. According to Ben Bagdikian, reporters and editors in the United States may be easily fired if they stumble in the private politics of the media owners. As he (1983, p. 39) concluded, "Even when such firings and demotions are clear interventions of corporate politics into the editorial process, the worst damage is not in one particular incident but in the long-lasting aftermath in which working professionals at the editorial level behave as though under orders from above, although no explicit orders have been given."

On the one hand, civil society is becoming increasingly invaded by the state "representing" collective interests. On the other hand, private corporations counteract by organizing private interests and using the "public" media. It is often argued that large media corporations accumulate enough power to resist state authorities and nonmedia corporations trying to influence editorial policies. They are defended as guarantors of free expression even though they jeopardize a genuine plurality of the public sphere. But this common defense of media oligopolies overlooks the fact that large media corporations are compelled to represent and promote their own partial interest rather than the public interest. Economic monopolies may turn easily into political ones, as political monopolies normally imply economic ones. As a consequence, public opinion circulating through the media is largely removed from civil society as its authentic form of expression and is transformed instead into massively ("publicly") distributed institutional (corporate) opinions.

At the same time, it is practically impossible for large populations in contemporary societies to participate fully in public business given the geographical and physical limits that constrain when and where people can meet together. In addition, the problems posed by coordination and regulation in contemporary societies are insuperably complex for any system of classical, or direct, democracy. Accordingly, the ideal of a democracy based on direct (face-to-face) communication, as, for example, that formulated by Jean-Jacques Rousseau, encounters too many elements that complicate processes of decisionmaking and thus destabilize the system. The only alternative seems to be representative democracy based on freedom of speech, the press, and assembly. In large-scale, complex societies, representative democracy is the functional equivalent of ancient Greek democracy. In such a democracy accountability ought to be combined with professionalism and expertise. Professionalism and expert knowledge also differentiate mass communication from all other, less complex forms of communication.

Contrary to the optimistic ideas and visions of democracy in the eighteenth and nineteenth centuries, conceptions of democracies developed beginning with Max Weber are much more restricted and even pessimistic, particularly because of the growing complexity of society, the plurality (division) of interests, and the sheer quantity of information needed for an effective administration and control of both the environment in general and the state in particular. As a result, the ideas of direct democracy have generally been rejected as inappropriate and ineffective, at least in the West, and new models of indirect democracy based on competition between different interests and rival political elites and parties have developed. Direct democracy has been (and still is) believed to be feasible only in organizations limited in the number of members and characterized by their relative equality. In complex, large-scale systems, bureaucratic administration becomes completely indispensable. Generally, the role of an ordinary citizen has been strongly delimited by his or her incompetence, lack of relevant information, and general depoliticization. Although rule by bureaucratic apparatus is not inevitable, bureaucrats necessarily have a considerable power because of their expertise and information.

It is interesting to note that Karl Marx, contrary to his early writings on freedom of the press where he passionately criticized Prussian censorship and strenuously pleaded for (the same kind of) press freedom that had been already established in France and England, in his later writings on (direct) political and economic democracy underestimated the significance of liberal ideals concerning individual liberty and the rights of free speech, expression, association, and belief and freedom of the press. This is even more significant because he stressed, together with Engels, in *The Communist Manifesto,* that only *written* history is the history of class struggles, which implies that the human ability to speak and write, or to communicate in any other form, is not only a *generic* ability but also a societally relevant ability. Or as Williams (1976, p. 11) put it, "The history of a language . . . is as central a part of the history of a people as its changing political and economic institutions."

Nevertheless, communication is not only a competence of human beings to learn and exchange ideas and experiences; it is also an instrument of power and profit maximization. Consequently, the mass media can be seen not only as a cornerstone of democracy but also as an important argument against direct democracy since they easily manipulate individual needs, desires, and choices or at least demonstrate their manipulability. As Ludwig von Bertalanffy (1971, pp. 122–123) argued, human behavior falls far short of the principle of rationality; "It is the job of an influential specialty—advertisers, motivation researchers, etc.—to make choice irrational. . . . Reading newspapers or listening to the radio readily shows that this applies perhaps even more to the twentieth than the seventeenth century."

This, however, does not imply that the majority of people are not capable of making valid (if not rational) choices—particularly political choices—and considering what is in their real interest. Although their individual capabilities, including communicative competence, along with the many inequalities in society are largely bounded by social forces, they are also "bounded" as a matter of principle by inner evolution. If people's knowledge, understandings, capabilities, and actions are indeed limited and "manufactured," it simultaneously follows that they can be developed, improved, and individualized in proper (ideal-democratic) circumstances. Among these circumstances, "proper" communication networks are inevitable.

One can hardly imagine a system, either on a local or national level, in which everyone would contribute to discussions and/or decisionmaking every time a controversial issue appeared. However, political systems can be transformed to make more citizens participation possible. Any democratic system that intends to enable citizen to develop and express themselves, help them determine the conditions of their association, protect them from the arbitrary use of coercive power, and expand economic opportunity to maximize the availability of resources (Held 1989, p. 270) must have an open information and communication system to ensure *informed decisions* in all public affairs. The question of how this condition can be secured and aspirations achieved remains largely unresolved.

Nevertheless, the very idea of society communicating freely was in the center of the democratic struggles in East Europe in the late 1980s. Particularly in Poland, this idea was closely related to those of civil society and an independent public sphere, "socialization of the media," and *"access to the media,* understood broadly enough to be almost equivalent to 'the right to communicate'" (Jakubowicz 1990, pp. 337, 341). The Polish project was "in its very foundations not a project to destroy, but to rebuild, not AGAINST the party-state so much as it was FOR society, i.e., for an *independent public sphere"* (Fedorowicz 1990, p. 79; italics added). In other words, the idea of the (re)construction of civil society and the abolishment of the system of distorted communication experienced for decades was an essential part, even the core, of this Polish conception of democracy.

These questions have no less relevance for advanced capitalist societies. As in socialist societies, the relationship among the state, private sectors, markets, and civil society profoundly changed during the 1980s. This change particularly applied to the communication sphere and the media, both old and new. In contrast to socialist societies, however, such changes in capitalist societies were based largely on new information and telecommunications technology, which affected the media industries in terms of economic restructuring, and on a new social and political environment, as reflected by media contents.

Civil Society and the State in the Information Age

Since the early 1980s a number of authors in both socialist and nonsocialist countries have discussed the question of whether a *socialist* civil society and a *socialist* public can exist, and what would be—in contrast to bourgeois society—their *differentia specifica.* I certainly believe that the two concepts cannot be linked to socialism in any intrinsic sense; both concepts clearly refer to the rise of capitalism and liberal bourgeois democracy (Splichal 1981b). Actually, with the decay of socialism, these controversies are of neither practical nor theoretical significance, so they can be left unquestioned here.

Nonetheless, the importance of civil society is certainly one of the central issues of democratization of both capitalist societies and societies in transition from socialism, although for different reasons. Is it possible to claim that civil society does exist in postsocialist countries? Is the concept of civil society even useful and valid? Do clear-cut boundaries between the state and civil society exist, and should they exist? These questions are legitimate for several reasons. First, the modern history of the idea of democracy is closely related to the idea of civil society, from which the state should be clearly delimited. At least since the nineteenth century, the two ideas have represented "eternal" concepts in the social sciences for describing social and political systems. Second, technological developments and the growing productivity of productive forces, the restructuring of capitalism, and the fall of sovietism (rather than socialism) also challenge traditional conceptions of the capitalist system and bourgeois democracy. Third, different approaches diverge from each other in interpretation (rather than definition, which in the strict sense does not exist) of the concept, particularly in terms of those relations and institutions that are supposed to form civil society and in terms of civil society's connection to state institutions. Fourth, apart from theoretical reasons, there are numerous political reasons for the recent popularity of the concept of civil society in the social sciences, both East and West. In industrialized Western societies these discussions intensified as a result of the rise of "invisible power" in the hands of capital and nonrepresentative institutions and the decline of the power of democratic institutions. In less developed, and particularly in the (former) socialist countries, the ideas of civil society and impersonal rules of democracy became popular with the fall of "scientific" socialist utopia and the decline of the socialist state.

An institutionalized distinction between state and civil society is normatively considered a fundamental precondition of pluralistic, parliamentary democracies in modern complex societies (Keane 1988, p. 25). At the same time, a number of authors believe that in postindustrial or information societies this distinction becomes more and more dubious because the institutions of civil society have become integral parts of a state structure that cannot be reduced to political-administrative functions. Whereas for centuries "society" usually connoted any relationship, company, or association (in the sense of deliberate association for some purpose), beginning in the eighteenth century the word acquired a far more general and abstract meaning of a system of common life. This meaning emphasized a state of social order, a state of "civility" in contrast with a state of barbarism. This extremely loose term has been made particularly indicative when used in contrast to the state. The division of human society into two spheres—the state and civil society—became in the nineteenth century a part of everyday social and political reality and a common concept among divergent social theories. The state and civil society were used to describe and even explain any form of sociopolitical system, particularly in terms of the degree of domination over, or control of, civil society by the state, which became an important practical and theoretical issue after World War II.

This conceptual transition was clearly related to the rise of the state as an organization of power in contrast to society as an association of free individuals.

Civil society meant the opposition not only to the barbarian state of nature but also, and particularly, the opposition to all forms of despotism, feudalism, and political interference in personal, family, and business life in general. Since the nineteenth century, the idea of the separation of the state from civil society has become a paramount conceptual framework in the social sciences. No theory of democracy can avoid the fundamental dichotomy "state–civil society," which is now "a central feature of any democratic political order" (Held 1989, p. 283), even if, as Boris Frankel (1987, p. 202) observed, this conceptual dichotomy is no more than "a caricature of the infinitely more complicated social interactions of everyday life."

Although the concept of civil society has a fundamental theoretical importance in the social sciences, at least one critical remark aimed at the traditional division into state and civil society is certainly to the point—namely, that there is neither an exact definition of nor an agreement about all relations and institutions that supposedly constitute civil society. In the "great dichotomy" civil society–the state, the former term is defined negatively in relation to the latter. Civil society usually means the part of social relations that enjoys a certain form of autonomy from its counterpart—the state. Although it is difficult to provide a positive definition of civil society, Bobbio (1989, p. 25) tries to define it positively in the following way:

> As a first approximation we can say that civil society is the place where economic, social, ideological and religious conflicts originate and occur and that state institutions have the task of solving them either by mediating or preventing or repressing them. The agents of these conflicts and therefore of civil society proper . . . are social classes (or, more broadly, the groups, movements, associations and organizations that represent them or declare themselves their representatives); as well as class organizations there are interest groups, associations of various types with social and indirectly political ends, ethnic emancipation movements, civil rights groups, women's liberation, youth movement and so on. Parties . . . in reality do not entirely belong either in civil society or the state.

Bobbio (1989, p. 24) sees three different approaches to the concept of civil society as the *nonstate:*

1. Civil society as the *prestate* is defined as the historical precondition of the state.
2. Civil society as the *antistate* is defined as the antithesis or alternative to the already existing state.
3. Civil society as the *poststate* is defined as the positive negation and dissolution of the state.

In the classical liberal tradition the state emerges as a consequence of civil society. Similarly, in Marxist tradition the state is a historical political-authoritative expression of civil society, particularly its class structure. In other words, civil society is first considered as constituting the (economic) basis of the state and preceding the formation of state, but the latter has the same class character in the sense that it represents the interests of the ruling (capitalist) class, mainly by political and ideological means. With the constitution of the modern (capitalist) state, civil society becomes the state's antithesis and a contradiction in itself: On the one hand, it is still the material basis of the state, but on the other hand, it is the site of the (re)organization and emancipation of social forces that should make the state historically superfluous. The state is considered a form of human alienation similar to the capitalist mode of production itself. With a genuine socialization of production and the abolition of private ownership, the state was expected to become unnecessary. After the withering away of the capitalist state, (civil) society would reappropriate the functions once captured by the state. In Lenin's (1949, p. 267) straight words: "At the time when all members of society, or the large majority of them, learn *themselves* to govern the state, . . . the need for any governing whatever ceases to exist. The more complete democracy, the closer the moment when it [the state] becomes unnecessary."

Marx's concept of civil society is actually a partial (re)interpretation of Georg Hegel's civil society. For the first time, Hegel (1981) defined civil society as the *antistate* (i.e., the state was excluded from civil society) but also as a moment in the process of the formation of the state. Hegel's idea that "civil society is the antecedent (or antithesis) of the state has so entered into everyday practice that it now takes an effort to convince oneself that for centuries the same expression was used to designate that collection of institutions which, as a rule, today constitute the state and which nobody would call civil society" (Bobbio 1989, p. 40). From Hegel onward, civil society by and large came to mean the domain in which those civil rights and freedoms protected from state interference and legally guaranteed by the same state were executed.

Whereas Hegel pioneered in defining civil society as the sphere of social relations not controlled directly by state authorities, Antonio Gramsci (1971) introduced a distinction between economic life and civil society by shifting civil society from the sphere of economic necessity to the sphere of social superstructure. In fact, Gramsci himself was not consistent in using the central terms of his analysis, particularly in relation to "hegemony" and "direct domination," which are central to his conceptual scheme. Nevertheless, his idea of civil society as a set of social relations "mediating" between the economy and the state and linked to, rather than separated from, both of them is important for the contemporary complex societies where no simplistic dichotomies—such as Marx's dichotomy between the economic structure and legal-political superstructure—exist, regardless of Gramsci's superficial understanding of economic relations in capitalism. Gramsci's idea of civil society is particularly important because it already represents a critique of a narrow Marxist concept of practice that "attributes an unambiguously emancipatory role *solely to industrial labour* and the development of the technology of productive forces" (Habermas 1991, p. 34; italics added).

In the classical idea of civil society, economic relations among private individuals represented its fundamental part. Early definitions of civil society, at least, were based on the perception that economic individualism in the liberal phase of capitalist production relations was central to the formation of civil society. However, oligopolistic and monopolistic tendencies, which started to supersede genuine competition among private entrepreneurs, transformed the economy into a site of substantially asymmetrical distribution of power and consequently rendered problematic and obsolete the assumptions that pluralism and free competition were two central features of civil society on which the economy was sited.

One (theoretical) solution to that emerging contradiction was to separate—as Gramsci did—civil society not only from the state but also from the economy (see Table 1.1). The economy and civil society are close to each other in that they are not controlled directly by the state; however, they differ significantly in terms of defining organizing principles. The state is financially dependent on the material base (economy), although it does not itself organize that base, and is politically dependent on citizens and their electoral support. In fact, the economy comes closer to the state (through either state interventionism or monopolization) than to civil society *as the antistate.* The same reasoning can be found later in Jürgen Habermas's (1982, p. 47) distinction between "socially integrated spheres of action within *civil society*" and the "system-integrated domains of the *economy and state.*"

Particularly in modern *hypercomplex* societies, social transformation cannot be reduced to either profit maximization (economy) or power maximization (polity) as an organizing principle. Another principle, that of *argumentative orientation,* coproduces "the development of individual and collective energies potentially volatile to the market and/or power structures" (Marz 1991, p. 43). The three principles—profit maximization, power maximization, and argumen-

TABLE 1.1   Gramsci's Model of Division Among the Material Base (economic infrastructure), Civil Society, and the State and Their Defining Characteristics

Material Base	*Social Superstructure*	
Economic moment	Political-ethical moment	
Necessity	Liberty	
Objectivity	Subjectivity	
	Civil Society	*The State*
	Consensus	Force
	Persuasion	Coercion
	Morality	Politics
	Hegemony	Dictatorship
	Leadership	Domination

SOURCE: Adapted from Bobbio 1989, p. 30.

tative orientation—operate within three different levels of society, which refer to the economy, the state (polity), and civil society (culture):

1. The *economic* level is dominated by the *profit orientation* of the economic subject.
2. The *political* level is dominated by the *hegemonic orientation* of the political subject.
3. The *cultural* level is dominated by the *argumentative orientation (Argumentationsorientierung)* of the cultural subject.

In contrast to this theoretical stream, and from another perspective—that of the contemporary informatization of society—some authors consider the new role of the "information economy" as denying the validity of traditional divisions between the state and civil society because the economy breaks down "the old spheres of 'civil society' and 'the state,' [and thus] the political objective of liberating 'civil society' from 'the state' becomes more and more dubious" (Frankel 1987, p. 203). The latter understanding of civil society is based on the normative presupposition that its autonomy resides functionally "outside the economy" and "outside the state." Frankel (1987, p. 235), for example, maintained that social movements based on workers employed within state factories or student movements in state-run universities cannot be considered a part of civil society because they "exist *inside* the larger state." This argument is not really persuasive, however: Because the state and the economy are interpenetrating (each performing several functions classically considered the responsibility of the other—e.g., economic corporations perform some important political functions, and the state performs economic ones), does it then follow that they do not exist?

Nevertheless, the contemporary restructuring of the capitalist economy should be considered of great theoretical relevance because it is the economy that intervenes in changing relations between the state and civil society and it is the (more productive) economy to which the idea of an *information society* primarily applies. However, the idea of economic individualism and liberty (which in its present corporate-capitalist form produces political inequality) and the idea of an information society and a new economic (information) sector are far from being noncontroversial issues themselves. Conceptualizations of social transformations spurred on by information technology generally do not concentrate on civil society as a specific entity in contrast to the state; rather, these conceptualizations focus on an information *economy* (marketplace) and its global consequences. This also holds true for a number of critiques of an information society.

The notion of (*information*) society in these new concepts is of society *and* the state as a whole, as *Gemeingesellschaft* or *Gemeinwesen*, without any clear-cut distinction between the two. Essentially, there is even no difference between information society and more general terms such as *information age* or *information culture*. In his 1988 book *The Information Society: Issues and Illusions*, for example, David Lyon (p. 5) critically discussed "features of modern societies" that "include military, commercial and governmental power," where "society" is obviously used as the most general term to refer to all institutions and relationships of a relatively large population.

As illustrated earlier, some information society theorists are even more explicit in denying the validity of divisions between the state and civil society. They argue that central to the information society concept is the growth of information technologies, information work, information workers, and the information sector, which pervades all parts of the (traditionally separated) spheres of family, economy, civil society, *and* the state. Whereas steam engines multiplied human physical power, information machines multiply the power of human minds. As steam engines in the past decisively influenced economic and social changes, now information and communication technologies are supposed to revolutionize social relations. On the one hand, the economy is becoming more and more complex and thus requires even more managers, researchers, administrators, advertisers, bankers—in short information workers. On the other hand, information management is being radically transformed by new information technologies. As a result, "information processing and flows need themselves to be controlled, so that informational technologies must continue to be applied at higher and higher layers of control" (Beniger 1986, p. 434). These processes are believed to be central to the information society, and the development of the information society is believed to account for "virtually all of the societal changes" (Beniger 1986, p. 436). Young (1982, p. 23) rightly claimed that the enthusiasm for this vision is informed largely by the logic of owners and managers.

What characteristics of new information and communication technologies have the power to make radical, or even revolutionary, changes in society, specifically in the relationships between civil society and the state? Or, to put the matter more generally, "how much productive power must increase for a consequent change in production relations to occur?" (Cohen 1978, p. 135). In Marx's analysis of capitalist society, he considered technology a productive force "responsible" for changes in social relationships: As the hand mill was typical for feudal society, the steam mill was typical for industrial capitalism because each of them presupposed a different social division of labor (Marx 1971, p. 499). From this point of view, it seems reasonable to maintain that information technology not only is one among many new technologies but also has a revolutionary character if it enables discontinuity (a "revolutionary leap") in (economic) development.

However, this assertion does not imply that it is possible to define generally (or even quantitatively) the extent of the development of productive forces (technology) needed for a radical change in production relations. This is even more the case because radical changes in production relations are not determined simply by technological changes. Rather, they *reflect the character of the productive forces* (including enrichment of *human* labor power) that challenge the economic structure to respond to their developments with its own transformations. In a purely technological sense of productive forces, there is no information revolution because "no fundamentally different technologies that will either *cause* a new social order or *reflect the essence* of a new social totality" exist (Slack 1984, p. 146; italics added). But this attitude does not imply, as Jennifer Slack believed, that new technologies are such an intrinsic "part of complex social formation" that, for example, "communication technologies are invented and innovated to generate surplus profit." If it were true that the existing social formation would in this way dictate all technological changes, how then would any revolutionary changes ever be possible?

According to Marx's theory, a given level of the development of productive forces is compatible with (and responsible for) a specific type of economic structure only: "Slavery, for example, could not be the general condition of producers in a society of computer technology, if only because the degree of culture needed in labourers who can work that technology would lead them to revolt, successfully, against slave status" (Cohen 1978, p. 158). From a different perspective, Christopher Freeman (1987, p. 14) maintained that technological revolutions or changes in the "techno-economic paradigm" (in analogy with Thomas Kuhn's scientific revolutions) are based on combinations of *"radical product, process* and *organizational innovations.* They occur relatively seldom (perhaps twice in a century) but when they do occur they necessitate changes in the institutional and social framework, as well as in most enterprises" (italics added). Is such a change marked by information technology?

Colin Gill (1985, p. 5) discussed three basic points in favor of information technology as revolutionary technology (or as a part of a new "paradigm"), that is, a technology to which only a new type of production relations can truly correspond:

1. Contrary to all technologies developed in the past, information technology involves an intelligence function.
2. Information technology is universal and can be implemented, in principle, in any kind of human activity.
3. Information technology developed in a period when the economic growth in industrial societies was exposed to serious limitations unknown to previous ages (e.g., ecology).

If there is no doubt about these radically new characteristics (greater power and specific context) embodied in new information technologies, it is worth asking, What are the social relations for which information technology is typical? What social changes does it necessitate? And what kind of social changes are typical for information society, which is the standard term to connote these changes?

Obviously, the concept of the information society is neither clearly defined nor unproblematic in itself. It is only vaguely related to technological changes that induce some social (or societal) consequences in developed societies and in those societies in which the most important social and economic activities are concentrated in the areas of information and communication. Such a vague notion of the information society is based only on a kind ("sector") of production that determines the position and the role of all other kinds of production. This notion neglects, however, the motives and goals of this production, its consumers and their needs and interests, and the difference between the use value and the exchange value of the new type of products—for example, the possibility that more and more information means less and less meaning, and that the information society is not by definition well informed.

In contrast, a number of authors argue that informatization does not mean a transition from industrial society to information society or postindustrial society but rather to "super-industrial society" (Kumar 1978), where all human activities are (still) largely industrialized. A society is considered superindustrialized when "not only production of material goods and evils is carried out by industrial means, but also the reproduction of the citizenry and labour force (household work, care, nursing, medical treatment, education and other forms of establishing or preserving more or less functional beliefs and attitudes)," when labor is extensively divided into discrete units, and when these discrete units of human actions are increasingly affected by nonhuman powers (Andrén 1993, p. 56). Similarly, Frank Webster and Kevin Robins (1989, p. 323) maintain that exploitation *and* the industrialization of information and knowledge are decisive for the shift from industrial to postindustrial society.

The idea of the information society is actually based upon an inductive generalization from particular *economic* trends in the restructuring of contemporary capitalism taking place in *advanced industrialized countries* where

> deregulation, crisis management, and stepped-up worldwide competition have led corporations, and their dependent units, to engage in cost-saving, product diversification, creation of new markets, and reorganization of the labour process, in order to increase profits and win market shares in a new and increasingly challenging environment. As a result, increasing productivity of both labour and capital becomes the bottom line on which will depend the fate of each corporate conglomerate in the struggle for survival. (Castells 1989, p. 168)

It is clear that such profound "global" economic changes—often referred to as typical for the information revolution, the information economy, or informatization—are related to, if not determined by, the totality of social structures in *specific* geographic and cultural areas. Indeed, the distribution of information resource endowments is historically determined by a country's experience of industrialization (Hepworth and Robins 1988, p. 330). The fundamental importance of information processing results from a number of changes in the spheres of production and consumption in advanced industrialized (capitalist) societies, where the emergence of large corporations, the growing importance of knowledge, tendencies toward profit maximization, the constitution of mass markets, different forms of collective consumption, and state support for international economic activities have led to the information economy. Informatization has appeared as a consequence of the convergence between technological and organizational changes in the context of a specific social, political, and cultural life; it is not merely a product of technological innovations ("technology-push" theories) or simply a response to new organizational demands ("demand-pull" theories).

There is no doubt that we are facing great changes in the organization and administration of everyday human life as a consequence of technological innovations and the development of the information sector. In the employment structure these changes indicate a process of deindustrialization and superindustrialization of developed capitalism, with information technology and information work as the new moving economic and social ("productive") forces. In all traditional economic sectors more and more information is needed for an effective control of more and more divided and socially combined work. If there is no doubt about these technological developments, there is much more doubt about the societal implications of telecommunications and informatics. How are these changes related to social and political inequalities, particularly practical inequalities in the realization of declared rights and freedoms? Are we facing a more equitable social redistribution of economic and political power or, perhaps, the rise of a new social class? What are the alternatives to these changes, if any? Are the growing differentiation and complexity of modern societies primarily a limit, or are they a new possibility for democratic restructuring? And, finally, what is the fate of the state and civil society, which are directly influenced by changes in organization and management?

For Gramsci, civil society connotes "the ensemble of organisms commonly called 'private,'" while political society is represented by the state. Although different interpretations exist in Gramsci's work itself, particularly in terms of differentiation among the state, political society, and civil society, it is precisely his understanding of civil society as all those relationships that cannot be *reduced* to economic activity, and that fall outside the public and administrative realm of the state, that seems to be the most important for contemporary critical thought (Giner 1985, pp. 252–253). Typical examples of civil society actors would be households, educational institutions, cultural institutions, churches, communications media, interest groups, and, to a certain degree, political parties. However, a conceptualization of civil society as being in contrast to both the state and economy is lacking in an (effective) organizing principle that would be competitive to the sorts of power held by the state and economy and that would make the autonomy of civil society viable. Moral power and the prestige generated by intellectuals do not yet seem able to "retaliate" against the state and economy.

In contrast to capitalism, the distinction between civil society and economy that has been traditionally subsumed under civil society is particularly important and also easily explicable from the socialist perspective. In state socialism (as well as in state capitalism), the economy became a part of an overwhelming central plan executed by the state. The merger of the state and the economy generated an increased tendency toward integration, centralization, and uniformity, thus repressing individuality, autonomy, freedom, and differentiation in society. As the events on the eve of democratic revolutions in East-Central Europe showed, however, this did not imply a total destruction of civil society. It emerged *on the border between the economy and the state;* it was motivated, not by profit or power maximization, but by moral efforts to recreate a public sphere. According to John Keane (1988, p. 5), civil society's ultimate goal was "the cultivation of solidarity among a plurality of self-governing civil associations capable of pressuring the state from without and allowing various groups to attend peacefully to their non-political affairs." In this context, the role of the media as critics of the monopolized power was similar to that newspapers had played in the period of transition from feudalism to capitalism in West Europe.

In a way, at least "in the last instance," civil movements against the dictatorship of the party-state in East-Central Europe, or formerly against the military dictatorships in south Europe and Latin America, converged with the role the "economic moment" played in the developed part of the world. In both parts of Europe, civil society was jeopardized by the growing power of the state and economy, but it reacted in very different ways. In the East, civil movements challenged morally and politically the ruling elites that tried to maintain the socialist system through an institutionalized ideology and state repression. In West Europe, however, the activities of social movements were largely antipolitical; although they challenged existing power relations, they were not aimed to transform them radically. Instead of an authoritarian state, traditional analytic approaches to civil society in the West confronted *technological developments* in communications, growing *productive forces,* and the *restructuring of the capitalist economy,* which challenged bourgeois democracy in all fundamental dimensions that were (are) constitutive of "any mature civil society." According to Salvador Giner (1985, pp. 255–257), the dimensions comprise the following:

1. *Individualism:* The ultimate unit of social life is the individual, and all social institutions are no more than associations of discrete individuals.
2. *Privacy:* A liberal utopia can be approximated by being bought or by being acquired through status, privilege, power, or social skill.
3. *The market:* This most salient structural feature and organizing principle of civil society allocates resources, honor, authority, goods, and services through interactions and transactions (supply and demand) among free individuals and their associations. However, "the market" does not equal "the economy"; neither is it an extension of the economy in the realms of ideology and polity. According to

Giner, the market is the "locus for the production of social life" without external intervention.

4. *Pluralism:* The diffusion of power throughout society generates a specific culture of "coexistence."

5. *Class relations:* Society is made up of unequal people, though "perhaps not of people unequal before the law."

Each of these dimensions is contradictory in itself because it generates counterprocesses that endanger the existence of civil society. All five dimensions, which predominate in civil society, actually represent an orientation toward *differentiation*, "anarchic competition," even conflicts, and *autonomy*. Civil society is based on the heterogeneity of the institutionalized social practices performed by *different* groups, which are constituted according to class, status, gender, race, age, religion, or nationality. In social systems, however, the development of systems always implies *integration* as a common counterorientation, which includes, for example, tendencies toward increased unity, order, collectivity, uniformity, and regulation (Gharajedaghi 1983, p. 13). The dialectic between differentiation and unity first clearly appeared in Hegel's division between civil society and the state: In civil society everyone is his or her own end, and the materialization of the private interests of individuals produces a split between the individual and the totality. The state, in contrast, comprises the *unity of differences* and is where, according to Hegel, the individual finds his or her true self and freedom. However, the dialectic between the state and civil society is more often considered a permanent *opposition* of the state to individuals, the state thus representing an external power limiting individual freedom (Park 1972, p. 64).

Specifically, the state as political system regulates the use of coercive power to prevent disintegration; we can consider it a "coercive order." In a systemic perspective, the contrast between civil society and the state might be also defined as the contrast between the formation of demands aimed at the political (sub)system (the state) and the capacity of state institutions to supply answers to these demands (Bobbio 1989, pp. 25, 51). One of the main problems in systems theory—that of the governability (and reduction) of complexity—can be easily translated into the dialectic (rather than dichotomy, as Bobbio suggested) between civil society and the state. Namely, if the lower-level opposing ends of civil society and the state are transformed into conflicting *means* that imply an interaction between, and a higher-level objective shared by, the state and civil society, we can speak of a dialectic rather than a dichotomy.

In the dialectic between civil society and the state, the counterprocesses of integration toward a differentiated *unity* are subsumed under the state, which intervenes in the processes of differentiation to reduce or even suppress them. However, integration processes are not alien to the logic of economic forces in the economy, which may—similarly to the state—penetrate the self-organized public based on solidarity and communication. For example, production means can be monopolized either by the state apparatus or by private capital; the control of the "marketplace of ideas" may be executed either legally by the state or privately by commercial measures. And economic monopolies often lead to political ones, and political monopolies turn into economic ones, which is one of the central issues to be discussed in relation to the media in East-Central Europe. Democratic life can be strongly limited by concentrations of ownership and control in the hands of individual or corporate, private or public proprietors. Although the market economy has been included—until Gramsci—in the core of civil society as its essential element, globalization and corporatization of the economy significantly change its relation to both the state and civil society and lead to the decay of the latter. This is the most important reason that the economy deserves particular attention in discussions about the changing status of the media in a more complex relationship between civil society and the state, particularly in the changing situation in East-Central Europe, where privatization efforts seem to constitute the basis of political democratization.

The relationship between civil society and the state is dialectically contradictory as it represents *dialectical interaction* between the opposing tendencies of *integration* (the state) and *differentiation* (civil society). According to Giner (1990, p. 261), in the information age this interaction is becoming "paradoxical": The state itself, in some senses the "worst enemy" of civil society, has become in the capitalist parliamentarian countries one of its safeguards. Although the state wants at the same time to dominate civil society and control it, the state cannot avoid protecting some of the fundamental dimensions of civil society—that is, by providing the overall legal framework for social relations not directly regulated by the state. No less paradoxical is its position toward the economy, in which the state has to intervene at least to provide finances; but at the same time, "it must maintain the accumulation process without undermining either *private* accumulation or the belief in the market as a fair distributor of scarce resources" (Held 1989, p. 211). As Habermas (1991, p. 34) claimed, the regulative devices of a market economy "cannot be replaced by administrative planning without potentially jeopardizing the level of *differentiation* achieved in a modern *complex society*" (italics added), which was one of the fundamental errors of the Marxist critique of capitalism.

As Bobbio (1989, p. 43) argued, the contradictory processes of *the state making society* and *society making the state* may be represented by the conflicting images of the *participating citizen* and the *protected citizen*. Whereas the citizen "through active participation always asks for greater protection from the state," he or she at the same time "through the request for protection strengthens the state which citizen wants to control but which ends up becoming his or her master. Under this aspect *society and state act as two necessary moments, separate but contiguous, distinct but interdependent, internal articulations of the social system as a whole*" (italics added). In contrast to critiques of the civil society–state distinction that stress the nonexistence of their mutual *independence* and argue for the withdrawal of the notion of civil society as a distinct entity or system, the spheres of the state and civil society should be understood as special *sub*systems of a social system that compete with and thus limit each other. According to Jamshid Gharajedaghi (1983, p. 13), competition implies compatibility of *ends* and incompatibility of *means;* in this conception, "the interdependence of the opposing tendencies are such that the seeds of the destruction of any system lies in the success (or the dominance) of one of the tendencies over the other."

This paradox or contradiction between the opposing tendencies originating from the state and civil society is the basis of any possible process of democratization. David Held and John Keane described the reform of the state, on the one hand, and the restructuring of civil society, on the other hand, as constituting a process of "double democratization," which is the only possible way "for democracy to flourish today" (Held 1989, p. 283; Held and Keane 1984) because both the state and civil society have to be reformed to increase the power and influence of the citizenry:

> The structure of civil society (including private ownership of productive property, vast sexual and racial inequalities)—misunderstood or endorsed by liberal democratic models—does not create conditions for equal votes, effective participation, proper political understanding and equal control of the political agenda, while the structure of the liberal democratic state (including large, frequently unaccountable bureaucratic apparatuses, institutional dependence on the process of capital accumulation, political representatives preoccupied with their own re-election) does not create an organizational force which can adequately regulate "civil" power centres. (Held 1989, pp. 282–283)

In other words, the rebirth of civil society is not possible without the corresponding reform of the state. As Andrew Arato and Jean Cohen (1984) claimed, a "dualistic strategy" for democratization is needed, involving movements from below and institutional reforms from above. In the long run, the processes of individuation and differentiation cannot be suspended; thus, a certain level of differentiation and independence of (civil) society from the state always exists. This is clearly proven by the sudden rise of civil society in East Europe. The same is true for the opposing processes of integration. Even if a certain form of integration, the state, is peculiar to class-divided societies, it is eternal in the sense of the existence of certain institutionalized forms of integration. In this sense, the belief in the possible (or even necessary, as for Marx) withering away of the state—through a fusion of civil society and the state as the "final act" of the processes of democratization to be achieved in communism—is not only utopian but also historically incorrect.

The modern state is not simply an apparatus of coercion or an instrument of the dominant economic class, as it was traditionally conceptualized—at least in a critical or Marxist perspective. Twenty years ago Umberto Cerroni (1983, p. 207) argued that the theories of the coercive state, imperialistic colonialism, and crisis as decay or the theories of "bourgeois democracy" and "proletarian dicta-torship" had lost all interpretative and organizational power. The state became autonomous in relation to production relations, rather than determined by them, although it preserved the power of institutionalized coercion. However, the "synchronization" of the activities of the state and class interests now has been replaced by a far more complex relationship. An *informational mode of development* mediates among (defines the relations between) the (political) *state* based on representative democracy, the *economic structure* of society (production relations), and (largely depoliticized) *civil society.* This new mode of development is essential for the contemporary restructuring of capitalism (Castells 1989, pp. 7–32).

A global system of information flows has developed that fosters organizational changes in the economy and the state and also makes possible the reemergence of civil society as a part of the process of double democratization. At least, the information revolution and the globalization of information and communication processes make total state control or even repression no longer possible, although authoritarian systems may exist locally and temporarily. External radio broadcasting and satellite television broke state monopoly on what citizens were permitted to know, and they forced state-controlled media to provide at least some information available from external broadcasts. Democratic changes in East-Central Europe clearly support this idea. The development of new information and communication technologies, particularly direct broadcast satellites, broadened the penetration of external television programs into socialist and other developing countries and posed an immense threat to national control of the media. However, these complex developments created a number of new contradictions involving the processes of social communication. What we are facing in these complex relationships is, not the withdrawal of the state, but the emergence of new forms of state interventions into different spheres, including communications—a kind of simultaneous de- and reregu-lation of social and communication systems.

Giner's five fundamental dimensions of differentiation constitutive for civil society versus the state have been challenged in the last thirty years by the development and deployment of information and communication technologies. New technologies are thought to enable greater *individualism* and *differentiation,* activities traditionally belonging to the sphere of civil society, and less unity and integration (see, for example, Naisbitt 1984, pp. 97, 128). As recent history indicates, the globalization of information and communication processes does not necessarily terminate the role of stratification systems based on caste, class, party, ethnicity, or religion. It is evident that even the reverse may occur: National and federal structures may fragment, decentralize, repluralize, or even self-destruct (Ferguson 1992, p. 72). At the same time, however, individualism and differentiation are challenged by the formation of collective power agents (corporations, political parties, unions, and state institutions) that "assert themselves in an utterly non-individualistic manner" (Giner 1985, p. 255).

The same sort of dialectic holds true for the marketplace (resulting in the restructuring of the capitalist economy) and (political) pluralism (the decline of the welfare-state model). While the state is becoming universal under the rule of representative democracy, civil society remains stratified and subject to the domination of capital. As Benjamin Barber (1992, p. 59) maintains, "In all this high-tech commercial world there is nothing that looks particularly democratic. It lends itself to surveillance as well as liberty, to new forms of manipulation and covert control as well as new kinds of participation, to skewed, unjust market outcomes as well as greater productivity."

It is more difficult to prove that the same applies to the two other fundamental dimensions of civil society—the relation between classes or privacy (e.g., new social movements, redistribution of power, politicization of society versus depoliticization of the state) and new information technologies. However, a number of discussions on *new classes* and new threats to the privacy of citizens point to some important, and contradictory, consequences of informatization, as we see later. Apparently, huge differences exist in this respect between the two halves of Europe and elsewhere. Nevertheless, it ought to be at least evident that the nature of civil society, as well as society in general, is decisively affected by these changes.

Although the processes of informatization and global economic restructuring are particularly relevant for the rebirth of civil society in West Europe, the importance of civil society in East-Central Europe is rooted in "radical" civil movements mobilized against the state-party system and its monopolistic economic and political power. "You may, if you wish, call it the transition from socialism to capitalism, or from totalitarianism to freedom, or from security to unemployment, or from Russian domination to West German domination. I prefer to call it an unfinished attempt to make the shift from autarchic *nomenklatura* state capitalism to *nomenklatura* private capitalism integrated into the world market. What it undoubtedly is in substance, however, is a *massive increase in the power of civil society relative to the state*" (Sparks, forthcoming; italics added).

In the West, the distinction between the state and civil society is normatively aimed at the restoration and revitalization of the already achieved level of democracy or, at least, against the erosion of an already existing civil society fostered by corporatization in economy and polity, state expansion, and the rise of information technology. In East-Central Europe, however, this distinction was and still is aimed primarily at legalization of democratic grass-roots movements, that is, at the (re)creation of civil society, which had been largely abolished by omnipotent socialist states. These efforts go back to the 1950s in Hungary, the 1960s in Czechoslovakia, and the late 1970s in Poland as well as to a number of democratizing projects in Yugoslavia. In different ways, these efforts represented the mobilization of social actors, particularly intellectual nonconformists and new social movements, either by bypassing the institution-alized "public sphere" (communist parties and parliaments) or by reforming it "from above." The importance of discussions about an autonomous civil society in East Europe is in the fact that they emphasized, in addition to human rights and liberties, the role of autonomous special interest groups and general polit-ical associations as a necessary infrastructure of contemporary pluralism (Bibič 1990, p. 10). In a way, as, for example, Ivan Bernik (1991, p. 10) argued, "the theory of civil society was the most elaborated version of the ideology of non-conformist intellectuals. They portrayed themselves . . . as representatives of the civil society before the authoritarian state."

The media had, and still have, an important role in this historic battle for democracy and pluralism in three senses:

1. In a number of countries, particularly Poland and Yugoslavia, the media were agents of revolutionary political changes.
2. At the same time, in all East-Central European countries, revolutionary changes in society were aimed at the transformation of the party- or state-owned media.
3. In one way or another, all the central questions of transition of these societies pertain to the media: the role of the state and civil society, the question of demo-cratic pluralism, problems of denationalization and privatization of the means of production, the quest for sovereignty, and, of course, the liberalization of the media systems themselves.

Although developments in different East European countries may be described as having a number of characteristics in common, one should avoid generalizing them too quickly and ignoring "disturbing details." Generally, all East-Central European countries proceed in the same direction, with the same ideas per-vading the media and society. However, democratic revolutions originate in dif-ferent social circumstances, they differ in their acceleration (or delay), and they do not always result in equivalent consequences. The question of meaningful equivalences between specific social phenomena and their broader conse-quences cannot be reduced to a merely nominal similarity, either on an ana-lytical or on a normative level. Analysts often fail to notice, for example, that there may be different assessments of the concept of democracy (let alone civil society) in different cultural settings. This fact makes comparisons, examination of differences, and generalizations a difficult task because the "countries" repre-sent highly complex systems that differ across a range of historical, political, and economic dimensions. Major differences among the former socialist coun-tries derive from historical and cultural specifics that existed before socialist revolutions and from circumstances that resulted from different paths followed by socialist revolutions and reforms. With some exceptions in eastern Yugo-slavia, the Commonwealth of the Independent States (CIS), and other states of the former Soviet Union, the old regimes were overthrown almost overnight, and the new authorities tried to stabilize political changes. But the nature of these changes and the pace of transition and restructuring of society set by the new power elites differ immensely.

The same applies to the media: Significant differences still exist both among national media systems in the region and among the media in a specific system. In terms of the role of the media and their relationship to the polity and economy, these differences may help us get beyond superficial revolutionary enthusiasm for the new elites. At the same time, such comparisons ought to provide us with some general principles about the nature of these developments and about the relationships between the media and their "environment," both national and international. The latter seems to be particularly important because of the increasing vulnerability of any kind of "subglobal" system: For example, democratic revolutions in East-Central Europe may not have succeeded without the globalization of the communication sphere. There is no doubt that all former socialist countries are witnessing an enormous development toward a less authoritarian or nonauthoritarian society, but many impediments to a genuine democratic restructuring of society and the media remain. Some important obstacles to democratization common to all postsocialist countries or specific to some of them are problematized in the following chapters.

2 Media and Democratization in East-Central Europe

Before the late 1980s, media policy throughout East Europe was rather simple. State responsibility for print and broadcast media was legitimized in terms of the political, educational, and cultural importance of the media to society (and, of course, to the state). Because of their educational and propaganda functions, the media represented a means of transmission (similar to other educational institutions) for an authoritative definition of reality. Broadcasting was severely limited by state restrictions and control, which the authorities justified as being necessary because of technical standardization, scarcity of frequencies, and special national priorities and interests (armies, police, etc.). National, regional, and local radio and television stations were directly controlled by the state and/or the Communist Party and were financed by license fees, advertising, and direct state subsidies. Yugoslavia was the only exception to this authoritarian model: Its media system was based simultaneously on a state-dominated, one-party political system and centrally planned economy and on self-management pluralism of (mainly nonpolitical) interests and a market economy that introduced some features of civil society.

All forms of external control over the media (including state censorship) and those internally generated within media organizations (e.g., self-censorship) were aimed at maximizing the role of the media in popularizing the ruling ideology and state policy. External control of the media was based on state ownership of all major forms of mass communication means. The "sponsors" of the media were not industries; rather, they were political organizations and state institutions involved in the budgetary distribution affecting the mass media. Although state control of newspapers was not so rigorous as that of broadcasting, "alternative" newspapers (i.e., those opposing the existing power structures) were marginalized. Opinions dissenting from official attitudes were repressed by preventive censorship and penal legislation. The legislation in most socialist countries provided a system whereby an author of opinions criticizing constitutional order, political institutions, and leaders or stimulating public disorder could be punished for publishing such criticisms.[1] No genuine public opinion in the sense of "the public expression of agreement or dissent concerning institutions" (Bobbio 1989, p. 26) existed; the sphere of civil society was almost entirely absorbed by the state. Only a few newspapers based in oppositional political groups were able to survive. Nevertheless, strong public political dissent,

generated within a rising civil society, progressively spread from the oppositional public sphere and its semipublic communication channels to the national
(official) media.

Although the formal structure of media institutions remained essentially unchanged after manifest social and political tensions in Poland (1956), Hungary
(1958), and Czechoslovakia (1968), some minor changes occurred. According
to Miklos Sukosd, (1990, p. 45), these changes were marked by a transition
from the *totalitarian* model to the model of *tolerant repression*. Indicators of
this change were the growth and diversification of publications and (professional) journals published by nonstate organizations and technological modernization (new radio channels and local radio stations and, particularly, the establishment of national television stations). The media remained largely state
owned and/or state controlled, but their contents changed from an aggressive
ideological propaganda into deideologized entertainment and mass culture.

After the late 1970s, in a number of socialist countries the party-state media
monopoly was broken, although a significant part of the new and independent
media remained illegal or semilegal. New (mainly print) media appeared as a
consequence of the development of the "second economy," which was, in contrast to the official, state-controlled economy, not dependent on or controlled by
the dominant communist ideology, the Communist Party, or the state. Liberalization of the economy and the rise of a new (economic) elite also affected the
official, state-controlled media, which started to import Western popular culture
and even to support nonconformist and dissident political views.

During the late 1980s, endeavors aimed at social liberalization succeeded.
Peaceful (r)evolutions in the region introduced radical political, and partly economic, changes and indicated the importance of autonomous social spaces devoted to communication as generators of democratization. The media became
of vital importance in the wake of popular movements that may not have
succeeded without them. As in all modern democratic revolutions, the call for
freedom of the press was vital. Democratic elections and legalized freedom of
the press, which located freedom of the press in an individual citizen rather than
in a nebulous "society," marked impressive political changes in these countries.[2]

Apparently, these changes could mean a break with the former media policy
based on party-state subsidies as the main economic strategy and party-state
control (and censorship) of the media as the main issue-oriented strategy. However, as Colin Sparks (1991b, p. 11) observed, one strategy does not necessarily
entail the other; "it is quite possible to combine a move away from subsidy with
an increase in direct censorship." A number of countries experienced this contradiction, which perhaps can be best exemplified by the military dictatorships
in Latin America. For example, the military government in Argentina that took
power in 1976 declared its belief in private ownership and freedom of the press
and removed advertising taxes introduced by the former Peronist government.
But at the same time, the government gave a free hand to transnational corporations, increased government advertising, forced the media to implement the

Doctrine of National Security, and placed them under tight political control. According to Heriberto Muraro (1988, p. 117), "The armed forces put into force a regime of terror for the media. The junta murdered journalists, closed newspapers and censored publications." As a consequence, the media limited their criticism of the government and passively accepted these repressive measures in spite of commercialization.

This is not to say that a similar situation occurred in East-Central Europe after the 1990–1991 democratic revolutions. Nevertheless, both the political and economic changes and challenges to democratization in East-Central Europe have contradictory consequences; what final shape the political and economic reforms will take is still controversial. Two years after the overthrow of nondemocratic governments many obstacles to a genuine democracy still exist, partly because of the persistence of the remains of previous nondemocratic environment and partly because of the reproduction of old patterns of behavior in the new political and economic environment. Again, the situation is at least partly comparable to that in Latin America after the overthrow of military dictatorships. "Even if the new democracies had the economic resources to implement communication policies and reforms, they did not have a clear idea of how to go about it. The leaders of the new democratic regimes had spent most of the last decade outside politics and removed from the daily exercise of government. They came to power without any new scheme to reorganize the mass media. Furthermore, they now depended on the same media to get elected" (Fox 1988, p. 29).

The ways in which new systems emerge in East-Central Europe are extremely dynamic, contradictory, and rapid, but they certainly have some essential features in common. Most of the current debates about the reorganization of the communication sphere, particularly broadcasting, are inspired and guided by similar debates in the West. Whereas most of the past forty years have witnessed socialist countries intensively engaged in trying to find their "own way," albeit not been very successfully (in Poland and the former Yugoslavia these efforts included the idea of a "socialist civil society"), the newest developments go in the direction of a mere imitation of industrialized countries. The policies of liberalization and privatization have already affected the press, but broadcasting is still largely state controlled. Government control of television and economic problems faced by the print press remain major obstacles to media freedom in East-Central Europe. These contradictory efforts toward defining a new role for the print and electronic media are also reflected in parliamentary controversies on de- and reregulation of the media and on the nature of democracy. Although freedom of the press is everywhere declared the legal foundation of the new democratic system, this principle encounters a number of difficulties in practice. But, as Williams (1976, p. 133) put it, "all proposals for new systems appear abstract, and at times unconvincing, because *it is only when they are put into practice that they can be felt to be real*" (italics added).

East European departures from previous socialist regimes are largely caught up in imitating West European practices in economy and polity rather than in reexamining the possible contributions of a "Western model" to the specific situations in East-Central Europe. Nevertheless, this does not mean that the key issues related to the nature of the reconstruction and democratization of former socialist countries are the same as those in West Europe. In West Europe, for example, the "civil society paradox" exists in the *parallel restructuring of the state and civil society,* where the state, although it wants to dominate civil society, cannot avoid protecting the autonomy of civil society (Giner 1985). On the one hand, the state pervades civil society by "publicizing the private" mainly through the regulation of economic relations. But on the other hand, civil society pervades the state as well, thus "privatizing the public" through the growing political power of large economic actors.

In postsocialist East-Central Europe, however, the revitalization of civil society is (again) blocked because of *the absence of corresponding reforms of the state.* It is paradoxical that civil society, after having overthrown the old undemocratic regimes, lost its own autonomy in this historical battle. Decisions of public consequence are, as they were in the former system, removed from the public, and citizens lose their ability to participate in political processes. The access of oppositional parties *and* autonomous groups from civil society to national broadcast media and mainstream print media is being limited. Nonpolitical issues are politicized, and the parliamentary mechanisms of party pluralism and formal democracy are considered the only legitimate way to articulate the interests and opinions in "society," while noninstitutional arrangements of civil society are ignored.

Economic restructuring and political democratization, two central issues in East-Central Europe, are also reflected in current media debates. The ruling parties "stand for a market economy and free enterprise system. Deregulation and (re)privatization are the order of the day. Foreign capital investments are being encouraged as joint ventures or in pure form" (Szekfu and Valko 1990, p. 2). However, these doctrinaire foundations of the new systems are easily used in practice as a cover for immediate pragmatic solutions that reproduce exclusivist ideology. In short, the question of economic restructuring is largely reduced to that of privatization of the means of production, and the question of democratization is diminished to that of the rights of nations (rather than of citizens). The two reductions could be considered major reasons for political polarization and conflicts in these countries.

The abolition of direct forms of state intervention into the economy makes the rebirth of civil society possible, but a partial disengagement of the state is not a sufficient condition for this rebirth. The new power actors (governments and political parties in power) in the former socialist countries still tend to reproduce the old form of hegemony based on the new but still exclusive (anticommunist and nationalist) ideology, not readily allowing adversary power actors and civil society to participate in decisionmaking and to control the activities of the state. The access of oppositional parties and autonomous civil groups to national broadcasting media is being limited. Like the old power structures, new authorities are not willing to surrender any part of broadcasting, particularly television, to groups they consider "oppositional," "leftist," or "communist."

The introduction of market mechanisms, new forms of management, and the inflow of foreign capital are considered the conditions of both economic restructuring/modernization and political pluralization/democratization. The new rhetoric of the privatized economy as the cornerstone of political pluralism and parliamentary democracy misses the point that, apart from market competition, there are other important elements of modern civil society essential for democratization. Particularly, it overlooks the fact that modern corporate capitalism, which is becoming the dominant model of the development, (re)-produces economic inequalities that prevent the majority of citizens from participation in decisions about public affairs.

Contrary to the new liberal philosophy, however, both economic and political activities are in practice still largely controlled by the state because of the absence of any indigenous commercial class. Liberalization and privatization in communications apply mainly to the press and local broadcasting. Some newly established newspapers and magazines are strictly private business; some are in limbo between state ownership and privatization; others remain firmly in state hands (Dennis and Heuvel 1990, p. 7). At the same time, national broadcasting organizations have been largely renationalized and put under direct government control. The same applies to printing facilities and distribution systems for both the press (e.g., the post) and broadcasting (transmitting facilities are state owned everywhere in East Europe). Apart from the privatization of newspapers in some countries, nothing really new has been institutionalized on a large scale. The reason for this contradiction between political/economic changes and the institutional stability of communication systems is quite evident: Privatization of the economy in East-Central Europe is not just a question of a more effective economy; nor is it only a question of ideological legitimation. Rather, it is a matter of the redistribution of political control over the economy. In contrast, denationalization of broadcasting would reduce the control new political elites have over it.

The current restructuring of broadcasting systems is aimed at establishing a *national, politicized, and quasi-commercial "public" broadcasting system* subordinated to the state authorities rather than to public accountability. A number of economic, political, cultural, and ideological reasons may be listed for this "delay" compared to West Europe: a lack of modern communication technology, a highly ideologized political scene, nationalist policies of new governments in multinational states, economic underdevelopment and an absence of a market economy, a need to "protect" national culture, legal vacuums in the economy in general and in communications in particular, and ideological opposition to "wild" privatization. These factors tend to support an increasing, or at least continued, penetration of the state into the media sphere.

The expansion of the state preserves traditional domination of the state over civil society in East-Central Europe, although the forms of authoritative penetration have changed as a result of capitalism-oriented politics. The marketplace is becoming a common denominator of pluralism and democratic restructuring. As a consequence of the state- and market economy—centered logic of social and media restructuring—inspiring one analyst to name these pervasive processes "privatization of democracy" (Maloča 1991)–paternalistic commercial media systems are emerging. These media reflect a tendency toward progressive privatization and commercialization of the media (particularly the press), on the one hand, and the exercise and maximization of the state's political power over broadcast media, on the other, where the highest power is concentrated in the hands of the state because officials consider the media (specifically journalists) politically "incompetent" and/or too partial.

A fundamental contradiction in the development of communications in East-Central Europe exists between the obvious tendencies of political and economic elites toward nationalist policies and privatization as means of power and profit maximization and the neglected development of public services as cornerstones of more democratic communication. In a way, this contradicition is comparable to the situation in Latin America, where "the strong memories of control and censorship under the authoritarian regimes made new regulation or public-service functions of the media anathema to the private sector and to many political parties" (Fox 1988, p. 28). A lack of money and demand, weak economies, and general economic decline caused by structural reforms make this contradiction even more acute.

In addition, turning to a market economy challenges the powerfulness of the states. They are increasingly becoming concerned about national sovereignty and their own peripheral position within the international community and thus try to strengthen state power, which is certainly not to the advantage of civil society and the autonomy of the media. The growing concern of the states with state vulnerability and, as in the case of nations living in multinational states, the need to establish national sovereignty are major reasons for national governments to neglect or even suppress the question of a "plurality of social identities" within civil society.

An important instance of the loss of sovereignty is represented—perhaps similarly to other smaller countries and nations in West Europe—by the growing penetration of foreign capital in the media and by satellite television programs. Both governments and journalists tend to argue, as Marvin Stone and Leonard Marks (1991, p. 5) reported, that strict media laws are needed "in order to prevent foreign interests from buying print and broadcast resources and driving out domestically-owned and -produced products." Hungary is the extreme example of the selling off of the wealth of national daily newspapers. In television, a decline of original program production and educational programming, transmission of satellite programs, and an increase in advertising exemplify the same trends. If these trends continue, and economic and power-maximizing reasoning prevail over cultural and civil society arguments, TV viewers in East Europe will be exposed to evermore commercial foreign programs in foreign language(s) because the costs of subtitles and voice-overs, not to speak of dubbing, are too expensive to be met. A change of emphasis in political and legal considerations from educational and cultural to political and economic issues will not only result in the decline of the public service system but may also lead to the decline of independent national program producers, which will not be able to compete with international giants.

Commercialization of the Press

The deregulation and privatization of the national economy and communications are considered by the new power elites in East-Central Europe as necessary conditions of both general democratization and media development. The breakdown of the state-regulated media (both broadcasting and the press) in East Europe is a part of a general tendency toward liberalization and privatization. In most postsocialist countries, the print media's creation of a more pluralist environment has constituted the most notable progress toward democratization. However, most papers are identified with different parties, particularly those in power, thus continuing the tradition of "advocacy press" rather than performing a watchdog function. Only a smaller part of newspapers and magazines, particularly those with foreign investors (in Hungary, for example), draw on Western business practice, try to achieve political independence, and "move from the former 'Leninist' model of journalism to the norms prevailing in the West, and in particular towards the 'Fourth Estate' model thought to characterise the Anglo-Saxon media" (Sparks 1991b, p. 12).

Changes in media policy remain highly politicized questions; political debates about legal changes in the media sphere attract as much attention as do the questions of constitutional changes. The authorities in power seem to be resolute about maintaining a firm control over (particularly television) broadcasting and national news agencies. In Serbia, for example, student demonstrations in March 1991 against the authoritarian national government concentrated on bias in media reporting and state censorship and forced the resignation of several high officials in the Politika publishing house (one of the largest in the former Yugoslavia) and national broadcasting organization, although reporting remained government controlled. In fact, media debates reflect key controversies within the general project of democratization, which I discuss in Chapters 3 and 4. Furthermore, these debates are paralleled (and to a certain degree even initiated) by increasing pressures toward liberalization and the abolition of the public service broadcasting monopoly in West Europe, which was motivated by an increasing belief in market-driven individualism and a decreasing confidence in public (state) regulation.

Most of the current discussions about the reorganization of the communication sphere in East-Central Europe seem to be guided by the political agenda of the New Right in the West. Conservative ideology "endorses the libertarian principle that private rights to property and choice are the most effective and efficient engines of economic and social progress" (Rowland and Tracey 1990, p. 13). It sees market competition as "the key condition of press and broadcasting freedom, understood as freedom from state interference, as the right of individuals to communicate their opinions without external restrictions" (Keane 1991, p. 53). Indeed, political arguments prevailing in contemporary debates in East-Central European countries are often little more than reproductions of what was already said and seen in West Europe before and after the take-off phase of private television networks. Political control and state interference, ideological monopoly, bureaucratic rigidity, and the economic inefficiency of the state- or party-owned media under the old regimes are the most commonplace allegations made by the new governments. At least implicitly it is assumed by these governments that a "natural" or "organic" development necessitates convergence on the type of society developed in West Europe and North America. A lack of historical perspective and a relative neglect of the existing social structure in East-Central European countries lead easily to such a fallacy.

The most excessive case of transplanting a Western model of deregulation to a former socialist country is the German "media unification." From the very beginning, an ideological war with West Germany was built into the East German political and media system as one of its cornerstones. Unlike Poland, Yugoslavia, and perhaps some other East European countries, East Germany did not have civil society movements capable of producing a popular antisystem opposition. East Germany was the most economically advanced socialist country, but it had the most dogmatic media within the Soviet bloc. It is not surprising, then, that the East German media were remarkably uniform in supporting and glorifying the achievements of the socialist state even during the last days of the Honecker regime, when hundreds of thousands of refugees sought asylum in West Germany. Even though other socialist countries were moving swiftly in the direction of *glasnost,* the East German media were resisting—together with the party-state authorities—the pressure for democratic reforms until the last possible moment (Willnat 1991, p. 204).

In the process of unification that started with national elections in March 1990, no regulation of the press was conceived. This brought the former East German newspapers into a competitive battle for readers, both among themselves and with the West German media. Thirty-one of thirty-four daily newspapers in the former German Democratic Republic (GDR) found West German partners. The press market in the former GDR became fully controlled by the twelve largest West German publishers, which owned more than 85 percent of former East German newspapers. However, the big four German media barons (Axel Springer, Gruner & Jahr, Heinrich Bauer, and Burda) were allowed to purchase only one newspaper each. The central battlefield is still Berlin. Newspapers from the western part, particularly Axel Springer's *Berliner Morgenpost* and *Bild Zeitung,* are successfully trying to extend their circulation to the eastern part. The former state-owned East Berlin newspapers that were privatized and almost entirely taken over by West German publishers are also expanding on the western side of the former iron curtain. However, Robert Maxwell, who linked up with the West German publisher Gruner & Jahr, took over control of the former Communist Party publishing house Berliner Verlag and its main daily, *Berliner Zeitung,* which is now edited by the former chief editor of *Der Spiegel* (IOJ 1991, p. 4). Maxwell also obtained 55 percent of the shares in the *Neues Deutschland* printing plant. Maxwell's rival, Rupert Murdoch, started together with the West German publisher Burda to build modern printing facilities for his new daily.

Nevertheless, privatization of the former GDR broadcasting was not foreseen for the transition period (until the end of 1991). The five radio and two television channels of the former state-owned broadcasting organization DFF (German Radio and Television) were transformed into the Independent Public Broadcasting Company, a semipublic organization funded from license fees and government subsidies and run by a broadcast committee of eighteen members, three each from the five new *Länder* and three from Berlin. However, the two West German networks, the ARD and the ZDF, are keen on integrating the former GDR state television and making it part of their cooperative national networks (Robinson 1991, pp. 10–14). At least at the present stage, the extent of private entry into the radio and television market is still less predictable. Nevertheless, it is clear—according to the Broadcasting Law that passed the former GDR parliament in September 1990—that the (West) German "dual system" of public and private broadcasters is accepted as the model and that the former GDR broadcasting will be rapidly integrated into the existing system of the Western part, although DFF wanted to become a third national public network in a united Germany. In 1991, some national (West German) companies, such as RTL Plus and SAT 1, already began the terrestrial (nonsatellite) distribution of their programs.

Another clear, and perhaps extreme, example of the imitative approach is the Yugoslav case of the *right to publish opinions,* which became a constitutional right in 1963. In the 1980s, this right—together with the right of reply and the right of correction—became widely used by citizens (mostly in the press). An important precedent was set in a 1985 lawsuit when the Supreme Court of Slovenia ordered the main daily newspaper in Slovenia, *Delo* (The Work), to publish an article by a citizen criticizing a high political functionary. This case became a rather celebrated one for editors, journalists, and (critical) citizens.

However, when in 1991 the Slovenian Ministry of Information proposed amendments to the former (and still valid) Law on Public Information adopted in 1985, it suggested cutting "out the provisions related to the publication of opinions." The ministry admitted that "this citizens' right represented a great achievement of civilization under the conditions of a one-party system." However, it argued that "in a plural society and developed information market such a citizens' right, or duty of the media, is an anachronism; the media will be forced to publish opinions important for the public primarily because of the pressure of competition" (Splichal 1991, p. 497).

What we have here is a version of the liberal theoretical argument about the free marketplace of ideas, which would create an informed citizenry able to make rational decisions. Although there is no doubt that these arguments are aimed at establishing a free press uninhibited by authoritarian interference from above, they underestimate the tendencies toward mental homogenization and monopolization inherent in a market-driven media system and the way in which media organizations do not make themselves accessible to nonprofessionals. (I discuss this issue, especially in relation to the East European "old-new journalism," in the last part of this chapter.) This latter characteristic is neither new nor specific to any particular system. Paul Lazarsfeld (1972, p. 123) considered the "nervous reaction to criticism" often exhibited by the media as an *institutional disease,* which is paradoxical because the media vigorously defend the right to criticize when their freedom is at stake and try to limit the same right when another social actor—either a citizen or the state—wants to have it.

Although there are some significant differences between the print and broadcasting media, the newest legal and practical developments are generally of little theoretical relevance because of the lack of any indigenous approach to the restructuring of the media sphere. Nevertheless, they certainly may be considered important changes in practical (political, economic, cultural) terms when compared with the previous system.

Under the old regimes, newspapers were owned mainly by the ruling parties, rather than by the state, but they often received state subsidies. Their position changed radically after the revolutionary political changes in 1989 and 1990. At least in some East-Central European countries (particularly in Hungary and Poland), the press was left to its own resources and to the marketplace almost overnight. Generally, commercialization of the press (based on the principle of profit maximization and on advertising as an essential source of income) and the suppression of governmental subsidies for newspapers and magazines caused painful consequences for large sectors of the press. Many formerly subsidized newspapers could not survive without external financial assistance. Although a large number of new publications were established during the early period of democratization, it is likely that oligopolistic tendencies similar to those in West Europe will prevail in the future. Newspapers based in political parties and factions are still dominant and partly subsidized, but these subsidies are far from being sufficient to enable these newspapers to expand in terms of their quality, circulation figures, and power. The processes of privatization and "colonization" of the East by the West could lead to "a stratified press in which the majority of the population will be effectively denied access to information about matters of public importance" (Sparks 1991d, p. 20). Only a limited number of small newspapers will probably survive, but they will remain marginal in terms of their social importance—as was the case with "alternative" publications in capitalist countries or "dissident" publications in the former socialist countries.

In fact, the present situation in East-Central Europe might be compared with that of mid-1800s in West Europe, when press owners and editors became politically respectable and influential and the role of the press was reinterpreted as that of an independent fourth estate. Many of the newly established newspapers in East Europe that have survived the economic earthquake still lack prestige and autonomy from political parties. Their lack of political independence is also a reflection of limited circulations. Consequently, the position of newspapers will probably undergo a fundamental change only if newly established newspapers acquire mass circulation.

Although the press normatively represents the cornerstone of emerging democratic media systems in East-Central Europe, it is under huge economic as well as political pressures. The majority of newspapers are denationalized or privatized, but printing plants and distribution systems are still largely owned or controlled by the state. Generally, there is a shortage of printing capacities, and printing is expensive, though of low quality. Distribution systems are ineffective and slow. Desktop publishing technology that could ease some of the problems of small publishers is hardly available. To avoid all these obstacles, some publishers try to attract foreign capital and technology. Although some—though limited—noncommercial loans from governmental agencies are still available, they are politically not attractive, at least not for publications that want to demonstrate an independent editorial policy.

Hungary was the first East European country with whole sectors of its economy sold off at bargain prices to foreign capital (see Table 2.1). For instance, the former leading Socialist Workers' Party "solved" the party's financial problems by selling its newspapers to Western companies, often for a very low price. Hungarian newspapers have also been seeking external financial support, and thus independence from the state, because the new leading Hungarian Democratic Party (MDF) tends to intimidate critical newspapers into more favorable assessments of government activities. In 1990 Axel Springer Verlag AG took control of seven Hungarian provincial dailies and 90 percent of their profits without even having to buy them; all the corporation did was assure the employees' salaries and pay the buildings' rent, the dailies' printing costs, and the national press agency's fees. After the "Springer Affair," the MDF became involved in acquiring foreign investors so that it could control foreign ownership

TABLE 2.1   Ownership of Daily Newspapers in Hungary, 1990

Newspaper	Hungarian Share	Foreign Share	Foreign Owner
National			
Népszabadság	60	40	Bertelsmann AG
Magyar Nemzet	60	40	Hersant
Magyar Hírlap	60	40	Mirror Holding Ltd.
Nepszava	100	0	
Esti Hírlap	60	40	Mirror Holding Ltd.
Mai Nap	50	50	Murdoch
Kurir	80	20	Deton Gmbh
Pesti Hírlap	100	0	
Regional			
Új Dunantuli Napló	0	100	Axel Springer Budapest
Somogyi Hírlap	0	100	Axel Springer Budapest
Tolnai Népújság	0	100	Axel Springer Budapest
24 Ora	0	100	Axel Springer Budapest
Új Nograd	0	100	Axel Springer Budapest
Új Néplap-Szolnok	0	100	Axel Springer Budapest
Heves M. Hírlap	0	100	Axel Springer Budapest
Pest M. Hírlap	100	0	
Délvilág	100	0	
Petöfi Nepe	60	40	Oscar Brunner (Standard)
Békés M. Népújság	60	40	Oscar Brunner (Standard)
Észak-Magyarorsz	51	49	FVB-Funk Verlag u. Druck
Csongrad M. Hírlap	50	50	Nice Press Invest
Fejer M. Hírlap	70	30	Westdeutsche Allgemeine
Kisalföld	51	49	Ass. Newspapers Holdings
Hajdú-Buhari N.	51	49	FVB-Funk Verlag u. Druck
Kelet-Magyaro	51	49	FVB-Funk Verlag u. Druck
Vas M. Néplap	51	49	Westdeutsche Allgemeine
Napló-Veszprem	51	49	Krone Verlag
Zalai Hírlap	51	49	Krone Verlag

SOURCE: Tamas 1990, p. 4. Used by permission.

of the media and make sure "that investor will have political views in accord with those of MDF. Presumably the investor will then use its influence within the paper on MDF's behalf" (Dennis and Heuvel 1990, p. 52). In 1990, the large majority of thirty-one Hungarian dailies became partly owned by foreign multi-nationals (Bertelsmann, Hersant, Maxwell, Murdoch, Springer).

Huge controversies related to the development of the private-sector press can be best exemplified by the case of *Magyar Nemzet* (Hungarian Nation). Early in 1990, an American investor wanted to purchase this anticommunist newspaper, but his offer was rejected as too low. After the Springer Affair, the newspaper entered into discussions with a Swedish investor, but the deal was blocked by the government, which wanted the paper sold to the French conglomerate

Hersant because the Swedish investor was politically too "liberal." Although the editors and journalists protested, a special committee appointed by the government to evaluate both proposals decided in favor of Hersant, which acquired 40 percent of the stock in *Magyar Nemzet*.

In spite of foreign investments, financial problems are still one of the main problems faced by Hungarian newspapers. An "explosion" of new publications with limited circulation have to deal with growing inflation, a reduction of average incomes, and lower effective demand. In 1990–1991 the readership of national daily newspapers dropped almost 10 percent. As a consequence, one hundred newspapers and magazines went under (Stone and Marks 1991, p. 9).

In Poland, major obstacles to the development of independent press are related to the long tradition of party-affiliated press, the precarious economic climate, and the state-owned printing facilities. The result may be that "the former Communist-controlled press will not become an independent press at all, but rather a press controlled by two new political parties," that is, Mazowiecki's Civic Movement Democratic Action (ROAD) and Center Alliance, which formerly made up Solidarity (Dennis and Heuvel 1990, p. 16). Despite pluralization of the press, newspapers are not truly independent; they serve largely as political organs of new political parties and their factions. There is a tacit agreement that the big newspapers should remain in Polish hands. Consequently, the penetration of foreign capital is far more limited than in Hungary, and six out of eight dailies in Warsaw were reported to be in financial difficulty. The largest Polish press trust in the former system, RSW Prasa-Ksiazka-Ruch, owned by the former Polish United Workers' Party, was not as "successfully" sold out as were the Hungarian dailies by the Hungarian Socialist Party.

In March 1990, the Polish parliament passed a law liquidating this huge publishing and distribution conglomerate, which had published and distributed virtually all newspapers under the previous regime. A special governmental liquidation commission was created to sell major newspapers and magazines to private bidders. The newspapers owned by the conglomerate were partly sold and partly handed over to cooperatives formed by their staffs, while several hundred publications were closed down, particularly those that wrote critically about the growing social problems (unemployment, the fall in production) under the new government, and two thousand journalists and newspaper employees lost their jobs (Sawisz 1990, p. 394). At the same time, however, a large number of new (mainly) local papers appeared, mostly on a nonprofessional basis. The main reason for their limitation to local or regional market is the absence of an appropriate distribution system because privatized kiosks—formerly owned by the party distribution network—now increasingly sell other, more profitable goods than newspapers (with the exception of pornography). Some newspapers—such as *Gazeta Wyborcza* (The Electoral Gazette), the pro-ROAD newspaper established by Solidarity in 1989 and now enjoying the largest circulation in Poland—are trying to establish their own distribution system, while others—including some foreign newspapers—prefer a new, independent national distribution system.

A similar trend was evident in the Czech and Slovak Federal Republic (CSFR), where in less than twelve months after the velvet revolution, the number of periodicals increased by more than 15 percent, although the selling prices of newspapers doubled during this period because of price liberalization and high taxation. Among others, the prestigious newspaper *Lidové Noviny* (The People's Newspaper), established in Brno in 1893, had already been reestablished in 1987. Newspapers and magazines pay a 20 percent tax on newsprint, an 11 percent "turnover tax," and a 55 percent tax on profits (Stone and Marks 1991, p. 21). It seems that for both economic and political reasons only state- and party-subsidized newspapers will be able to survive the period of transition. As in Poland, the newspapers criticizing the government are exposed to discriminative economic conditions. The Communist Party daily *Rude Pravo* (Red Right), which was the largest daily under the previous regime, has remained one of the most influential newspapers, although its circulation has decreased by 50 percent to roughly a half million copies. Its main competitors are *Lidové Noviny* in Prague and *Národná Obroda* (The National Revival) in Bratislava, which are formally independent but closely connected with the governing parties.

At least in some East-Central European countries, the extension of the market is combined with increased selective government intervention, which led some journalists to strike for independence from the government—e.g., Television Slovenia in Ljubljana and *Svobodné Slovo* (The Free Word) in Prague. In Slovenia, for example, the fifth daily newspaper, *Slovenec* (The Slovene)—the first privately owned daily, with a clear Christian democratic orientation—was established in June 1991 with substantial governmental financial support not available to other already existing newspapers or new projects. Everette Dennis and Jon Vanden Heuvel's (1990, p. 34) assessment that "in the murky legal waters of the Czechoslovak media, there is no substitute for knowing people in high places" can be extended without qualifications to other East European countries. Or as the Slovak writer František Benhart (1991, p. 7) remarked for the CSFR: "Connections blossom. The Spring of Connections. Can we be surprised that Czech journalists severely protest against the newest decision of the federal government that the tax (22 percent) on all periodical publications will remain unchanged, but the government will subsidize *some* newspapers, according to its own judgement (need)?"

Unlike Hungary, newspapers in other East European countries generally do not experience such radical changes toward privatization and Western "colonization." However, a lack of domestic capital, and often a legal vacuum, seem to be attractive to some West European investors. Apart from having bought 40 percent of the shares in two Hungarian newspapers, the daily *Magyar Hírlap* (The Hungarian Newspaper) (with a circulation of 100,000 copies) and *Esti Hírlap* (The Evening Newspaper) (260,000), Maxwell bought shares in Bulgarian TV and financed some media projects in the former USSR. He also printed the English version of *Moscow News* in Russia and negotiated with the Croatian government to buy the Vjesnik publishing corporation in Zagreb (which would also publish the Croatian edition of his new weekly, *The European*, as in Hungary). Maxwell also launched, in association with Merrill Lynch Capital Markets and a British commercial bank, the Maxwell Capital Partnership, a special fund for investments in East Europe and the USSR (mainly Russia), and expressed an interest in buying a share in the national Croatian Television, which is now state owned. After Maxwell's death in 1991, a number of his East European media projects fell into severe financial difficulties. His shares in the two leading Hungarian dailies were bought by the government. Murdoch bought 50 percent of the shares in the *Mai Nap* (Today) daily and the *Reform* magazine in Hungary. In addition, Murdoch aimed at establishing a third television channel in Romania. French publisher Jean-Louis Servan-Schreiber signed a joint venture agreement with the influential Polish economic magazine *Gazeta Bankowa* (The Bank Gazette).

In contrast to radical *economic* changes in the press systems in Poland, the CSFR, and particularly Hungary, Romania represents primarily an *ideological* break with the former authoritarian system. Many Romanian journalists played an important role in the political struggles that led to the overthrow of the Ceauşescu dictatorship in December 1989. However, soon after the revolution it became evident that many former collaborators of Nicolae Ceauşescu were reappearing in top political positions. The long expected freedom of the press did not materialize not only because of extremely unfavorable economic conditions, but also because of the impediments imposed on press distribution by the government, including a temporary suspension of oppositional newspapers (*Mass Media* 1991, p. 2). A number of newspapers changed their names, but they remained closely related to the government. The former press organ of the Communist Party, *Scienteia* (The Spark), for example, changed its name to *Adevarul* (The Truth), and the organ of the Union of the Communist Youth, *Scienteia Tineretul* (The Youth's Spark), became *Tineretul Liber* (The Free Youth). Nevertheless, their circulations dropped significantly. At the same time, a number of new periodicals appeared; from the prerevolutionary five hundred publications their number rose to some fifteen hundred but all were confronted with growing financial difficulties.

A similar pattern of slow transition exists in Bulgaria, where the former leading communist newspaper, *Rabotnichesko Delo* (The Workers' Cause), renamed itself *Duma* (Thought) and remained the most influential daily, with a circulation of some 500,000 copies. Although the press explosion in Bulgaria was not as strong as in Poland and the CSFR, a number of new (at that time oppositional) newspapers were established, including *Demokraciya* (Democracy; 250,000 copies) and *Svoboden Narod* (Free People; 70,000 copies).

The process is even slower in the former Soviet republics, where both the former rulers and the new governments want to control the media, although not in such a direct form as in the past. Nevertheless, the prime minister of the Republic of Byelarus openly stated that "the government gives credits to newspapers and magazines which maintain correct positions. What is the use of crediting a newspaper which attempts at subverting the stability of our country? I shall support all the press, *except publications opposing the government"* (quoted in Manaev 1992, p. 9; italics added).

The declaration adopted by the Parliament of Yugoslav Journalists (established for a short period of time in 1991 in the then-still-existing federation) revealed some of the controversies typical of the process of liberalization not only in Yugoslav society but also in East-Central European societies in general. The parliament requested that the director be elected by all the employees and that the editor in chief not be nominated without the consent of journalists; it protested against "the transformation of the old monopolies over the press, radio and television into new ones; against banning of newspapers and programmes; as well as against firing of journalists and editors' replacement on political, religious, ethnic or other non-professional grounds" (Vogel 1991, p. 239).

The above examples indicate that the new systems still carry with them some important characteristics of the former totalitarian model. The governments still try to control the media either directly or indirectly. The existing and potential media laws tend to "protect" the state (government) rather than civil society, citizens, and journalists. The most bizarre is the case of the democratically elected government of Slovenia, which "approached USIS [United States Information Service] several times to ask for assistance in drafting legislation 'to control the media'" (Stone and Marks 1991, p. 25). However, the vast majority of citizens are very much opposed to these tendencies. In a survey conducted in Slovenia in July 1990, when the government drafted a new press law that would actually legalize a form of state censorship, 35.5 percent among 606 interviewed citizens were "absolutely opposed" and 43.9 percent were "opposed" to government control of the media; only 7.9 percent agreed (*Delo*, 1990). After a strong public dissent supported by the media, the government revoked the draft law, but a few months later it resubmitted a slightly amended version of it. As in other East-Central European countries, the law is still in a state of flux. Indeed, the questions of citizens' freedoms, democratic institutions, media autonomy, and the control of society over the state are no less relevant now than in the late 1980s.

In the field of the press, there is as yet no evidence of a willingness among new governments to provide public support to minorities and groups not capable of exercising their rights. Such support could include reduced taxes and postal and/or telephone charges, redistribution of advertising revenues or spectrum usage fees, and subsidies and specific aids to newspapers to maintain a sufficient diversity and quality. In West Europe, "there is no country in which no State favors are conferred on newspapers, if only reduced postal charges or alleviations of VAT" (Ardwick 1982, p. 21). However, one should not neglect the danger hidden in different forms of "public support" controlled by the state. At least two state strategies to reduce press autonomy and diversity can be identified in subsidizing policies. One strategy is to give sizable financial aid to the press, which encourages dependence because individual enterprises cannot cover their production costs. This was certainly the case in the former socialist countries, but a similar strategy was adopted in some other countries, such as Greece. The other strategy is based on the "trickle-down principle" (Hummel 1990, p. 313): Subsidies are distributed among all newspapers in equal shares regardless of their market share, circulation figures, and advertising revenues. Austria typically exemplified this approach until 1992, when the subsidy system was partly changed. In the former case, the press becomes directly dependent on the state. In the latter, however, the state supports market-driven oligopolization. But both strategies clearly pervert the idea of public support to the press to strengthen its plurality and diversity in terms of interests and views (re)presented in the public.

Deep economic crisis in the former socialist countries makes the question of an appropriate legal and financial encouragement of independent media even more urgent. Because of a lack of capital, entry costs for new media organizations in East-Central Europe are prohibitively high even to commercial investors. However, governments are not yet reacting to alarmed voices, as in Hungary, saying "The government should find a way of subsidizing those newspapers and press products which cannot be profitable, but nevertheless cultivate important cultural values" (Terestyeni 1990, p. 415). Governments are not considering different regulatory strategies to protect the media from state and market censorship. On the contrary, some governments (e.g., in Romania, Serbia, and Bulgaria) are still more willing to control and supervise them. A typical case is that of the discriminatory financial support of the press established in Russia in February 1992 by Boris Yeltsin's decree. As the daily *Izvestiya* (News) reported, the largest finanacial support was assigned to governmental publications, particularly to *Rossiyskaya Gazeta* (The Russian Gazette) (Manaev 1992, p. 19).

It is not surprising, then, that initiatives to support media autonomy and to safeguard the democratic principle of plurality are originating in civil society. Polish print journalists, for example, decided to set up their own Free Press Fund to support the founding of newspapers and to assist those in danger of closing down. Prague saw the establishment of the similar Foundation in Support of Independent Media. Unfortunately, both funds are lacking the financial resources to make their policies feasible. Obviously, these are rare exceptions in the development of new press systems in East-Central Europe, which are likely to be dominated by an externally capitalized "free market" rather than become genuinely plural.

As in some Western countries, however, the fetish of market-based freedom of the press is severely contaminated by various forms of state intervention. Five "ideal types" of political censorship directly or indirectly performed by the state—"emergency powers," "armed secrecy," "lying," "state advertising," and "corporatism" (Keane 1991, pp. 95–109)—continue to exist in a number of countries. In March 1991 the Romanian government introduced in parliament a bill that called for heavy fines and prison terms for journalists found guilty of slandering public authority, the president of Romania, and the army—provisions typical for the old communist system (Stone and Marks 1991, p. 13). Although the bill was withdrawn ten days after its introduction because of strong dissent among journalists and other independent groups, the government still tends to control and censor the media. According to the Law on Radio and Television Broadcasting, which passed the Romanian parliament in May 1992, a journalist can be punished with up to seven years of imprisonment for "defamation of the Country or the Nation, instigation to war of aggression, national, racial, class, or religious hatred, incitation to discrimination, territorial separatism, or public violence" (Articles 2, 39).

In Croatia, the Agency for Economic Restructuring and Development, a government body that actually behaves as the "private owner of the whole country" (Maloča 1991, p. 9), has established managing boards in both the print and broadcast media to protect "social property." In fact, the main rationale of these boards is to compel the obedience of the media to state and governing party authorities or even to produce the collapse of "disobedient" media. The list of such government efforts began growing after the first, though not successful, attack on *Slobodna Dalmacija* (The Free Dalmatia; published in Split), the leading Croatian independent daily newspaper, with a circulation of 130,000, soon after the 1990 elections. "Public" demonstrations of "exasperated readers" organized in Split to overthrow the leading staff did not succeed. In August 1991, the editorial offices of a Slavonian local daily newspaper, *Glas Slavonije* (The Voice of Slavonia), were simply occupied by soldiers of the National Guard to "protect social capital" (Maloča 1991, p. 9; Vasle 1991, p. 3). After the 1992 elections and the victory of the Croatian Democratic Community (HDZ), the government finally succeeded in nationalizing *Slobodna Dalmacija*. The Agency for Economic Restructuring and Development simply nominated a new managing board "to protect social capital," but the new board was not able to displace journalists and editors mainly because—perhaps ironically—*Slobodna Dalmacija* was the only profitable daily in Croatia. However, it was strictly independent of the government in editorial matters and (thus) extremely popular, but it was considered by the government a "communist remnant." As a former leading ideologue of the new ruling party, Letica, argued, the nomination of a new governing board was an example of "state and party terrorism in the media" (Letica 1992, p. 36).

Even a more direct form of terrorism was used in 1990 in the province of Kosovo, where Serbian police occupied all the Albanian-language media and expelled all journalists and editors from their offices. The media were completely closed down and the equipment confiscated. Similar measures were applied to discipline "badly behaved" Hungarian-language media in the province of Vojvodina. A number of local radio programs in Hungarian were reduced or even eliminated. A more cunning trick was used to discipline journalists of one of the leading critical magazines in Croatia, *Danas* (Today), which had permanent clashes with the former socialist authorities as well. The managing board appointed by the agency simply decided to initiate bankruptcy proceedings to shut up critical voices. Although the bankruptcy idea failed, the agency was "successful" because a number of critical journalists left the magazine.

Finally, the decree issued by President Yeltsin after the anti-Gorbachev coup represents one of the most direct forms of the limitation of freedom of the press. By Yeltsin's decree, a number of newspapers (published by the Communist Party) that did not detach themselves explicitly from the coup d'état were banned. Another widely used form of suppressing newspapers' autonomy in Russia and some other postsocialist countries is an administrative distribution of print paper among publishers, which was also largely practiced by the former socialist regimes to control newspapers.

All these obvious violations of the principle of press freedom make clear that the slow implementation of market mechanisms does not yet guarantee the autonomy of the press from the state authorities. Often the new economic "laws" are little more than a camouflage for an indirect state interventionism and restrictions of freedom of the press.

Reregulation of Broadcasting

Whereas political changes have had immediate consequences for the press in the form of newly established private newspapers and/or privatization of formerly state-owned newspapers, discussions on the reregulation of broadcasting have not yet generated significant practical changes in terms of democratization. Again, there are important differences among countries, and the situation is rapidly changing everywhere. Nevertheless, at least some common tendencies are easily recognizable. In all postsocialist countries, new broadcast laws are at some stage of a generally slow legislative process. The traditional West European public service broadcasting is the most attractive model. But contrary to the West where questions about how well extreme marketplace models work, the cultural function of the public media, and "the slower-than-expected pace of new media development" at least partly reverse deregulation processes (Rowland and Tracey 1990, p. 9), commercialized "public service" broadcasting in East-Central Europe is unanimously advocated by new political elites for very pragmatic political and economic reasons—to maximize their power through the winning of support and to make public service profitable. Consequently, rapid staff changes and replacements of editors and directors are not followed by broader and more fundamental structural changes. As Wolfgang Kleinwächter (1992, p. 4) reported, for example, after the replacement of the director of Latvian Television immediately after the political (r)evolution, the new director got the order from the government to schedule two of the four TV cameras for the daily activities of the new prime minister and the president of the parliament. At the same time, there is an immense increase in foreign and entertainment programming, despite a shortage of foreign currency. National networks are trying to attract foreign investors and program suppliers. Commercially based private radio and TV stations are also emerging, but only to a limited degree.

The most prominent sign of (potential) changes in broadcasting in East-Central Europe is probably the decision to close down the East Bloc broadcasting organization (L'Organisation Internationale de Radiodiffusion et Télévision, or OIRT). In 1992, three OIRT members—the national broadcasting organizations of the CSFR, Poland, and Hungary—were admitted as associate members to the European Broadcast Union (EBU) formed by West European public broadcasters. Yugoslavia, the only socialist state included in the EBU, was never a full member country of the socialist OIRT. It was decided that the EBU would accept the former European OIRT members and the newly established independent countries individually in full membership, while those outside Europe would become associate members of the expanded EBU (Walker 1991, p. 42).

Legally, censorship has been abolished in all former socialist countries in East Europe but not yet in the state regulation of broadcasting. Although the new media laws are apparently more liberal than the old ones, they still have "loopholes that offer governments the opportunity to influence the media or define what constitutes 'responsible' journalism or determine who is a professional journalist and therefore eligible for accreditation" (Stone and Marks 1991, p. 5). The new governments do not hesitate to use regulations and strategies of the old authoritarian regimes to retain control of national broadcasting—either a direct control through appointments of boards, directors, and editors or a more indirect control through budgets and other economic instruments (e.g., state advertising). In some countries, such as the former Yugoslav republics, the existing broadcasting acts have been changed to (re)establish state control over radio and television organizations. Whereas in the former self-management system the right to participate in appointments to managing and editorial positions in the media was granted to media workers, the amended broadcasting acts in all former Yugoslav republics have abolished this workers' right and made it a privilege of either the executive government (e.g., in Serbia, Vojvodina, Kosovo, and Croatia) or the parliament (as in Slovenia and Bosnia-Herzegovina).

Similarly, limited changes were adopted in Poland and Hungary. Before parliamentary elections in 1989 in Poland, Solidarity demanded that national radio and television be controlled by society and that "our fundamental right be respected to express our views and opinions in our newspapers and in independent radio and television broadcasts" (Goban-Klas 1990, p. 51). But Solidarity changed its attitude after winning the elections and insisted on direct control by the government (Sawisz 1990, p. 399). In Hungary, the presidents of the national television and national radio are appointed by the president of the state on the recommendation of the prime minister; there is no board or similar kind of pluralistic managing institution in these companies. This reregulation violates the basic principle of independence and responsibility for content of program sources that protected "traditional" public service systems from state and party political interference (Blumler 1991, p. 12). Whereas in the "BBC model" the board of governors "functions as a buffer between government and the broadcasters, appointing the Director General, the chief executive of the BBC, and the Deputy Director General, and has a responsibility for overall policy" (Meech 1990, p. 233), reregulation of broadcasting in East-Central Europe has brought broadcasting companies again under direct state control both at national and local levels. National "public" radio and television stations are politically controlled by authorities because of their competencies in appointing directors, editors, and managing boards; local stations are either not yet legalized or impeded by the political partisanship of those local authorities entitled to issue transmission licenses to private companies.

Nevertheless, new broadcasting policies differ from the former ones in at least one important respect. After the democratic changes in 1989 and 1990, East-Central European countries became increasingly influenced by Western radio and TV broadcasting not only "theoretically" but also practically. Three types of Western broadcasting penetration into East Europe can be distinguished:

1. Direct broadcasting satellites facilitate direct penetration of East-Central Europe by Western television programming.
2. International media corporations and other private companies are trying to gain market share by supplying capital and broadcasting technologies.
3. Some Western governments (e.g., France) have made arrangements with the new political authorities in East-Central Europe whereby Western radio or television programs are broadcast on national broadcasting organizations that are still state controlled.

Two among the most successful West European corporations in East-Central Europe are the French television network La Sept and Radio France Internationale. Specifically, French corporations are interested mainly in exporting programs rather than capital. La Sept has negotiated retransmission agreements for its programs in Hungary, Poland, and the CSFR, and Radio France Internationale has propelled the creation of "bi-cultural radio" in Poland, the CSFR, and Romania (Semelin 1991, p. 17).

Contrary to contemporary deregulation tendencies in West Europe, the current restructuring of broadcasting systems in East-Central Europe is still aimed mainly at establishing a national, politicized, and quasi-commercial public broadcasting similar to those in West Europe during the last decades before the successful breakthrough of satellite and cable television. Although the public service model is advocated for broadcasting, in practice broadcast organizations are neither noncommercial nor independent of the state. In fact, public broadcasters heavily depend on the advertising income that became an important source of financing after the reduction of state subsidies.

At the same time, broadcasting is still, as it was before the political changes, largely subordinated to state authorities and party elites rather than to public accountability. Political parties, parliaments, or even governments usually act as the only representative of the public, thus having the right, for example, to appoint both the board and directors and editors of broadcasting companies. Although the new systems differ from the "socialist" one in that these functions were transferred from the Communist Party to the democratically elected state organs, this does not change the fundamental relation of the dependence of the media on external political authorities and the reduction of the public to a mass of passive consumers. Broadcasting administrative boards and other bodies or institutions established to control broadcasting activities are mainly—or even exclusively—composed of representatives of the government and political parties. Independent experts in arts, education, or industrial and economic life and representatives of different social and ethnic groups are usually not elected to these bodies. As Kleinwächter (1992, p. 5) critically remarked, "Although many politicians in these countries have studied among others the German experiences, the German 'Rundfunkrat,' which limits the membership of representatives of the government and the parliament to one third, was not taken as a 'model.'"

Even worse, practical decisionmaking often belongs to the sphere of *invisible power* of informal political elites, which are beyond democratic and jurisdictional control but may strongly influence the decisions formally taken by the government, parliament, managing boards in media organizations, or even editors and journalists. This *déjà vu* approach is hardly affected by the newest trends toward liberal deregulation of the media taking place in West Europe. A number of economic, political, cultural, and ideological factors cause such a "delay" in comparison to the West and at least partly explain why the regulation of broadcasting in East-Central Europe was—and will probably be in the near future—held up for a longer period of time.

1. Technological innovations resulting in new media opportunities in the developed world do not reach East Europe, with very few exceptions. The availability of services such as teletext, videotex, electronic mail, cable and satellite TV, and even telephones is still extremely low. There is an immense lack of modern communication and computer technology. With rare exceptions, there is

no market for electronic equipment, and its quality is not up to Western standards. An information society is much more a dream—or even a nightmare—than an emerging reality in East Europe (Splichal, 1990b).

2. The present political scene is highly ideologized. Contrary to West Europe, where a rather stable balance of power among political parties exists, the new governments in East Europe are burdened with anticommunism and antibolshevism and with a fear of losing power. In particular, they consider the most influential national media as the footing of the former power elites, and they justify the authoritative control of, and penetration into, the media in terms of "democratization." Although censorship has been generally abolished and new democratic press laws have been adopted, the interference of governments in the media continues informally (e.g., discrimination in state subsidies, nomination of political leaders for directors and editors, persecution of journalists for their political beliefs) and, in the case of broadcasting, formally through (non)allocation of frequencies.

3. The nationalist policies of the new governments and parties in power may get much benefit from the state-owned broadcasting (particularly television) monopoly in mobilizing the population in their favor. At the same time, the predominantly national media policy, concerned mainly with ideological and cultural questions, is itself in opposition to the commercially oriented supranational policy developing particularly within the European Community (EC) countries and supporting current changes toward deregulation.

4. All media are faced with financial problems, particularly a lack of advertising revenues. In broadcasting, a total commercialization that would imply the suppression of license fees is not (yet) feasible. Advertising income is limited, partly because of the absence of *a market economy* and particularly because of the general underdevelopment of the region's economies, which therefore cannot advertise their products and services. For the same reason, "the advertisers who support satellite channels beaming from Astra, with its coverage of the whole continent, will rarely be interested in reception there if it costs anything" (Baker 1991, p. 18). Generally, the commercial potentials of broadcasting in East-Central Europe are still very modest.

5. A lack of the indigenous private capital needed to privatize the existing media or invest in new private media makes "cultural" arguments against privatization even more convincing. It is largely believed that national interests and national culture might be endangered by foreign investments and internationalization of programming without strict national (i.e., government) control. The broadcasting sector is particularly sensitive because it deals directly with questions of cultural identity. Not only are private media unable to challenge "the cultural and political mainstream" because they have to maximize their audiences to survive economically; even more important, private broadcasters are also not interested in program production of their own and rely instead on imports (Sepstrup 1989, p. 35).

6. In all former socialist countries, changes in media laws have been initiated, but the legislative process is slow and controversial. Paradoxically, the legal vacuum caused by rapid political changes makes the proclaimed politics of economic liberalization and deregulation even more complicated, particularly in the media sphere. Although the new governments favor privatization, they hesitate to legally transform the formerly state- or socially owned media into privately owned enterprises. In addition to the uncertainty regarding privatization and regulation, an absence of competent commercial and legal personnel makes the introduction of foreign capital into East European markets very difficult. Meanwhile, because an appropriate legal framework does not exist, privatization often implies a mere stealing of the former public property.

7. Finally, as in West Europe (McQuail and the Euromedia Research Group, 1990), different ideological actors, such as public broadcasting bodies, established cultural institutions, and different (but not necessarily oppositional) political parties, are opposing media commercialization and internationalization. Recently, for example, Jan Stern, editor in chief of the Czech weekly *Forum,* made clear that a foreign investor such as Rupert Murdoch would not be acceptable because this would imply that the former political dictate was being replaced by another, commercial one (*Mass Media,* 1990b).

No one of these factors could be considered the dominant one in all East-Central Europe. Even from a Western perspective, as Dennis and Heuvel (1990, p. 3) observed, "in this crazy-quilt media system it is important to recognize that there are differences and variations between and among the several countries." For example, there are significant differences between Poland or Hungary and other countries. Poland and Hungary had comparatively long democratic traditions before World War II; the process of postwar democratization started in the 1950s in Hungary and in the 1980s in Poland, though not successfully. Both countries are nation states similar to those in West Europe and are not burdened by nationalistic conflicts; as a consequence, they are considered relatively safe for foreign investments. They are both opening the door for commercial newspapers, radio, and TV stations, which are not under the control of state authorities. It is not surprising, then, that Hungary and Poland are attracting the greatest interest among foreign investors. As in West Europe, large transnational media companies (e.g., Murdoch, Maxwell, Berlusconi, Springer, Bertelsmann) try to enter the field with "denationalized" contents, programming, and advertising.

Privatization of broadcasting, which followed the establishment of the first independent radio station, Radio Solidarity, in Warsaw in 1989, took the fastest course in Poland. The process is controversial, however, mainly because of the diverse interests of political groupings. The former Polish Radio and Television remained essentially unchanged as a state-owned monopoly until spring 1993. Solidarity took control of the management of the corporation, as has happened with the new governments in other East-Central European countries; the two leading factions of Solidarity, ROAD and the Center Alliance, "have inherited the mindset of the Communists" and try to influence television to their own advantage (Dennis and Heuvel 1990, p. 24). One consequence of the controversies between different political parties was a moratorium on the allocation of radio and television frequencies, which was adopted in July 1991. This decision significantly slowed down the development of the private broadcasting sector.

The broadcasting bill has been postponed several times, so that until December 1992 the legal status of broadcasting was essentially the same as that defined by the 1960 Broadcasting Act. This indicates how complicated the changes are. The Mazowiecki government did not get parliamentary support for its draft of the broadcasting law. In October 1991, under the Bielecki government, the law was adopted by parliament, but President Lech Walesa vetoed it, and parliament approved his veto in January 1992. A new version drafted by the Olszewski government in 1992 did not get a majority in parliament. Both versions attempted to provide the government with considerable authority over the national broadcasting system. However, several other acts adopted by parliament modified the situation: Censorship was abolished in April 1990, and the amended Press Law (originally adopted in 1984) regulated, among other things, citizens' right to reply and media access to information from public institutions. Finally, both houses of parliament adopted the new Broadcasting Act in December 1992.

At that time, over 600 applications to set up commercial radio and over two hundred applications for television licenses had been filed with the Ministry of Telecommunications, including nine applications for national television networks. Since no institution was empowered to award broadcasting licenses (only three private radio stations and one private television station were given experimental licenses), a number of private stations started to operate illegally. The first private radio station, Radio Małopolska-Fun, a joint venture of a Polish corporation and the Fun Radio network owned by French media conglomerate Hersant, went on the air in Kraców in February 1990. It transmits programming beamed from France via satellite. Soon it was followed by another station, Aleks, established in Zakopane, and Solidarita Mazowsze and ZET in Warsaw. In Wrocław, the first private TV station, Eho TV, was established by eight former employees of national television in February 1990. It broadcasts mainly pirated Western satellite programs such as "Film Net," "Eurosport," "Sky News," and "Veronique 4." By the end of 1992, six more private television stations had begun illegal operation: Top Canal and Independent Television in Warsaw, ES in Poznan, More in Szczecin, Independent Television in Lublin, and TELE–24 in Lodz. Some of them were established in cooperation with foreign (mainly Italian) capital. Private stations recently formed the Federation of Private Radio and Television Stations.

The only legal exception from the moratorium on frequencies' allocation is for the Polish Catholic Church, which has, according to the Catholic Church Act of 1989, a special role and privileges in broadcasting. The Church has the right to obtain broadcasting frequencies and licenses on a priority basis. Although the parliament introduced a moratorium on the allocation of broadcast frequencies, eighteen radio stations around Poland are legally operated by the Church. The Church also asked for licenses to operate two national television networks. In addition, Article 21 of the Broadcasting Act determines the responsibility of Polish public radio and television to "respect the Christian system of values that adopts as the basis the universal principles of ethics."

The new broadcasting bill that finally passed parliament in December 1992 envisages the establishment of a national regulatory agency for all broadcasting—the National Broadcasting Council. The council consists of nine members, three appointed by the president of the state, four by the Diet, and two by the Senate. The president of the republic appoints the chairman of the council. Membership in the council is incompatible with membership in a political party or a civil-servant position. The council's main tasks are to grant licenses to broadcasters and cable distributors, to supervise their activities, to determine license fees and fees for granting licenses, and to advise state authorities in matters of broadcasting (see Table 2.2).

On the basis of the Broadcasting Act, the former Polish Radio and Television was split into two state-owned companies—Polish Radio Ltd. and Polish

TABLE 2.2 Composition and Tasks of Broadcasting Councils in Poland, the Czech Republic, Slovakia, and Romania

	Poland[a]	Czech Republic[b] and Slovakia	Romania[c]
Members of the councils are appointed by			
Parliament	+	+	+
Government	−	−	+
President of the republic	+	−	+
Tasks/responsibilities of the councils			
National communication policy	+	+	+
Issuing broadcasting licenses	+	+	+
Issuing cable licenses	+	+	+
Determining license fees	+	−	−
Fees for broadcasters and cable operators	+	+	−
Imposition of fines	+	+	+
Organization of research	+	−	−
Advice to the state	+	−	−
Appointment of directors of public radio and TV	+	−	−

[a]Polish Broadcasting Act, December 1992.

[b]Law on the Operation of Radio and Television in the CSFR, October 1991. After the split of the former federation (December 31, 1992), the provisions of the law remained in force in both new independent states.

[c]Law on Radio and Television Broadcasting, May 1992.

Television Ltd.—both operating under the direction of a board of directors (appointed by the National Broadcasting Council) and controlled by a board of management (appointed by the board of directors). Polish Television operates two national television channels and Polish Radio operates four principal national radio stations, which all take advertising. In addition to a production center in Warsaw, there are eight regional television studios managed by the central authorities; for several hours a day they broadcast their own programs, which are financed almost exclusively by advertising. All seventeen regional stations of Polish Radio broadcast twenty-four hours a day. Regional television stations are to be turned into separate state-owned companies as local subsidiaries of Polish Television Ltd. The concept of granting autonomy to regional TV stations and transforming the second national TV channel into a commercially based network of regional stations was not accepted by parliament. Although parliament rejected the idea of privatization after two years of debate, primarily because a national channel was considered too expensive and threatening to public television, political considerations clearly also played an important role: If local politicians could get effective control over local "public" TV stations, the eight local stations could distribute their particular kind of programming nationwide.

Although privatization of the second national television channel was finally rejected, over one hundred private companies were licensed to establish cable television systems. A private radio station based in Kraców offered its program on satellite (Astra 1A), and another private company launched a satellite television channel Polsat, showing mainly films and entertainment (Jakubowicz 1993b, p. 6)

Generally, the Polish authorities hesitate to accept foreign investment without achieving a satisfactory price: They do not want to repeat the "Hungarian mistakes." They did not want to sell broadcasting time on national TV to Berlusconi and Murdoch, but the government seriously discussed privatization of the second national TV channel: The British European Communication Industries was interested in becoming the owner of 30 percent of the shares (*Mass Media* 1990a, p. 24). In addition, Polish Television signed a contract with the U.S. company Conduit International Film, which supplies programming for the second channel. The main reason for at least some support for privatization is that eight regional stations are in financial trouble. However, the idea of privatization of national television is meeting strong opposition, although private (foreign) investments in cable systems are regarded as less dangerous. David Chase, owner of Chase Enterprises, which seems to be the only U.S. corporation investing significantly in East Europe, signed a joint-venture agreement with the Polish government to construct a cable system with a 70 percent share in ownership (Dennis and Heuvel 1990, p. 15).

After 1989, when the Hungarian Law on Broadcasting was drafted (the fourth draft was presented to parliament in May 1992), limited changes occurred in the

Hungarian broadcasting system, although the first Hungarian commercial radio station, Radio Danube, had begun operating in the German language as early as the mid-1980s. Another foreign-language radio station is Radio Bridge, which mainly relies on the programming of *Voice of America* and was founded with Swedish and Canadian capital; it is mainly aimed at the Hungarian business community. The most popular programs are transmitted by Kalipszo Radio (Radio Calypso), a twenty-four-hour commercial FM radio station in Budapest. State-owned radio broadcasts via three national channels, Kossuth, Petoefi, and Bartok, and six regional stations.

The former license system for the press as well as for radio and TV was abolished in January 1990, and it is now formally possible for any legal entity or private person to establish either a newspaper, radio station, or TV station. Close to sixty radio and fifty television license concessions were requested in 1990 (*Mass Media* 1990a, p. 20), a number of which have been sought by foreign investors. However, after the liberalization introduced with the amended Press Law, the government decided to impose a moratorium on the allocation of broadcasting frequencies. Only two commercial TV stations succeeded in getting frequency allocation prior to the moratorium.

Nap TV (Sun TV), a privately owned commercial station connected with Murdoch, who is one of the owners of the newspaper *Mai Nap,* was the first independent commercial television channel that, in August 1989, started to broadcast news and magazine programs for a short transmission period (some three hours daily) in the early morning hours on the state-owned MTV (Hungarian Television) Channel One (Szekfu and Valko 1990, p. 6). It was founded by the Ribbon Ltd. publisher (58 percent of founding capital), the afternoon tabloid *Mai Nap* (14 percent), the Hungarian news agency MTI (14 percent), and the film and video company MOVI (14 percent). However, MTV canceled the agreement in 1991 when it started its own morning program, so that Nap TV went off the air for a couple of weeks. Another commercial TV station that managed to get registered before the moratorium was Sio TV, owned by the municipal council of the town Siofok, which is based in the holiday region of Lake Balaton. It mainly broadcasts entertainment programs in German and Hungarian during evening and night hours in the summer, primarily for German-speaking tourists.

In spite of commercial broadcasting initiatives, MTV and Hungarian Radio (MR) still have a total monopoly of the airwaves. MTV operates two national channels (which are relatively independent of each other in terms of programming and management) and two regional stations, and MR has three national programs. Daily news bulletins on the first TV channel are edited by a new progovernment newscast department, while some of the former editors and journalists produce the ten o'clock news ("Evening Balance") on the second channel. A clearly political division between the two channels resembles the Radiotelevisione Italiana (RAI; Italian public broadcasting system) model in

Italy, where Christian Democrats control RAI Uno; Socialists, RAI Due; and the former communists, RAI Tre.

Both MTV and MR are directly controlled by the government. As elsewhere in East-Central Europe, the government is trying to retain control over national broadcasting. In September 1991 two leading "Hungarian" daily newspapers— *Népszabadság* (The People's Freedom; Bertelsmann) and *Magyar Hírlap* (Maxwell)—released the minutes of a closed meeting of the parliamentary fraction of the MDF, held on August 24, 1991. MDF leader Imre Konya pleaded for radical changes in the government media policy to "transform radio and television." According to Konya, there is no need "to continue to avoid confrontations in order to create a favorable image of our country" because Western countries have largely acknowledged the changes in Hungary toward "liberalism, democracy, freedom of the press, human rights, and market economy." Thus, the time has come for "radical transformation of political attitudes and ideas on the Hungarian radio and television" (*Delo*, 1991).

Like the press, Hungarian national TV is in severe financial difficulties. Allegedly, it has been under pressure to cut back to only one channel and to raise more money from advertisements (Mytton 1991, p. 4). As in Poland, a new broadcast law with a Federal Communications Commission–type organization to regulate both public and private broadcasting was drafted, but it is not likely to be enacted in the near future in light of severe controversies among different political parties and groups. Nevertheless, the majority agree that Hungarian Radio and TV should remain state-owned companies. A special body is envisaged to allocate frequencies and licenses to all private and public broadcasters.

A restrictive broadcasting policy is apparent in the development of cable systems, too. More than sixty privately owned local cable systems exist in Hungary, but the majority of them transmit no more than two or three hours of "homemade" programs in a *week*. Usually a cable "system" means a network of up to one hundred households that may receive up to twelve TV programs (two Hungarian and ten retransmitted from satellites). To prevent the establishment of a third (privately owned) national channel, the government does not allow these local cable systems to connect. Nevertheless, an American-Hungarian joint venture, led by Chase Enterprises, was formed in the beginning of 1990 with the goal of wiring local cable systems into a national system similar to that in Poland (Dennis and Heuvel 1990, p. 56).

In several East-Central European countries, the pace of broadcasting reforms is much slower than in Poland and Hungary either because of slower political changes (as in Romania and Bulgaria) or because of nationalist tensions that support a paternalistic or even authoritarian media system (e.g., in Serbia and several republics in the former Soviet Union). Whereas the CSFR, which was one of the last East-Central European countries to reinitiate political liberalization in the 1980s, succeeded in creating democratic forms out of the disintegration of the former federal state, Yugoslavia, with the longest postwar tradition of democratic restructuring of society, lost its democratic way in violent nationalist clashes and civil war.

Apart from that, democratic revolutions against the "proletarian dictatorship" in the former Yugoslavia and the former CSFR did not overthrow all paternalistic or even authoritarian modes of governing. In the former CSFR, for example, the new governing coalition strove to replace the president of the national parliament, the late Alexander Dubček, who was the leading figure in the Prague Spring in 1968. The new parliament "democratically" decided that former state and party functionaries had no right to be elected or appointed in the new, postsocialist era. In the Republic of Slovenia, the three conservative parties in the governing coalition were trying to replace the more liberal ministers from other parties in the coalition. The most bizarre case occurred in April 1991 when the former minister of information, a journalist, was replaced by the deputy minister of defense. Newspapers cynically commented on this change in the Slovenian government "as natural due to the fact that there is a media war in Yugoslavia" (Belič 1991). In the Republic of Croatia, the new presidential system often reminds one much more of the former gerontocratic system than of a true democracy.

After the 1989 velvet revolution, a completely new leadership was appointed for the national broadcasting organization in the former CSFR. The federal broadcasting law, which was adopted in October 1991, broke down the monopoly of state radio and television and formally introduced a dual system of broadcasting. However, the law failed to restructure essentially the (former) federal radio and television stations, as well as the new national—Czech and Slovak—public radio and television companies. Contrary to the principles of the dual system developed in West Europe, the companies and stations in the former CSFR continued to operate as state-run institutions. Some significant changes appeared in the Czech system after the split with Slovakia on December 31, 1992, and the termination of the federal radio and television companies determined by the Broadcasting Liquidation Law. The federal law on broadcasting remained in force in both new states, with the exception of the provisions related to the Czech and Slovak Federation and its parliament, the federal broadcasting system, and the federal broadcasting council.

Although the state broadcast monopoly has been officially abandoned, only limited changes have been introduced in television. In April 1991, the first private station, NTV (Nezavisla Televize—Independent Television), went on the air in Prague, but after a few weeks it ceased to transmit because of immense financial difficulties. Cable TV and satellite delivery were not regulated (nor are they now in two separate states—the Czech Republic and Slovakia), but all these distribution systems without their own production facilities operate on a very limited scale. The former centralized broadcast system was partly decentralized during the period of the peaceful dissolution of the former federal state. In addition to the first television channel broadcasting the "federal program"

(CST or F 1), two national public programs (Czech and Slovak) were broadcast on the second TV channel, and an international commercial program, OK 3, consisting mainly of West European entertainment programs, was broadcast on the third channel, although this was available in only one-third of the former federation. A number of potential foreign investors (CNN, Berlusconi, Maxwell, and Murdoch) expressed their interests in this channel, and so did the new national association of independent TV broadcasters that forced the government to end the state monopoly.

The Czech amendments to the former federal broadcasting law limit the broadcasting of Czech Public Television (CPTV) to only one channel. The OK 3 channel is temporarily operated by CPTV until the broadcasting council rewards a license to a private operator, which is expected to happen after 1995. The second channel has been privatized already: a twelve-year license was granted to Central European Television for the 21st Century (CET 21)—a joint venture established by several Czech banks and the Central European Development Corporation, a U.S.-Canadian firm—that is obliged to be on the air by the beginning of 1994.

According to the federal broadcasting law, radio was also no longer a state monopoly. In addition to the popular federal program transmitted by Czechoslovak Radio, national Czech Radio (CR), based in Prague, and Slovak Radio (SR), based in Bratislava, transmitted three kinds of programs: (1) news and popular music, (2) regional programs (a network of seven stations in the Czech Republic and three stations in Slovakia), and (3) arts and culture. Fifteen new radio stations, some of them in cooperation with foreign partners, have been created since the velvet revolution, but there were still more than eighty radio and fifty television license applications pending at the time of the dissolution of the country. As Jan Carnogursky, the vice president of the Slovak government stated, the state will hold back granting private broadcasting licenses for a time to "facilitate recovery in the state sector" (Walker 1991, p. 40). In 1992, among the total of twenty-four radio stations in the country, seventeen were state owned, three were in joint public and private ownership, and four were entirely privately owned (Evropa 2, Radio 1, Radio Country, and Radio Plus—all in Prague). Radio 1 was the most interesting not only because of its popularity among listeners but also because of its "history." It had been established illegally as Radio Stalin in 1990: illegally, because private radio stations were not yet allowed at that time, and as Radio Stalin, because the station was located under the pedestal of the removed Stalin monument in Prague. The provocative program was on the air for only a week because the police discovered and confiscated transmitting facilities. In February 1991, the station was reestablished as Radio Ultra—illegally again and for a short period of time. Finally, the station was legalized as Radio 1, although the broadcast law was still in preparation.

A number of the applications for radio and television licenses in the former

CSFR are of foreign origin—for example, CNN, NCL, and ICT from the United States; Berlusconi's Fininvest from Italy; and the Voice of America. Global Cable Systems from Canada and Heartland Ventures from the United States are engaged in cable television (Walker 1991, p. 38). Some foreign radio corporations (Radio Free Europe, BBC, and Radio France Internationale) were granted special permissions by the federal government for terrestrial (re)transmission in the CSFR in Czech and foreign languages. In Bratislava, SR in cooperation with the Austrian firm Drehscheibe established a commercial radio station (Radio CD International) that transmits its German-language program toward neighboring Austria, where no local or commercial stations were allowed before July 1993. However, the proposal to allow ethnic minorities (especially Hungarians) to broadcast in their own languages was blocked in the federal parliament. Although ethnic tensions are not as strident as those in the former Yugoslavia and the former Soviet Union, they obviously play an important role in the licensing of independent stations.

The principle of decentralization did not apply to the management of the federal, Czech, and Slovak radio and television stations. In fact, the federal and Czech stations were not different entities; they were fused under the same roof with Czechoslovak Television and Czechoslovak Radio. The director general was appointed by the government (since the revolution, three directors have been dismissed), and all other directors and editors were appointed by the director general. Journalists were often exposed to pressures "from above" in such a hierarchical organization. The new federal broadcast law adopted in October 1991 established the Federal Broadcasting Council, which consisted of representatives of parliamentary parties: three elected by the federal parliament, three by the Czech parliament, and three by the Slovak parliament. (Since the split of the CSFR, all nine members of the new Czech council are elected by the Czech parliament, and the nine members of the new Slovak council by the Slovak parliament.) Although there was a tendency to establish a kind of public service radio and television, it was limited to the representation of parliamentary political parties in the governing bodies. The debate about political (or societal) control over radio and, particularly, television that was going on in the CSFR, and now continues in the two succeeding independent states, exemplifies the key arguments in the debate all around East-Central Europe.

> Some argue that the Parliament is Czechoslovakia's most representative body and that a representative oversight board ought to be composed of individuals whose political affiliations are roughly proportionate to those that exist in the Parliament. But others argue that Civic Forum, with its Slovak equivalent, the Public Against Violence, has an absolute majority in Parliament, and giving it the same majority in the television oversight board would in effect give the governing party control of Czechoslovak television. The interests of minority parties and groups could well be overlooked. (Dennis and Heuvel 1990, p. 36)

An important departure from the largely paternalistic broadcast model was represented by the endeavor to establish "independent production units" to cooperate with Czechoslovak Television (CST). The idea was actually borrowed from the British Channel 4 model and aimed at separating broadcasting and program production. However, contrary to that model, foreign producers, public producers in the CSFR, and private producers were not expected to produce programs to commission. Rather, the "center for cooperation with external producers" established within Czechoslovak Television was a kind of "free market" for independent producers to supply their programs. As a result, less than 1 percent of the total CST (both Czech and federal) programming originated from independent producers in 1991, including some propaganda programs for the ruling party.

Even before the federal council for radio and television was established, a form of governmental commission started to grant licenses to commercial private radio stations without any legislative background. Until the end of 1992, eight licenses were granted to applicants from Prague and one license to an applicant from elsewhere. After the split of the federal state, this "illegal" task was performed by the Czech Ministry of Culture (in the Czech Republic only), which issued twenty-seven licenses, twenty-two of them to applicants not from the capital. This is now causing severe difficulties, which are mainly related to attempts by private owners of local stations to extend their activities beyond the local area—a tendency well known from the beginnings of "local" television in Italy. Curiously enough, after the Council of the Czech Republic for Radio and Television Broadcast finally was established to regulate broadcasting and, particularly, to grant licenses for broadcasting, there were no frequencies left to be licensed.

A situation similar to that in Poland has occurred in several Yugoslav republics, where some new frequencies for private local TV broadcasters were allocated in the year after the democratic elections (Channel A in Ljubljana, Slovenia; two private TV stations in Sarajevo, Bosnia-Herzegovina; and Marjan Television in Split, Croatia), but there were numerous applicants waiting for government concessions. Channel A, the first independent television in the former Yugoslavia, was established as a joint-stock company by 150 shareholders in 1989 but did not start to broadcast its mainly movie programming before May 1991. Its main owner is a private entrepreneur, B. Polič, with 63 percent of founding capital; apart from him, only Television Slovenia has a significant share (10 percent). Channel A began to transmit for a short period (some three hours daily, which was soon doubled) in prime time on its own channel, but not with its own transmission facilities; rather, it has a contract with Radio and Television Slovenia. In Serbia, two commercial local TV stations went on the air in Belgrade. One of them, Politika Television, was founded by Politika. The other one is Nezavisna Televizija—NTV, an independent TV company founded by the local radio station Studio B. However, these new stations were not allowed to become members of the Yugoslav Radio and Television Association (JRT). Contrary to broadcasting, cable TV is not subject to licensing, but because of high installation costs, it does not seem to be very attractive for either private or public investors, although there are some successful experiments.

A number of political (and even military) confrontations in the former Yugoslavia are related to the fact that "communism is not necessarily out, nor democracy in," as Stone and Marks observed. Even in those parts of the former Yugoslavia where communist parties were voted out of government, "Communist-like means of media control survive and thrive in the minds of some of the new ruling parties" (Stone and Marks 1991, p. 24). Paternalistic media policies in all republics and divergent political interests are the key reasons frustrating potential private broadcasters in their plans. In the old Yugoslav system, privatization of broadcasting was further complicated by the parallel existence of federal and republic communications regulations by which broadcast companies were required to obtain frequency allocation from the federal authorities and transmitting license from their respective republic. (The same kind of parallel regulation existed in the CSFR until its split on January 1, 1993.)

New national authorities hesitate to adopt new regulations. Expectations that the period after the velvet revolutions would bring a further blossoming of democracy in the media were premature. In 1990, the new noncommunist ruling coalition in Slovenia tried primarily to establish as strong an influence as possible over the media and to subject them to party will. In substantiating the legal changes on Radio and Television (RTV) Slovenia in December 1990, the government stated in its proposal to the parliament that a new law was necessary to change "the present structure of the Assembly of Radio and Television Slovenia in favor of the representatives of the so-called civil society (the public)." This was certainly a desirable idea because its realization would strengthen the autonomy of the media and the influence of the public. However, the "realization" of this idea in the law was in a complete contradiction with any possible understanding of civil society because the "representatives of the public" to the council of Radio and Television Slovenia were chosen by parliament from among prominent leaders of political parties (including members of parliament). After the 1992 parliamentary elections, however, the new governmental coalition consisting of Christian democrats, liberal democrats, and former Communists proposed amendments to the law on Radio and Television Slovenia to exclude party elites from the council and to open it to representatives of civil society.

Similarly to the early "revolutionary" changes in Slovenia, in 1991 the new parliament of Bosnia-Herzegovina changed the 1989 Broadcasting Law, which, in accordance with the principles of self-management, had given workers the right to manage the company, including appointments to managing and editorial position. The new ethnic parties decided in parliament to split Radiotelevision Sarajevo among the three—Serbian, Croatian, and Muslim—parties. Surprisingly enough, the supreme court passed judgment in favor of the journalist of the RTV station who objected to the amendments. Nevertheless, ethnic pressures on the station continued until the ethnic war and the demolition of broadcasting facilities. In Croatia, the national parliament adopted a new law on the media in April 1992, but it does not apply to broadcast media, which are still regulated by the former "socialist" law and totally controlled by the new anticommunist government. Finally, everywhere in the former Yugoslavia, as in other postsocialist countries, existing transmission facilities are totally controlled by national television stations, which may not release a part of the facilities to potential competitors, as was the case with Euro 3 TV in Slovenia in 1991. In 1992, Television Slovenia decided to establish a "third national channel" in cooperation with a number of privately owned local companies. According to the contract, local companies established local TV stations as joint ventures with Television Slovenia (with 49 percent of the shares) and broadcast their programs only locally. However, the new government that came to power after the 1992 parliamentary elections eliminated the moratorium on frequencies to private radio and TV stations and a governmental commission started to grant licenses without any legislative background, as was also the case in the Czech Republic.

In addition to six national radio and TV stations having operated in the former Yugoslav republics, the two stations of the autonomous provinces of Kosovo and Vojvodina in Serbia, and radio and television stations in Koper/Capodistria in Slovenia (which broadcast in Italian language), a federal television news program "YUTEL" (Yugoslav Television) was founded in 1990 by the federal government. It main aim was to broadcast news alternative to the nationalistically biased programs produced by the national TV stations in different republics. However, this two-hour program produced in Sarajevo could be broadcast, not on separate (new) frequencies, but as part of the already existing national programs—if the national stations were willing to sell "their" program time. In most of the republics, however, this program was not welcome to the new governments.

Contrary to the programs of national television stations, "YUTEL" was financed not by license fees but by advertisements and federal government support. Except for Bosnia-Herzegovina, where the "YUTEL" studio was located, no other republic carried the program at its inception. It never succeeded in penetrating Serbian Television (Belgrade), and after having been present for a few months on Croatian Television (Zagreb), "YUTEL" was abrogated by the Croation authorities because, as the former Croation minister of information asserted, "it excites suspicion that the news program of Croation Television is not objective, not complete, and closed for information from certain parts of the country" (Krstulovič 1991). In other republics, "YUTEL" was usually transmitted after midnight on second channels.

The case of "YUTEL" clearly shows how freedom of the press as one of the fundamental democratic liberties can be easily threatened by the nation-state to "protect" national sovereignty and national security—as happens in the West, where different forms of "state interference in the process of publicly defining and circulating opinions . . . warrant critical attention" (Keane 1991, p. 95).[3] Facing up to this situation, the Parliament of Yugoslav Journalists declared that journalists should, in accordance with their professional and ethical norms, refuse to obey the initiators of the "media war" and disengage from spreading hostility and battles and that the "political blockade of 'YUTEL' should stop and its transmission be permitted in Serbia under the same conditions as in other Yugoslav republics" (Vogel 1991, p. 238). However, these protests against "military liberalization," which set national security above any limitation on the sovereign power of the state, were in vain. A few months later, when the Serbian army invaded Bosnia-Herzegovina and heavily bombarded Sarajevo, broadcasting facilities were among the first "victims" of the war, and "YUTEL" was shut down.

Finally, Bulgaria, Romania, Albania, and the eastern Yugoslav republics (Serbia and Montenegro) seem to have the longest way to go economically and politically before they can establish genuinely democratic media systems. In all these countries broadcast media are still totally state controlled. In Albania and Bulgaria, private broadcasting companies are de facto not allowed, and even those (public service) organizations that are entitled to apply for radio frequencies have to surmount huge bureaucratic and political barriers. Although they are partly based on an extremely underdeveloped telecommunications infrastructure, they can certainly not be justified on these grounds.

Romania is closer to the development of a dual system, at least in legal terms, although the Iliescu government drafted a very restrictive broadcast law that, after long discussion, was adopted by parliament in the spring of 1992. The law established the National Council of Radio and Television as the main "regulatory" body, with broad competencies in terms of appointments and control over content. It consists of eleven members delegated by the government (three members), by the president (two members), and by the two chambers of parliament (three members each). The national radio and television stations are officially independent, but they are under tight government control. To mention just one example: The director general of Romanian Radio and Television is appointed by the president of the state. Generally, restrictions to broadcasting and cablecasting are still mainly political, whereas cultural and commercial regulations are still missing. For example, there is no protection of national programming as in other European countries, no limitation to cross-ownership, advertising time, and advertised products (which may include alcohol and tobacco).

During the Ceaușescu regime, there was only one TV channel, which broadcast three to four hours of programming per day. The second national channel, established in February 1990, reaches no more than 20 percent of the population. Apart from one national radio station, the state-owned Radio Bucharest, there are several local stations that provide coverage of larger towns. Potential private broadcasters are faced with immense "technical" problems because all transmitters and repeaters are state owned. As a consequence, private media companies hesitate to enter these markets. A number of private initiatives are limited to "participation" in the existing state-controlled television channels: Several local TV companies (twelve by the end of 1992) may broadcast their programs locally on the first or second national channel in late evening hours after the "official" programs. They started with an average one-hour program a day and have reached as much as thirty-two hours a week by the autumn of 1992. However, only five of them were granted licenses by the National Audio Visual Council that was established on the basis of the 1992 broadcasting law. The only major cities where private stations received licenses were Iasi and Bucharest, whereas the already operating private stations in Timisoara, Oradea, Brasov, and Constanza were not given licenses—obviously for political reasons. The Association of Local Private Television Stations in Romania (UNTELPRO) is not (politically) influential enough to challenge the politically biased decisions of the members of the council who are expected, according to the law, not to be "members of political parties or other political groupings" or to have "public or private functions, except the academic ones in university education" (Article 28 of the Law on Radio and Television). Cable TV operators are in a relatively better position in relation to the council, as illustrated by the fact that thirty-six received licenses and "only" thirty-two did not receive them.

For two main reasons—economic underdevelopment and nationalist clashes—the new Commonwealth of Independent States is in the most unfavorable position, although the CIS's political and military importance in international relations and immense (potential) market give rise to an inflow of international capital, particularly in Russia. The Soviet media law adopted in June 1990 and the replacement of the former USSR State Committee for Radio and Television Broadcasting (Gosteleradio) by the All-Union State TV and Radio Broadcasting Company have not introduced radical changes in the Soviet media practice.

The most important departure from the previous system is represented by partial decentralization. In a number of former Soviet republics, the governments formed their own radio and TV stations to break the monopoly of the national All-Union channel controlled by the central government and funded through its budget. Apart from that, regulatory changes opened the way to some independent stations established on commercial bases, but in cooperation with Gosteleradio because this is the only way for a commercial station to get a frequency from the Ministry of Communications (Androunas 1991, p. 199). In 1988 the first cable sets appeared in some Moscow districts, and some independent cable networks, such as NIKA-TV, were formed. By 1990 some five hundred cable systems with more than 1.5 million subscribers in two hundred cities were in operation (Muratov 1991, pp. 177, 181). However, the army-backed attempted coup d'état in August 1991 easily suspended all democratic legal changes overnight, though, fortunately, only for a short period of time. The August coup in Moscow, or the Bloody Sunday in January 1991 in Vilnius—where several people died defending a republican television station against Red Army troops—

clearly show that democratic procedures have a long and thorny road to travel before they become an intrinsic value in these societies and that the struggle for control over the former Soviet media, particularly television, will continue. The institutional disintegration of the Soviet Union formally accorded by the agreement in Alma Ata in December 1991 and the establishment of the CIS does not guarantee that similar attempts could not take place in the future.

Similarly, Bulgaria and Romania are attempting to introduce one or another limited form of commercialization. The second channel of Romanian Television was sold to the British company Atlantic Television Ltd., which bought 80 percent of the shares, while the remaining 20 percent remained with national TV. Another form of private-public partnership in television is the abovementioned "participation" of local Romanian TV producers in the national network. Six commercially oriented independent radio stations and the first independent cultural television station, Antenna Independenta TV, which was established by students of the Institute of Dramatic and Film Arts and the Faculty of Film and Television, began to operate recently. They have established the National Federation of Independent Radio and Television in Romania. In Bulgaria, the popular "Every Sunday" commercial program on the state-owned Bulgarian Television went on the air. In addition to the first (information and entertainment) and second (educational) national channels operated by state-owned Bulgarian Television, a third channel is planned, with the backing of foreign companies that will also provide programming (e.g., Viacom International and Maxwell as joint owners of MTV Europe and some other foreign broadcast organizations, such as CNN, Worldnet, and the Voice of America).

Generally, broadcast companies in East-Central Europe are still under strong government control. Efforts to democratize national media systems are limited by severe political, technological, and financial restrictions, which, however, often stimulate a "wild privatization." Western media moguls see great possibilities in the "redefinition" and privatization of the media in postsocialist countries because these moguls can easily compete with national actors lacking in capital. As the editor of a Slovenian daily newspaper stated, "Germans or Austrians would buy it in fourteen days, if they were allowed to" (*Novinar* 1991, p. 4). Foreign "investors" are particularly interested in taking a share of advertising industries. Berlusconi started the process of discovering the East European media market and succeeded in getting a license from Gosteleradio to gather advertisements from Western enterprises. "While it is too early for commercial advertising for traditional mass market products, considering the difficult distribution and supply conditions in the Soviet Union, 'business to business' advertising and 'corporate image' communication of enterprises [are] liable to contribute in creating an advertising culture without giving rise to resistance and negative trauma" (Richeri 1990, p. 13).

Soon after Fininvest entered the emerging advertising market in East-Central Europe, other Western competitors took the same course. In Slovenia, for example, in 1990 a semiprivate, joint-venture IP founded by the highest managers of Television Slovenia and affiliated with the French Havas, signed an extremely beneficial agreement with Radio and Television Slovenia. They received an exclusive license to gather television advertisements for national television. It was later found that the agreement bypassed legal regulations, and it was suspended by the new Council of Radio and Television Slovenia in 1991.

Apart from foreign operations within East European markets, all postsocialist countries are experiencing another form of externally driven deregulation. Foreign television programs broadcast via Direct Broadcast Satellite (DBS) can be received either with individual satellite dishes or community antennas distributing these programs by cable. Although the availability of DBS television programs in East Europe is still low, it is constantly increasing. In addition, some national television systems, such as Television Slovenia, decided to transmit DBS's (almost exclusively entertainment) programs on its own channels. The members of the former JRT have concluded agreements with some European satellite TV services—CNN, BBC TV Europe, Sky News, Euro Sport, TV 5, Super Channel, and MTV—for free experimental broadcasting. Similarly, Bulgaria broadcasts free of charge the program of the French station TV 5—Europe eight hours a day. In the CSFR, the former Soviet TV program on the third channel was transformed into an "open channel," *OK 3*, transmitting a selection of West European satellite programs (TV 5—Europe, La Sept, Worldnet, CNN, Screensport, RTL Plus) and the "Vremya" news program of Soviet TV, mainly without dubbing or subtitling. This program covered about 27 percent of the national territory (*Mass Media* 1990a, p. 12). In all these "new" channels, English is the most widely broadcast language. As Simon Baker (1991, p. 18) put it rightly, the central question is therefore, "When will channels be introduced in the national languages? This is the real test of overseas interest. It is a commercial question because the West-European public service broadcasters on satellite, notably the French and German, are unlikely to launch services in another language."

Direct foreign investments do not yet affect the broadcast media in this part of East Europe, but the proclaimed commercialization and privatization of the media sphere will probably open the door for the import of capital in the future. However, because of general economic decay and low effective demand, it is unlikely that new media companies could attract the number of subscribers and/ or advertisers necessary to make their operation in national languages profitable. Stone and Marks (1991, p. 6) made clear that "East Europeans are under the false impression that U.S. dollars are the answer to their problems. Many are ignorant of the strict business criteria applied to loans and grant support. They fail to appreciate fully that private investors are unlikely to underwrite projects that lack legal protection and proper management. On the other hand, they see German, Austrian, French and British firms moving in and wonder why Americans are so skittish about taking a risk."

Since foreign entrepreneurs are not likely to be interested in investments with unsafe returns, it is more realistic to expect that in the near future East European countries will be much more exposed to a direct inflow of foreign *media products* (via DBSs, mostly in English, including subscription television) than of foreign *capital.* For example, MTV Europe, a partnership among Maxwell's Mirror Group, Viacom International, and British Telecommunications, reportedly reaches about 160,000 homes in East Europe, which are officially getting MTV programs, and this number is expected to increase ten or twenty times in the near future (*Telecommunications Update* 1990, p. 2).

New Journalism, Old Journalists—or the Other Way Around

Apart from political pressures; the state monopoly over paper supply, printing plants, and distribution of newspapers and broadcast signals; a legal vacuum; and financial problems, *journalists* are often considered by both foreign observers and domestic governments as an important impediment to press freedom. In a recent study by the International Media Fund, the authors (Stone and Marks 1991, p. 4) observed that in Eastern Europe "the journalists themselves often are unable to cast off practices ingrained under the old regimes where subservience was a virtue. Second, the very definition of 'journalist' differs from that of the West, and gatherers and reporters of information take a back seat to the columnists, essayists and editorialists who, in the minds of many, constitute the 'real' journalists." Similarly, Dennis and Heuvel reported in their 1990 study that "much of the printed press practices advocacy journalism, blurring reportage and opinion. Quality is generally quite low, both in terms of physical appearance, writing, scope of coverage and orientation to readers' needs" (Dennis and Heuvel, p. 4). One of the main reasons for the low quality of East European journalism is that in many cases "the same journalists are producing the same newspapers and news programmes today as two years ago" (Sparks 1991b, p. 11). This argument is often used by new ruling elites to justify their attempts to dismiss editors and journalists from editorial offices that are still state controlled. The argument is similar to that often used in the former regimes, when the system was considered faultless, but, unfortunately, the people acted inappropriately.

With the help of such arguments, the old party press is also generally marginalized, although it is still influential in some (local) environments. The new elites would like further to minimize its importance. At the same time, trends toward both commercial and critical journalism are becoming apparent. Whereas the former fits in perfectly with government efforts to privatize economy, the latter produces many more controversies because it is often associated with partisan and/or investigative journalism critical of the dominant agents of power. But these assessments are often partisan as well. In Slovenia, for example, a 1990 survey revealed that almost two-thirds (61.9 percent) of citizens considered the media "objective" and "not partisan" (*Delo* 1990). Similarly, two years later, only 15 percent of respondents believed that the national television newscast program was party- or politically biased.

However, the complaints of the new elites are not really related to the imperfection of journalists who fail to report "objectively." What they are really concerned about is the way objectivity is applied by journalists in the mainstream media: which events should be assigned for coverage, which observations should be reported, or which story should be prominently displayed. Governments largely consider critical voices in the media as an opposition to democratic changes rather than as a critique of specific policies and decisions taken by those in power. Governments' understanding of democracy is similar to that often prevailing in developing countries, where democratic rights and citizens' freedoms are limited by the vague and undefined "national interest"; these views are also close to those of the former system, where the Communist Party controlled the media to protect the "class interest." Indeed, the collapse of control by the Communist party did not introduce autonomous media and journalism. Paradoxically, new political elites and parties are likely to see a total control over the media as "the precondition for the arrival of real democracy. . . . In a sense, before the elections the politicians attempted to replace a 'one-party dictatorship' with a 'multi-party dictatorship'" (Kovats and Whiting 1992, p. 19).

More generally, the kinds of political pressures that can be easily found in East-Central Europe often appear in developing countries as well as in the developed world;[4] it would be difficult, then, to relate such pressures mainly to the socialist heritage of the postsocialist systems. Jae-Kyoung Lee (1991, p. 157) argued, for example, that power elites in newly industrialized Asian countries claim that it is necessary to sacrifice freedom of the press because of national development, at least during the period of modernization. Zahorom Nain (1991, p. 39) reported on similar attitudes of the Malaysian government: "So long as the press is conscious of itself being a potential threat to democracy and conscientiously limits the exercise of its rights, it should be allowed to function without government interference. But when *the press obviously abuses its rights by unnecessarily agitating the people,* then democratic governments should have a right to control it" (italics added). Criticisms of journalistic practice are further related to the education and training of journalists because it is believed that most journalists are "hereditarily infected" by the fact that, under the former regimes, they were "educated at universities or journalists' associations, where they received a heavy dose of Marxist-Leninist theory but little of practical value" (Dennis and Heuvel 1990, p. 8).

However, controversies related to the problem of the professional quality of journalism and journalism education cannot be reduced to contemporary developments in East-Central Europe. In the classical sociological sense, journalism is not a "profession" anywhere in the world, which is one reason that the social status of journalists differs from one country to the next. This does not mean that journalists are trained and recruited randomly; only those who "show solid signs of reliability and commitment to the prevailing ethos" are selected (hired) by media owners or managers (Downing 1980, p. 174). As a consequence, journalists in different political and cultural settings vary widely in their occupational commitments, social status, ethical principles, standards of qualification, autonomy and responsibility (Splichal and Sparks 1992). For the same reasons, journalism education varies widely throughout the world. Thus, the "quality" and "objectivity" of journalistic practices and the nature of education in journalism are not simply a question of, and directly related to, the skills and political beliefs of journalists (and their educators), although the professional orientation of journalists is usually related to the degree of their education and middle-of-the-road political leanings (cf. Windahl and Rosengren 1978; Hennigham 1984).

From the point of view of the quality—in more precise terms, the specificity—of journalism, the social and the political structures in which journalistic practice is embedded are even more important because such practices, which are supposed to be fundamental to any model of democracy, are directly and/or indirectly influenced by their political and economic environment. A number of cases have clearly demonstrated that much news reporting is determined more by the internal logic of media organizations and external power actors than by objective reality. As the editors of *Culture, Society and the Media* maintained, media organizations exist in a "symbiotic relationship" with their environment, drawing on it not only for their economic sustenance but also for the "raw materials" of which their contents are made (Curran, Gurevitch, and Woollacott 1982, p. 20). In the case of East-Central Europe, it is at least questionable whether the economic and political environment, forms of external control, and internal organization of the media can be, and have been, remarkably changed in such a short time.

I do not intend here to discuss the question of the professional ideology of journalists or the question of status identification and its relatedness to the total process of the socialization of journalists. I do wish, however, to distinguish between the indigenous characteristics of journalism as a profession (though they differ among specific environments) and those emerging from the broader social and political context. There is no doubt that the power and autonomy of journalists, and the kinds of journalism they perform, are constrained and channeled—though neither directly nor apparently—by other, mainly political and economic agents of power in society. These structural constraints are implicit in the "organizational system" in which the journalist works: "Although structural considerations partly, at least, determine both the nature of mass media operations and the approaches adopted in their execution, in the main they impinge more on the general organization of communicators' activities than on the day-to-day implementation of individuals' roles. These are affected at least as much by immediate, operational considerations as by their structural location within the organization" (Gallagher 1982, p. 163). In short, it would be shortsighted to claim that the "old" journalists ought to be simply reeducated (if not fired) to "improve the quality" of journalism, regardless of traditions, political and social relations, legal environment, and the structure of the media, which cannot be reformed as rapidly as, for example, the system of education.

In former socialist countries, journalists were civil servants ("sociopolitical workers") with relatively high occupational prestige, which is generally the case in less developed countries. Particularly in their role as publicists, journalists were seen, not as journalists, but as public relations persons for the state and the party. For quite a long period of time, the political elites even believed that the press should be written by party officials rather than professional journalists, a belief congruent with the dominant conception of the media as means of education and propaganda. In fact, editorial posts represented an important rung of the party mobility ladder. As John Karch (1983, p. 119) observed, "For upward mobility . . . journalists and commentators have to be unchallenged experts in conformity. They are among the higher echelons of society in terms of creature comforts and prestige." Nevertheless, journalism education at universities was permanently criticized—just as university-type journalism education in Western countries was, although for different reasons. In Yugoslavia, for example, journalism schools were constantly subjected to ideological suspicion even though they had been established by the Communist Party. Only later were they included in universities, which made them much more autonomous. In all East-European countries except Hungary and Romania, where no university system of journalism education was established, journalism schools joined universities.

Under the old regime, a person had to be in good relations with the party *nomenklatura* to work in a high position at national newspapers or radio and television stations. In a number of East European countries, this practice continued after the fall of socialism. Political credentials were often still more important than professional qualifications. Even for newcomers, university or professional education was not obligatory for entrance into a journalistic occupation. As in West European countries and the United States, many editors openly scorned journalism education as too theoretical and vocational and as failing to provide students with journalistic skills. These criticisms continue in East-Central Europe, but now they are focused mainly on the kind of social "theories" (Marxism-Leninism) formerly taught at journalism schools.

It is true that these criticisms of the nature of journalistic education were, and still are, justified in a number of cases. Nevertheless, these issues are not simply a question of what degree, what kind of journalistic skill, and what kind of ideology students acquire in the period of education. They also reflect general attitudes toward the *nature* of journalistic education. Contrary to the "craft apprenticeship model" of training that is conducted on the job and is directly controlled by the employer, university education places considerable stress on self-development and independent thought. University education implies the development of specialized groups of university teachers and researchers who are to some extent distanced from the daily practice of the profession itself (Splichal and Sparks 1992). The same holds true for students themselves, who tend to be more critical and hold higher professional norms and ethical standards than "skilled professionals." It is not surprising, then, that such differences may—and actually do—produce tensions and conflicts between the two groups. Critical voices coming from editorial offices in East Europe and elsewhere should be taken with a grain of salt: There is no evidence, for example, that a large number of young journalists who have graduated in recent years and found jobs in the media have intrinsically preserved the Leninist model of "revolutionary propaganda."

Current support for "Western training and instruction . . . channelled through media enterprises rather than through universities" (Dennis and Heuvel 1990, p. 8) is not really specific to East-Central European countries. Rather, it is a part of more general conflicts between the active (older) members of the profession and university educators that appear elsewhere as well. Apart from that, a constant tension exists between the tendencies toward elitism of the profession and the amateurism inherent in a free access philosophy. The tension between the media institutions and universities is a general feature of the professional education of journalists. A recent study into patterns of professionalization among first-year journalism students provided some evidence that a number of controversies now emerging in East Europe are far more complex than they appear at first glance and that these controversies are shared by very different systems (Splichal and Sparks 1992). Let me take just a few examples.

After political changes in 1989 and 1990, the faculty of journalism at Charles University in Prague was closed down completely, and a new department of journalism was established at the new faculty of social sciences, with roughly forty new professors *elected by students.* (A similar process in the former GDR was different in its nature because it was legislated by "external" authorities of the Federal Republic of Germany). Such a rigorous action in Prague (but not in Bratislava in Slovakia) was justified by the government as inevitable because of a close cooperation of the faculty with the pro-Soviet, or "socialist," International Organization of Journalists (based in Prague) after the Soviet intervention in 1968, when a large part of the former teaching staff and those active in the Prague Spring were expelled from the faculty.

After the establishment of parliamentary democracy in Hungary, a new school of journalism was established in Budapest within the framework of the (old) Association of Journalists. Soon it was subjected to criticism by the new political elites, which considered it inimical to the new authorities. The controversies resulted in a split of the Association of Journalists; some two hundred members of the association established a new, progovernment association, in contrast to the majority of six thousand journalists who remained "loyal" to their professional organization. The large majority of them did not want to attach themselves to either new or old political parties, less because of high ethical principles than because "they had no way of knowing which party [was] going to win the elections and what sanctions might be placed upon those who backed the losers" (Kovats and Whiting 1992, p. 20).

A similar situation may be found in Poland, where the journalistic community is deeply divided in two clusters, both of which—although for very different reasons—practice a kind of advocacy journalism (Jakubowicz 1993a, p. 71). After the collapse of the socialist system, former journalists, editors, and publishers of the underground press uncritically supported their political comrades and allies from the 1980s, who now constituted the new government. The old (communist) journalistic "cadre" toed the new government line to avoid any adversities or at least to minimize them. Obviously, the basic *political* preconditions for an autonomous, watchdog journalism do not exist yet, although more than 90 percent of Polish journalists believe, according to a 1991 poll, that their "main mission" is to inform about events, to serve as a watchdog of government, and to inform authorities about the views of citizens (Jakubowicz 1993a, p. 70).

In the newly emerging democracies in East-Central Europe, privatization of the media is often considered the most important prerequisite for press freedom. For journalism students in twenty-two countries surveyed in 1987–1988[5], however, forms of ownership, while often perceived negatively as the dominant threat to press freedom, were not considered a positive element in any hypothetical formula for a free press—with the exception of *public ownership of the media.* In addition, the majority of students in twelve countries (including Australia, Austria, Canada, Germany, the United Kingdom, and Norway) wanted to work for publicly, rather than privately, owned media systems. The preference for the public service media in East Europe was not related to a specific, supposedly Marxist, "mentality"; among three East-European countries included in the study (Bulgaria, Poland, and Slovenia), only Bulgarian students defined their political orientation as predominantly "Marxist", while Polish students belonged to "middle-of-the-road" orientations (social democrats, democrats), and students in Slovenia adhered to "alternative" orientations (mainly ecologists).

I am not saying that economics (and the form of ownership) is the sole determinant of media behavior and specifically of journalistic practice. However, even this foregoing survey suggests that the dominant form of media ownership is ultimately "responsible" for the kind of the media, including their contents, we find in a specific society. In principle, it is possible to distinguish nowadays between two dominant media systems—the commercial and the paternal. Beyond doubt, the democratic system is "firmly against authoritarian control of what can be said, and against paternal control of what ought to be said" (Williams 1976, p. 133), and thus it is closer to a "commercial system," although it is also against commercial control of "what can be profitably said." However, the nature of a media system (controlled versus free) does not determine the kind of journalism performed in a specific country. Similarly, it is not possible to advance any firm hypothesis about the relationship between the nature of the education systems for journalists in different countries and the nature of media systems (Splichal and Sparks 1992).

The (still) dominant practice of advocacy journalism in East-Central Europe that deliberately supports the governments in power and avoids criticism (Dennis and Heuvel 1990, p. 7) and preferences for columnists, essayists, and editorialists, rather than reporters (Stone and Marks 1991, p. 4), are, at least in terms of students' preferences, far from being specific to East Europe. On the contrary, a preference for news reporting was the most popular in the countries with typically paternal media systems, for example, in Brazil, Poland, Tanzania, and Slovenia, as well as in *some* commercial systems. Similarly, preferences for columnists and editorialists are distributed between paternal and commercial systems without any clear tendency; this kind of journalism is highly respected by students in Japan, Spain, the United Kingdom, Bulgaria, and Ghana. Even in the United States, "the voice and judgment of the journalist may have to be more honestly acknowledged. . . . Journalists used to speak sometimes in the first person. . . . Perhaps it wouldn't be a bad thing if that practice came back" (Hallin 1992, pp. 20–21). Students everywhere generally prefer the "Western definition of journalism" and choose as the most preferred career that of reporter, followed by columnist and presenter, but in what environments they have an opportunity to practice the career of reporter is another question. The case of "a certain schizophrenia in Polish journalists who go to the West," as reported by Dennis and Heuvel (1990, p. 23), seems to be very representative: "They go to intern at a Western publication, absorb Western journalistic techniques, write in a Western style during their internship, but then return to Poland and immediately revert to writing in the familiar opinion-laden style. The problem . . . is that these journalists see Poland *as needing a different journalistic approach*" (italics added).

Another example of the influence of the broader social context, rather than the system of forming journalists, is that of *Slovenec*, the daily newspaper established by government subsidies in Slovenia after democratic elections. Journalists were selected from among those not "contaminated by communism," and the chief editor was even "imported" from Argentina. However, after three months he was displaced by a new editor because he neither met the government's expectations of implementing a straight anticommunist editorial policy nor succeeded in achieving the circulation figures expected by foreign (i.e., Slovene emigrant) investors. The crisis continued with the resignation of the second editor at the end of 1991. "New journalists" are still producing an old-fashioned newspaper that does not really report news but mainly advocates a conservative progovernment political line.

There are, however, some cases in which the former leading communist newspapers became reliable sources of information. One such case, reported by Dennis and Heuvel (1990, p. 40), is *Rude Pravo*, the organ of the old Communist Party in the CSFR, which became after the revolution "one of the better sources of daily news. It has many *competent* journalists, and now that they are *less constrained* by the need to convey the party line, the quality of the paper has improved greatly" (italics added). Dennis and Heuvel found this transformation of *Rude Pravo* to be "ironic," which clearly reveals their partial knowledge about both journalism and East Europe. Such "ironic" cases (not only exceptions) may certainly be found in other postsocialist countries as well.

The Polish, Czech, and Slovene cases of a new old journalism clearly illustrate that the question of a new journalistic doctrine is not only (or not at all) a matter of a universally measurable "quality of journalism." Paolo Mancini (1991, p. 138) gave another case in point in relation to South European journalism:

> The sacred texts of journalism ... have taken as models several specific public spheres (above all, the Anglo-Saxon countries) and mainly have defined the functions of journalism in relation and in opposition to the political systems in force in those countries. ... When a public sphere of a different system is referred to, such as, for example, Italy, it is judged in terms of backwardness, blaming delays and malfunctions on the lack of journalistic professionalism, on the overall degeneration of the parties as a whole, on the historical distortions of the relations between the party system and the media in which the latter have always been considered greatly dependent on the former.

The "new" doctrine of objective journalism to be learned by journalists in East-Central Europe is related to a specific libertarian ideology of Western journalism that "celebrates the canon of professional objectivity, with its stress on disinterested detachment, the separation of fact from opinion, the balancing of claim and counterclaim" (Curran 1991, p. 32). Its basic principle is the separation of news from editorial policy because "an 'imprudent' pursuit of the paper's policy might offend and limit its market" (Gouldner 1976, p. 96). In the early 1920s, when the idea of journalistic objectivity was adopted as a professional norm, it represented "a rigorous reporting procedure growing out of the broader cultural movement of *scientific naturalism*" (Streckfuss 1990, p. 973; italics added). It was also related to the need for a professional education in journalism, as advocated, for example, by Walter Lippmann. At that time, many newspapers were closely linked to political parties, and objectivity represented an alternative to politically partisan journalism. After that period, however, cultural, political, and economic environments changed considerably. Mergers of newspapers became an everyday practice after the decline of the traditionally politicized party press. The new type of "objective journalism" was based on the growth of a mass media monopoly and the spread of mass advertising, both of which neutralized information because too specific news, personal views, and interpretations consonant with the attitudes and beliefs of one part of a large audience might have affronted those with different opinions and thus reduced the size of the readership on which advertising revenues depended. At the same time, the separation of news from commentaries was blurred by the subordination of both to entertainment, a practice that fundamentally limited diversity and fostered superficiality. As Streckfuss (1990, p. 982) argued, "By the time *objectivity* became enough a part of the working vocabulary of journalists to make its way into textbooks, its meaning was diluted." "Given the insistent pressure to maximize audiences and revenues, there is not surprisingly a consistent tendency for the commercial media to avoid the unpopular and tendentious and to draw instead on the values and assumptions which are most familiar and most widely legitimated, which almost inevitably means those which flow authoritatively downwards through the social structure" (Murdock and Golding 1977, p. 38).

Of course, media owners and advertisers do not always exercise such ideological control over the media in a direct way, nor does the pattern of ownership and control over the media always have a direct impact on their contents. But the media have to, and do, respond to changes in economic and political systems both in terms of their organization (for example, private versus public media) and contents. The property system, for example, "will, in part, construct news that helps reproduce the property system, sustaining the power and privileges of those already controlling the media" (Gouldner 1976, p. 109). As indicated, the doctrine of Western journalism fits in perfectly with the prevailing ideology of privatization in East-Central Europe, although more normatively than practially. Whether this doctrine fits in with a genuine democratization of those particular societies is another question.

One should not overlook the fact that objective reporting privileges stereotyped news, prefers "official voices[,] and tend[s] to leave unreported large areas of genuine relevance that *authorities chose not to talk about. . . .* It widened the chasm that is a constant *threat to democracy*—the difference between the realities of private power and the illusions of public imagery" (Bagdikian 1983, p. 182; italics added). This liberal perspective considers the media mainly as a channel of information between the government and the governed, although it rejects a direct advocacy journalism. John Downing (1984, p. 5) pointed to that liberal perspective by quoting James Reston's assertion that in practice "the responsible government official and the responsible reporter in the field of foreign affairs are not really in conflict ninety per cent of the time" and then asking, "Is this independence, pluralism, public access, balance, and objectivity? Or is it a constituent factor in the continuance of government of the people by a relatively cohesive—'ninety per cent of the time'—minority?" Journalists and politicians must treat their audience as a homogeneous entity to maximize the number of recipients and potential voters on whom their careers depend. As Richard Sennett (1978, p. 284) claimed, "Treating one's audience as equals becomes the means of *avoiding ideological questions,* and leads to a focus on the politician's person, the perception of his motives being something which everyone can appreciate and share." In fact, the more "natural" the process of "objective" news reporting seems, the greater is the ideological influence of the media.

Jerry Mander (1978) produced a list of thirty-three "miscellaneous inherent biases" to show what kind of world (Western) television must *inevitably* transmit. One bias is clearly related to the objectivity doctrine: "When there is a choice between objective events (incidents, data) and subjective information (perspectives, thoughts, feelings), the objective event will be chosen" (Mander 1978, p. 324). The principle of objectivity further implies that the one (e.g., personalities, charismatic leaders, symbols) is preferred to the many (e.g., a philosophy, political movements); hierarchy to democracy or collectivity; superficiality to depth; the conclusion to the process; doing to being; the specific to the general; quantity to quality; the finite to the infinite; and death to life. Indeed, "facts concerning the moon are better television than poetry concerning the moon. *Any* facts work better than *any* poetry" (Mander, pp. 326–327). Such a stereotyping of news obscures the existence of different perspectives and values and perpetuates the *illusion of objectivity*. As David Paletz and Robert Entman (1981, p. 23) argued, "The mode of presentation is designed to persuade the audience of the credibility of the news stories and the legitimacy of the media which present them." But "as news reports, it therefore also censors and occludes aspects of life; its silences generate a kind of 'underprivileged' social reality, a social reality implicitly said (by the silence) to be unworthy of attention" (Gouldner 1976, p. 107). What, then, should be considered a real or objective journalism is not simply a question of quality standards developed in the past century in the capitalist world. It is mainly a question of the social role of the media in society and the nature of society itself—that is, the *social* characteristics that influence the specific nature of journalism and its quality and objectivity.

The comparative study into motivations for studying journalism in twenty-two countries revealed, perhaps surprisingly, that news reporting was more attractive to female students, particularly in less developed countries. The next most likely group to choose reporting was the sons of poorly educated parents in commercial systems, whereas highly educated male students from both paternal and commercial systems were most likely to desire work as columnists. Thus, students' aspirations seem to have been channeled by family background and gender: Students from relatively prosperous families were most likely to aspire to the relatively high status of commentator or editor, while students (particularly females) who did not have this background looked disproportionately, and realistically, toward less prestigious roles. Generally, students' estimation of the prestige of journalists depended mainly on the economic status of their parents: The lower their economic status, the higher was the evaluation of the prestige of journalists.

At least in terms of students' attitudes in this study, neither political commitment nor political engagement were central to the journalistic profession in *both commercial and paternal systems* (with the exception of Bulgarian students). On the contrary, students quite explicitly considered political involvement to be incompatible with professional journalism. This finding is even more important because the same students did not share the same opinions about the most important qualities of and specific talents needed by "good journalists" as well as about the importance of university education! For example, students in paternal systems (including the former socialist countries) rated more highly university education and general knowledge and put less stress on the individualized talents of journalists and the need to be critical than did their colleagues in commercial systems, but both groups renounced political involvement by journalists as unimportant, unnecessary, and/or unprofessional.

Similarly, the profiles of the individual goals and social roles of journalists differ widely across countries. This obviously challenges a simplified belief that the idea of the media and journalists as either agents of social changes (e.g., the Leninist model of journalism and the media as the tool of the avant-garde) or agents of control (e.g., the Fourth Estate model) is restricted to a specific sociopolitical, cultural, or historical setting, such as that of East-Central Europe. Although there is no doubt that the vast majority of socialist models of journalism and the media were less *democratic* than those dominant in the capitalist world, we have not yet experienced—either in socialism or in capitalism—the democratic system "in any full sense" (Williams 1976, p. 133). To democratize a whole communication system means to transform mass communication from a process of *legitimation of power* (either political, as in paternal systems, or economic, as in commercial systems) into a process of *self-expression* of different social actors, which goes far beyond the question of the nature of journalism itself.

In fact, there is no such a thing as Western, American, socialist, or any other politically or geographically defined journalism. Specific journalistic practices (not a single practice) within a country result from a number of factors that some countries have in common and from a range of unique influences. Even in the former socialist countries, there was no single model of journalism. On the contrary, even the dominant models when put into practice changed considerably at least in some socialist countries (e.g., Yugoslavia and Poland), particularly beginning in the late 1970s. In Yugoslavia, for example, the former propagandistic model of an ideological-rhetorical journalism was replaced in the 1970s by a "distributional model" stressing the importance of information (news) for decisionmaking and reducing the role of journalists to that of information distributors rather than commentators (Splichal 1986, p. 1414). In addition, alternative models of journalism emerged and started to compete with the dominant model:

> One of the most significant changes in most Communist countries has been the appearance of a phenomenon external to the press apparatus—an unofficial press. In most cases, dissident media have chosen not only to challenge the official press

version of the truth but also the official ideology's assumptions about how truth is to be found. . . . At its extreme, this more neutral approach to the news, this preference for information over argument, can make for a style of journalism somewhat like the Western, so-called objective approach to the news. (Mills 1983, p. 169)

Another important, and paradoxically alternative, departure from the Leninist model of journalism was certainly that of producing special *news bulletins* containing mostly uncensored news on world events and relying both on Western news agencies and correspondents of domestic news agencies. Although this type of information service was intended, not for the general public, but for party and state functionaries and thus represented a form of highly restricted and privatized communication, it also meant an alternative to the kind of journalistic practice typical of and required from the "normal" media. This rather neutral approach to the news came very close to a Western conception of objective journalism—but only in terms of genres, not in terms of social functions and goals.

Instead of trying to define *the universal* hypothetical model (or typology) of journalism in terms of democracy or "quality," we should scrutinize rival theories and models of journalism. James Curran (1991, p. 28) identified four alternative normative judgments about the practice of journalism: (1) *disinterested* journalism, which is associated with the traditional liberal perspective on the media; (2) *subaltern* journalism, which is defined within a Marxist critique of the media in capitalism; (3) *didactic* journalism, which is part of the traditional communist conception of the media, and (4) *adversarial* journalism, which is emphasized by the radical democratic approach. But there are also differences within each of these streams, and each is more an ideal type (*normative judgment*) than an exhaustive description of an actually practiced journalism. In my discussion of the comparative study, I tried to look more closely for some empirical evidence of existing differences among specific models or norms of journalism. The empirical evidence reveals three specific conceptions of journalism:

1. The *Enlightenment conception,* which basically considers journalism a vocation—that is, journalists are believed to be called to and qualified for a specific kind of communication activity. This conception stresses the importance of objective information, education, and the development of a critical consciousness and considers journalists a part of "progressive social forces."

2. The *entertainment conception,* which considers journalists to have no social power and to constitute no specific social group, though they are independent. Their main goals are to entertain audiences and to advance their own beliefs, provided that someone is willing to pay them for their products.

3. The *power conception,* which relates the social position of journalism mainly to the production and reproduction of social power.

The first model is close to Curran's *didactic* journalism, but it differs significantly in proclaiming the importance of objectivity. In terms of Curran's alternative perspectives of media, Enlightenment journalism represents the convergence between traditional liberal and radical (including Marxist) perspectives. The entertainment conception is close to Curran's *disinterested* journalism, and the power conception is analogous to *adversarial* journalism. However, none of these conceptions is exclusive in terms of either theory or practice; all, for example, stress the importance of *news* reporting. Even as ideal types they are not totally exclusive, and in practice they often merely represent "different ways of looking at the same journalistic reality" in different media systems (Splichal and Sparks 1990, p. 169). The best exemplification for this point is Curran's differentiation between *disinterested* and *subaltern* journalism: Both refer to the very same practice of journalism in capitalism, but they evaluate it from totally different perspectives.

In the former socialist countries, the entertainment conception of journalism was obviously less popular (and even suppressed), but the other two conceptions are far from being "typical" for socialist countries only. In terms of the practical democracy (leaving aside theoretical controversies) developing in East-Central Europe, the democratic "solution" to be looked for is not Western training and instruction or Western-style journalism, as some Western observers believe, but rather the development of an indigenous pluralistic model of journalism that would enable different conceptions to compete in practice. Forced changes toward one single "best" model of journalism (i.e., the Western one) and a corresponding (single) model of education may cause painful consequences because sudden moves toward the full development of the market can be easily combined with increased government intervention (as in the case of nationalisms spreading in some postsocialist countries) and a shift from freedom of the press as an individual (though entrepreneurial) freedom to "freedom of *corporate* speech" performed by either large industries or political parties. In particular, the rapid commercialization of the media as a part of the privatization strategy of East-Central European governments may lead to both *external marginalization* of these countries because a large part of the media are likely to be owned by a small number of transnational conglomerates and *internal marginalization* of minority groups unable to compete with the state, political parties, and large industries—regardless of the quality of journalism and the nature of the educational system.

3 Economic Restructuring and Democratization: Privatization as the "Magic Key"?

The new power elites in East-Central Europe consider deregulation and privatization of the national economy and the media, particularly the press, as fundamental prerequisites for solving the weaknesses of bureaucratic control and achieving a higher level of productivity *and* as necessary conditions for general democratization and thus for the autonomy and development of the media. Arguments for such changes are similar to those prevailing in West Europe (cf. Keane 1991) and already *domesticated* in some developing countries. In the classical liberal model of the media, their primary democratic role is defined in terms of a watchdog function; accordingly, the media ought to control, and limit the power of, state authorities. It is precisely this function that determines the forms of ownership and organization of the media. Since the main problem in the model is to safeguard the autonomy of the media from the state, and since only private property is said to ensure such an autonomy, the fundamental condition for a democratic media system is its firm and exclusive foundation in a free market. Any state or public regulation essentially limits the critical role of the media. Although such regulation was "acceptable" in broadcasting in the period of technological limitations (e.g., because of the "scarcity of frequencies"), contemporary developments in communication technologies (e.g., satellites and cable systems) now support a complete independence of the electronic media from the state, too.

The classical liberal model is based on several (partially implicit) normative historical conditions, which are completely neglected by the new East European (de)regulation endeavors. At least four reasons making this model obsolete should be mentioned here:

1. In accordance with the traditional conception of the relationship between the state and civil society, where the latter include citizens as the owners of the means of production, the critical role of the media as "instruments" of civil society is understood in terms of limiting, and preventing the abuses of, state power. The task of the media is to control and limit the principle of maximization of political power.

2. Before the rise of the mass press on the eve of the nineteenth century (Splichal 1981a, p. 99), the press was highly politicized and clearly related to party interests. The growth of the mass press, particularly radio and television, in the twen-

tieth century generated depoliticization of the media and their commercialization based on the growing importance of their entertainment function. This trend obviously challenges traditional liberal conceptions focused on the political role of the media.

3. Traditional divisions between the state and civil society are challenged by the development of new media functions—entertainment and advertising—and the economic restructuring of advanced capitalist societies. Like the state, agents of "invisible power" (capital), their transnational agglomeration, and the principle of profit maximization they tend to advance jeopardize the independence of the media and journalists and the freedom and equality of citizens.

4. Processes of oligopolization and monopolization in the economy and specifically in the media have changed the traditional relationship of independence among the state, capital, and the media. Whereas traditionally the state wanted to avoid public media control and penetrate the media (e.g., by legal regulation), now it cooperates with media conglomerates, which for their part try to influence governments and get government support for their projects.

The controversies related to these developments make the validity of classical liberal conceptions of the media dubious. In this chapter I am going to consider those contemporary changes in the global restructuring of capitalist economy that affect relations between the state and civil society and thus the (in)dependence of the media from both the economy and polity. Although the criticism of the East European "New Deal" is partly emotive—similar to that of "Americanization" of the media in West Europe and developing countries—and does not (yet) result in a viable policy to solve enormous economic problems in the media sphere and elsewhere, it brings into the arena some evidence that contradicts the liberal fetish of the "superiority" of private ownership and market forces in the media sphere and of the "strictly economic goals" to be achieved by state-regulated privatization.[1]

In addition, this criticism is directed at a widespread fallacy in East-Central Europe that development entails convergence on the forms of economy and polity dominant in the developed capitalist world. In fact, this criticism contradicts the imitative approach represented by the "cosmopolitan models à la Klaus, Balcerowicz and Sachs" (Zeleny 1991, p. 4) advertised by East-Central European governments because that approach is not economically viable and leads to the colonization of East European economies. As Milan Zeleny (1991, p. 4) argued, "Its theoretical and practical value is zero." As he also argued (p. 3), the new government in the CSFR caused an economic fall in 1991:

It is not only a communist heritage, but a new and more dangerous heritage of the 1990–1992 interregnum of dilettantes. An irreplaceable destruction of capacities, dissolution of working teams, selling off the social property to nomenklatura and foreign speculators are happening every day. We are firmly and resolutely walking up the Only Possible Way to the Third World of economic dependence, to humble waged workforce. We are not producing national capital and capitalists; instead, traffickers and haberdashers' bazaar are springing up, we are stealing from each other and we do not mind that we are all robbed by the cosmopolitan ruling elite and geopolitically motivated foreign countries.

In other words, as, for example, Barber (1992, p. 63) demonstrated, "importing free political parties, parliaments, and presses cannot establish a democratic civil society; imposing a free market may even have the opposite effect." Uncritical imitation of democratic institutions developed in older democratic institutions may be a risky business. Instead, as Dahl (1991, p. 15) suggested, the countries in transition to the inauguration of democratic institutions should "discriminate between the aspects of the mature democratic countries that are essential to democracy and those that are not only *not* essential to it but may be harmful."

There is no doubt that a centralized socialist economy based on state ownership was both *economically inefficient* and *inimical to democracy.* But it would also be mistaken to believe that "free markets" and private property are the only (or, at least, the best) alternative in both respects. Although an advocacy of any form of socialized markets and social ownership is regarded with considerable suspicion where the laissez-faire doctrine is proclaimed, in East-Central Europe it should be acknowledged, as Robin Blackburn (1991, p. 234) claimed, that "the imposition of narrow commercial criteria menaces the integrity of civil society and hands the initiative to rapacious commercial interests." The question of an alternative to laissez-faire is particularly important for such vital activities in civil society as education, science, culture, and communication. Such a critical view is particularly needed, as Jörg Becker (1992, p. 13) argued, not only because the extent and forms of privatization of the mass media in East Europe exceed what has been practiced in Western capitalism until now, but also, or even primarily, because East Europe is becoming an experimental zone for those strategies of privatization activated by Western media capital, which are still held back by the social responsibility doctrine in the West. A policy not willing to restrict the operation of the free market in the media is clearly in favor of *corporate speech* rather than *free speech;* it is far from being a continuation of the ideas of the former democratic opposition in East Europe. Jakubowicz (1993a, p. 72) even maintained that "the results of the Solidarity revolution and the rule of post-Solidarity forces are almost the reverse of what was originally intended."

Paradox Number One: State Property Privatized by the State

The (re)construction of multiparty parliamentary democracy and a market economy in East-Central Europe points to the radical changes from socialist statism (sovietism) toward capitalism. The communist parties in East-Central Europe failed to reform their systems, which denied "any difference between political and social power, public and private law, and state-sanctioned (dis)information and propaganda and freely circulated public opinion" (Keane 1988, p. 2). "By abolishing the market, socialism reintegrated the economy into the body politic. The command economy fully met the requirements of political organization. Independently of the doctrine that called for dictatorship, and an end to private property, and the introduction of a bureaucratically managed economy, group interests of the new political elite pushed it in the direction of a garrison state" (Kaminski 1991, p. 346). The merger of economic and political power in the hands of the state produced a totalitarian, self-obstructing "command" system that was not even able to generate valid information about what was going on in society and in the economy. In short, the autonomy of civil society was "replaced" by an all-in state, a state that exists everywhere and penetrates into everything. At the same time, the ineffectiveness of socialist economies led to the decay of these countries as typical *peripheral* entities unable to collaborate (let alone compete) with the core of the developed countries.

Another typical example of the same process of exhaustion of peripheral growth is the fall of nonalignment as a movement aimed at restoring whatever limited control is possible over one's own system. Political, economic, and cultural cooperation among nonaligned countries is more and more substituted by a deliberately developed dependence on the core of the advanced capitalist countries (e.g., through different forms of financial, economic, technical, and other kinds of assistance).

Both instances clearly falsify the idea of (economic or cultural) "dissociation" (independence of the periphery from the core) as a feasible developmental strategy. It certainly would be difficult to speak of East-Central European countries as "newly industrialized societies" (in contrast to "advanced industrial societies" in the West), although industrialization was one of the basic goals (political and ideological even more than economic in the strict sense) declared during the early phases of socialism. Socialist economies were effectively protected from "Western imperialism" not only because of political or ideological measures but also because of economic frontiers (i.e., limited financial possibilities to import foreign goods). Strong protectionism resulted in high prices of and limited access to protected goods and services and increased the gap between socialist and advanced capitalist countries.[2]

New political elites in East-Central Europe generally rejected state socialism and tried to introduce capitalism. Consequently, we may expect a total reorganization of society around the logic of capital and the marketplace. A few years ago, the entry of private capital in the arena was politically and ideologically unviable. When discussing "informatization and restructuring of Soviet society," Dimitry Chereskin and Mikhail Tsalenko (1989) still pointed to "possibilities and specific features of socialist economy" and rejected a capitalist market economy. Now, however, it is believed by the new political elites that these tasks may be assumed only by private companies prepared to supply telecommunications services and to satisfy the demand, which far exceeds the supply.

Although the new East European governments are not seeking full-scale privatization at once, *denationalization* and *privatization* are considered by the elites to be the necessary and essential conditions for increasing the level of productivity and the amount of surplus, for helping governments spend less money on public welfare and services, for achieving disengagement of the state in the economy, for attracting foreign capital, and for decentralizing and diversifying the economy. Private property is mistakenly considered by the new elites to be "the most important factor of production" (Bajt 1991, p. 454). Reforms include new forms of management systems, (semi)autonomous government institutions to replace former ministries, and the granting of permissions to enter the evolving market to private companies, including foreign capital, which ought to be encouraged by the guarantee of repatriation of profits.

Hungary leads the way in the restructuring and privatization of the communication sphere. Privatizing and selling off newspapers to foreign entrepreneurs are only one example. In January 1990, the Hungarian Post, Telegraph and Telephone (PTT) split into three independent companies—postal service, telecommunications, and broadcasting. While the postal service will remain state owned, the Telecommunications Company is expected to be transformed into a joint-stock company and will be partially privatized (Datapro, 1990). Similar plans to allow private domestic and foreign operators to compete with the national PTTs exist in other postsocialist countries. Although there is no coherent policy for foreign investment in and ownership of national broadcasting, there already exist some private local stations (Nap TV, a commercial station connected with Murdock, and Balaton TV Channel in Hungary; TV Echo in Wrocław, Poland; and a number of private radio stations in Hungary and Poland founded with some foreign capital) and joint-venture agreements between governments and foreign investors to construct cable systems (e.g., with Chase Enterprises in Poland). Berlusconi, Hersant, Maxwell, Murdoch, and other West European media corporations are allegedly trying to invest their money in existing or new broadcasting systems and newspapers in East Europe.

The new East European economic policy resembles those implemented in a number of developing countries in Latin America and Southeast Asia. No fundamental difference exists between the official policies of East-Central Europe and those geared toward the corporatization of, for example, the Malaysian economy in the 1980s. "The Mahathir years have seen greater concessions being made towards international capital, where new government policies such as 'Look East,' 'Malaysia Incorporated' and 'Privatisation' have been introduced supposedly to transform the Malaysian economy into a more competitive one on the world stage" (Nain 1991, p. 40). Even the policy of "looking East" is not completely replaced by that of "looking West." At least in some smaller East European countries, the model of development implemented in countries such as South Korea and Hong Kong seems to be even more attractive than that of Westernization of backward national economies.

Leaving aside the question of the feasibility of the new economic policies, we can challenge contemporary processes of denationalization and privatization in former socialist countries from four main perspectives:

1. The nature of privatization with the dominant role of the state ("centralized privatization") contradicts the proclaimed quest for democratization of society and the state. Although "the public interest" is the keyword that governments use to justify their efforts toward privatization, it is not a guarantee of an extension of citizens' rights and freedoms. The new key right to private property and private ownership of economic enterprises may support political liberty but certainly not political equality. It may be that free enterprise is a prerequisite for a free press, but market mechanisms cannot guarantee the diversity and quality of information needed by citizens in a democratic society. As Barber (1992, p. 59) put it, a free market does not equal an open and democratic society.

2. Privatization is often considered an almost universal solution for improving the efficiency of former socialist economies. However, privatization is motivated more by the need to fill the state treasury than by economic efficiency, which could be improved without privatizing (e.g., by introducing competition among public enterprises) (Przeworski 1991b, p. 45).

3. Denationalization and privatization forced by the state are primarily aimed at redistributing wealth and power (for example, redistributing control over systems of communications) rather than at making a more effective economy. Instead of a means to rationalize the economy, privatization and denationalization are implemented as *the* (political) goal.

4. Transplantation of Western capitalism and private ownership to postsocialist countries is limited by the indigenous social structure and superstructure of these societies. Developmentalists in the late 1950s and early 1960s believed that press freedom correlated with and spurred on economic growth, but they largely ignored the cultural and historical context that often plagues political development in developing countries toward a Western-type democracy.

In contrast to capitalism, political and economic activities in former socialist countries are still largely monopolized by the state. In practice, for example, the policy of liberalization and privatization in communications applies only to the press and local (or regional) broadcasting; at the same time, national broadcasting organizations have been largely renationalized and put under the direct control of the government. The reason for such a contradiction is quite evident: "Privatization" is often used as a metaphor to indicate some (and to conceal other) dimensions of much more complex sociopolitical realities. As Sparks (1991a, p. 24) argued, "privatization" explains only a small part of contemporary restructuring of media systems in Western Europe: "The most substantial changes in the electronic media have nothing to do with a shift from the public to the private. Rather they are the result of a series of *policy decisions* which cut across the structure of privately and publicly owned broadcasting institutions alike. In the case of the press, the search for privatization leads us to ignore the real changes going on" (italics added).

Some authors even believe that these changes should be attributed to "a *con-*

spiracy" that grows from "the patterns of life, the social and political systems, the narrowing style of thinking about the world and the technologies that both result from and foster these trends" (Mander 1978, p. 117). At any rate, privatization of the economy is not, and cannot be, only a question of a more effective economy because private ownership of the means of production is certainly not the most important factor of production (Bajt 1991). It is also an illusion to think of economic transactions exclusively in terms of private economic actors. As Atle Midttun (1990) made clear in an analysis of the complex, structured markets of European aviation, space technology, and export financing, economic transactions involve a set of both commercial and political negotiations on state and company levels and open the gates for a "politicized economy."

Nor is privatization only a question of ideological legitimation, as Nicholas Garnham (1985, p. 13) argued in the case of the government decision to sell a majority shareholding in British Telecom to the private sector, a decision that had, according to Garnham (1985, p. 13), "everything to do with the *ideology* of the Conservative government but nothing to do with its *telecommunication policy*." This does not imply that the ideological dimension of the question is irrelevant. On the contrary, the ideological dimension of privatization can be proven by the French case, where, contrary to that of the United Kingdom, the public service model has a long tradition (e.g., centralized education, France Telecom); "this involvement is a central issue in public policy: *ideological* and *political* faith in the efficiency, both political and economic, of the public sector is so strong that it is very difficult to imagine the next move toward deregulation in France" (Colas 1991, p. 87).

Nevertheless, in addition to ideological legitimation, it is even much more important that contemporary privatization policies in East Europe are mainly concerned with allocative control over the economy rather than with the question of ownership itself or with operational control aimed at an effective use of available resources. Privatization policies are mainly related to the question of the *redistribution of political power and control* over the economy and aimed against the "red managers" (Mencinger 1991a). They are—once again and in a manner similar to the nationalization performed by the former socialist states—aimed at establishing a new social structure by political force and placing that structure in the hands of the state and the new *effective* owners. As Zeleny (1991, p. 3) argued, "The selling off of social property in the CSFR has been misused for political purposes," which is but "a propaganda in an election campaign for a new totalitarianism."

The new state is trying to "reform civil society" from the top down without institutional reforms of the state and without autonomous restructuring of civil society from the bottom up. Whereas in Western countries private ownership was—together with the market—the most prominent characteristic of civil society, privatization of property in postsocialist countries is primarily a *political* feature, *the* question of revolutionary changes toward a future "ideal society" designed by the political will of the revolutionary avant-garde to materialize its "historical project." It is not surprising, then, that "new order" ideologues argue that a period of paternalistic control is necessary to implement "democracy," where the prime function of the media ought to be legitimation of the new social order.

In this respect, no fundamental difference exists between the former socialist (or, generally, developing countries) and the new postsocialist ruling elites. This may help us understand why the new political elites everywhere in the former socialist countries are so eager to regulate the transition from the former (socialist) into the new (postsocialist) systems "mechanically" rather than "organically" (Rus 1991, p. 510). As formerly the (socialist) state planned in a very "exact" way the periods of time needed for transition from one stage of the socialist development to another, now the (postsocialist) state would like to break with the old system overnight, regardless of the consequences this shock therapy might have for society.

Contrary to the West, new East European governments still operate in the same way as did previous communist governments—as the dominant political and economic actors because no indigenous commercial class exists; nor does a genuine process of privatization within civil society. Political and economic activities are still largely monopolized by the state. Consequently, no clear borderline is established between political (power) and economic aims (profit), and this is typically the case with the process of privatization. In Russia, for example, close to one hundred thousand state officials prepare the privatization of state-owned companies. The process of privatization conducted by the state may be considered a kind of *social engineering* that is compatible neither with the legal state nor with civil society. "Legal state is legal inasmuch as it protects the individual and the whole civil society against unlawful actions. And vice versa: Civil society is civil inasmuch as it is—under state protection—being constituted and changing according to the principles of *spontaneous and autonomous self-organization*" (Rus 1991, p. 509).

As a matter of principle, efforts to privatize the whole economy by the state intervention are paradoxical. As Zhiuyan Cui (1991, p. 64) observed, the historical process of transformation of ownership is *asymmetrical:* Although it is possible to nationalize the private sector by state intervention, it is impossible to (re)establish it by the same means. State-directed privatization is as voluntaristic as was the nationalization of the means of production by the revolutionary socialist state. Nevertheless, new East European governments want to renationalize former state or social property first—to achieve political control over industrial privatization and over the economy in general. This "ought to assure them, in accordance with the Marxist doctrine of production relations and social superstructure, the permanence of power" (Mencinger 1991a).

In a way, it is also paradoxical that, whereas in the West, as Raboy (1989, pp. 7–8) remarked, obstacles to democratization are seen in developments related to the shrinking of public space, the growing influence of private capital, and the ensuing difficulty of popular access to the media, in East-Central Europe a promise of democratization is seen in private ownership and market mechanisms to be introduced by the state. In other words, what is considered a fundamental contradiction and an obstacle to democratization in the West is seen as its fundamental prerequisite in the East.

The question of the paradoxicality of *revolutionary privatization by the state* is "transformed" by the new ruling elites into a question of loyalty to the postsocialist state. Criticisms pointing to the *paradox* of the state as the agent of privatization are "transformed" into advocacy of the old regime. Nevertheless, the question of private ownership as an obstacle to (in capitalism) versus private ownership as a prerequisite for democratization of communications (in postsocialism) is not completely paradoxical. As was found in a recent international comparative study, respondents tended to identify as the key obstacles to the free practice of journalism the *dominant forms of ownership and control* in their own country—that is, private ownership of the media in capitalist commercial systems and state ownership of the media in socialist paternal systems (Splichal and Sparks 1990, p. 156).

Another comparative study into the importance of the Fourth Estate function of the media revealed the same tendency: Political pressure on the media and political advantage were considered two of the least important obstacles to the exercise of the Fourth Estate function in Western countries, while they were by far the most important in socialist countries. In Western countries the critical obstacles were economic constraints, pressures from owners, and commercial advantage, which do not play any significant role in socialist countries (Sparks and Splichal 1990, p. 10). Indeed, different dominant forms of ownership in different contexts may be functionally equivalent in relation to communication freedom and the autonomy of civil society.

That the nonexistence of the marketplace and private ownership of the means of production was one of the fundamental features of "socialist economy" and "socialist democracy" in East Europe—and thus the reason for their failure— may help us understand why privatization is largely believed to be essential for the democratization of these societies. Although for many years East European media built an unfavorable image of the Western capitalist system, now they often propagate it in the most idealistic form. The ideological purpose is rather obvious: The change in media contents is aiming at stabilizing and legitimizing political and economic transformations taking place in the postsocialist countries and at burying the last remnants of socialism.

In addition, privatization of ownership and the opening to foreign capital are considered by Western observers as the only way for East European countries to modernize their economies. Undoubtedly, these changes (will) have positive effects for international capital and its attempts to increase sales and profit on global level. As Peter Havlik (1989, p. 3) believed, "Information technologies form one of the few powerful tools which the West has at its disposal" to exert influence on the development of East European societies.

It is another question, however, whether the developmental tendencies of privatization and consumerism in East Europe will and can result in genuine democratization. There are two main reasons for skepticism: first, because bureaucracy is not directly influenced by the mode of production and second, because the big business that is expected to develop is not traditionally the site where democratic decisionmaking takes place. As with state ownership, private ownership of economic corporations does not foster economic democracy. This is important because the economy is apparently one of the key areas of policy-making. If, however, we reverse the question of how major economic changes influence political life, the answer remains in principle the same: "The impact of democracy in the political realm on economic development remains unclear" (Przeworski 1991a, p. 23).

Although privatization in postsocialist societies is firmly against the former authoritarian or paternalistic (state) control, it cannot genuinely democratize communication processes because it retains control in the hands of a minority, rather than the people, and reduces the public interest to interest in the maximization of profit. In addition, "the management of the economy mainly belongs to the sphere of *invisible power* in that it is beyond the compass, even if not in theory, then in practice, of democratic and jurisdictional control" (Bobbio 1987, p. 94; italics added). New arguments of the "liberal solution" that favor privatization may, however, imply "social regression, not only by reducing the process of equitable distribution, but also by indirect support to a strong state which could confront any revolts that may arise among the deprived population" (Rosanvallon 1988, p. 200). Unfortunately, East-Central European developments in 1991 represent a very accurate vindication of this thesis, including "revolts" of journalists because of the penetration of the state into the media. Thus, Dahl (1991, p. 17) was right to warn East European reformers not to embrace uncritically the belief that "corporate capitalism, in the form of unregulated markets and privately owned corporations, is economically the most efficient alternative [to state ownership and central direction] and the most compatible with democracy," particularly because once established, the structures that produce economic inequality, and thus political inequality, among citizens and a constant threat to democracy are very difficult to change.

For several reasons it would be extremely oversimplified to believe that the East European "rediscovery of capitalism" per se will increase the productivity and the level of surplus, as it was misleading to believe that the introduction of socialism forty or seventy years ago would provide formerly backward societies with general prosperity. As Manuel Castells (1989, p. 16) argued, that the "informational mode of development" developed in capitalist societies does not imply that "market forces are innately superior in steering development in information technologies." On the contrary, channelling public resources into education, developing national infrastructure for communications and other public-sector services, and reregulating (including removing barriers) import, foreign investments, and so on, can help the national economy survive in an increasingly competitive and international marketplace. Neither state nor market has any monopoly on efficiency, innovation, or responsiveness. For Geoffrey Mulgan (1991, p. 248), "At different times under different conditions both have acted either as liberating forces, opening communications and dispersing power, or as constraints and fetters."

The current global economic restructuring implies important and complex changes in production, consumption, and management that cannot be reduced to privatization of the means of production. The extension of privatization in the developed capitalist societies—for example, the shift from the public to the private in the electronic media—explains but a small part of the present restructuring. The obvious correlation between advanced capitalism with private ownership of the means of production and high productivity does not necessarily imply a causal relationship. For example, the development of a country's infrastructure in general (and telecommunications in particular) is even more perfectly correlated with per capita gross national product (GNP) regardless of the dominant form of ownership. This means that the state of telecommunications reflects the level of general economic development rather than the dominant mode of production (Kudriavtzev and Varakin 1990, pp. 107–108). In the case of either the dominant form of ownership or GNP, however, it is difficult to determine which is the cause and which is the effect. At least, this falsifies the belief of developmentalists that communication systems themselves are agents of social change and makes clear that "no unified body of theory is capable of explaining economic development" (Przeworski 1991a, p. 23).

A Western-type capitalism cannot be simply transplanted to East Europe because of huge cultural and ideological differences that are certainly not known to and understood by "irresponsible foreigners who do not distinguish between Mongolia and Slovenia" but have nevertheless been invited by postsocialist governments as economic saviors (Mencinger 1991b, p. 25). In both political and economic terms, East Europe is often closer to developing, rather than developed, countries. Thus, the concepts and strategies that may well apply in the developed market economies of the West are not wholly or directly appropriate to the former socialist countries. Even more, there is a great variability in patterns of change in developed countries themselves. Japan, for example, is a typical case of successful "domestication" rather than transplantation or imitation of Western capitalism, with a significant economic role for the state and a weak civil society (Morishima 1990, p. 62). Accordingly, Cui (1991, p. 65) concluded that "when we think of reforming state ownership in existing socialism, we need not search for a single 'best' form of ownership and adopt it once and for all. The most important lesson of human progress is 'experiment space' for innovation should be kept open. It might turn out that state ownership is still an 'efficient' form of ownership in some sectors of economy." Similarly, Lee (1991, p. 155) argued that historical developments in newly industrialized countries in Asia (e.g., South Korea, Taiwan, and Singapore) do not lend empirical support to the modernization theory formulated by developmentalists in the United States—at least not in the sense of a *universal* theory: "Economic development and media development indeed have gone hand in hand in these countries, but neither press freedom nor other political freedoms have kept up. The fundamental assumption, therefore, that economic growth will translate into a concomitant increase of press freedom must be either abandoned or radically modified."

On the contrary, it is easy to demonstrate that a consumer society and democracy are not synonymous: The free market flourished in junta-run Chile, in military-governed Taiwan and Korea, and earlier in a variety of autocratic European empires as well as their colonial possessions (Barber 1992, p. 59). Authoritarian temptations are even inevitable in newly democratized countries in East-Central Europe, Przeworski (1991b, p. 64) argued, because radical economic reforms are likely to limp under democratic conditions. As is already the case in a number of the former socialist countries, the new political and technocratic elites are becoming impatient because of democratic procedures that take a lot of time and are trying to "suppress *glasnost* in order to continue with *perestroika* of the economy." But tragically "democracy in a hurry often looks something like France in 1794 or China in 1989" (Barber 1992, p. 63).

Generally, a large proportion of populations in East Europe—in the abstract—support privatization of the economy as a means of achieving a more effective economic system. However, the contemporary erosion of consumers' standard of living, the rapid rise in prices, high inflation rates, the lack of investment potential, and growing economic inequalities have made many people, including journalists, hostile to the market economy that was supposed to "save them from poverty" and more hospitable to statism. According to Vladimir Shlapentokh (1990, p. 161), the new policy toward private business is disapproved by close to one-half of the population in the former Soviet Union. According to a 1991 survey conducted by the United States Information Agency in Romania, 54 percent of respondents believed that "some businesses should be privately owned and the government should continue to run the *majority* of businesses," while only 42 percent felt that "virtually all businesses should be privately owned" (*Economic Reform Today*, Fall 1991, p. 25). Similarly, in a public opinion poll taken in Poland, 91.4 percent of workers and 95 percent of managers accepted private initiative in crafts and services, but only 23 and 12.5 percent, respectively, approved of the same in heavy industry (Kozminski 1990, p. 138). Such a strong dissent has not only practical but also ideological grounds. For decades, the superiority of public ownership of the means of production over private property has been one of the cornerstones of socialist ideology and propaganda. According to a recent Hungarian study (Csepeli and

Orkeny 1992, p. 2), people rejecting "socialist identity" tend to favor classical social democratic solutions in terms of state intervention in health care, education, social policy, and housing and dislike market economy principles.

In capitalism, which stimulated the contemporary information revolution, a higher general level of productivity and thus a higher rate of profit were achieved without a significantly higher degree of exploitation in terms of lower wages and/or reduced social benefits (but certainly with some significant regional disparities and a generally increasing problem of unemployment). In the former state economies in East Europe, however, workers are much more severely affected by the shift toward privatization. It not only dramatically increases exploitation and unemployment but also decreases the purchasing power of the population in general. Structural reforms in East Europe are even predicted to cause economic decline (EESTR 1990).

It is clear, then, that private ownership of the means of production, which is going to replace state ownership in former socialist countries, is not the sufficient (even if necessary) condition for transplanting a profitable Western economy from advanced industrialized societies to the collapsed economies of East Europe. As Mark Raboy (1989, p. 8) remarked from his "admittedly western perspective, it seems . . . that there is a real danger that buzzwords like 'privatization' and 'perestroika' can end up meaning the same thing." Whatever the role of the "invisible hand" of privatization and market forces, many more factors producing contradictions and inequalities have to be "controlled" to establish more effective economic systems or to explain the role of civil society in recent political upheavals in East Europe. The ideas of the reformability of socialism into "market socialism" (Przeworski 1991a); the traditional role of the absolutist state in East Europe, which in contrast to Western Europe developed earlier, lasted much longer, and "nationalized" society (Szucs 1988, pp. 316–318); significant cultural differences; and rising contemporary nationalisms and chauvinisms are certainly such factors. As Veljko Rus (1991, p. 510) pointed out, "A mechanical inauguration of a new ownership structure has no chance to produce positive results unless it is accompanied by the emergence of a new culture—as we cannot imagine the emergence of capitalism without a simultaneous, or even previous, birth of the spirit of Protestantism and liberal culture."

Even more, as Aleksander Bajt (1991, p. 454) argued, "private property is the *only factor* whose absence still makes production possible," while it is not possible without labor, land, management in commodity-based economy, or invention. In particular, the form of property cannot be the most important economic factor under conditions of a forced transformation of state and "social" property into private property, where private ownership is primarily a political, rather than an economic, aim. And even more important, the idea that socialist countries simply need to "catch up," imitating the patterns of development known in (some) capitalist countries a century ago, conveniently ignores all the specific endogenous (national) and exogenous (international) factors in the development of modern "information societies." Such an idea is simply ahistorical and too contingent to explain the peculiarities of former socialist countries and their differences compared to ideal-typical Western democracies.

Paradox Number Two:
Political Communication Rooted in Economic Relations

A fundamental contradiction in the democratization of communications in East-Central Europe exists between the obvious tendencies of political and economic elites toward privatization and commercialization as a means of power and profit maximizing and the neglected development of public services as one of the cornerstones of more democratic communication. The lack of money and demand, a weak economy, and the general economic decline caused by structural reforms make this contradiction almost unsolvable, although both East European governments and Western observers largely believe that there exists a "magic key": liberalization and privatization. A liberal economic policy is considered inherent in the processes of making the economy more productive and social relations more democratic. This assumption can certainly be challenged on the basis of experiences in developed industrial societies. Some reasons showing that private ownership and free market philosophy cannot guarantee the quality and diversity of information needed for an active citizen participation in decisionmaking were discussed earlier. However, critical voices arguing that too close ties of the media to private capital will inevitably skew their contents in the direction of the interests of capital are largely overlooked.

The fetish of market competition among private individuals (the new dominant ideology in East Europe) and uncritical trust in the administrative state (the former dominant ideology) are in fact *complementary* perspectives. Both encourage the fragmentation of the social bonds of civil society (Keane 1988, p. 11; Rosanvallon 1988, p. 199). They support the logic of "developmental dictatorship" (Lee 1991), which emphasizes the necessity of strong centralization of authority and resources in order to implement the restructuring and modernizing of the economy.

One of the most persuasive examples of the complementarity of these two perspectives is probably that of Austria, with its fully regulated, highly centralized, and state-controlled broadcast system and its powerful oligopolies in a totally unregulated private print sector. Although the new broadcasting law adopted in July 1993, supported mainly by the Newspaper Editors and Publishers Association, foresees regional private radio stations in addition to the state-controlled radio, television remains in the hands of the state. On the other hand, the plurality of the party press has deteriorated in the past forty years into a "market-driven" monopoly system with only seventeen newspapers in the market, which are loosing "sovereignty" because of a massive inflow of foreign, mainly German capital. The German media concern Westdeutsche Allgemeine Zeitung bought 45 percent of the two newspapers with the largest circulation, and the Springer concern holds shares in another two Austrian dailies. Two-thirds of daily newspaper circulation—represented by conservatively oriented *Neue Kronenzeitung* (The New Crown Newspaper), *Kurier* (The Herald, or The Messenger), and *Kleine Zeitung* (The Little Newspaper)—are distributed by the same company and absorb two-thirds of branded goods newspaper advertising expenditure (Hummel 1990, p. 313). These trends brought the leftist-liberal *Arbeiter Zeitung* (Workers' Newspaper) close to the concourse; it was saved from wreck only with the help of its readers, who paid their subscriptions in advance and thus became its shareholders. Another strategy of newspapers' socialization is that accomplished by the privately owned French press company Ouest France, which was transformed into a nonprofit organization to resist both external and internal commercial pressures.

Generally, we may support, and the new governments in East-Central Europe should consider seriously, Rosanvallon's (1988, p. 201) thesis that "we have to overcome our misconception that public service = state control = nonprofit-making = equality, and that private service = the market = profit-making = inequality. The forward for the welfare state requires a new combination of these different components." In a similar way, Mulgan (1991, p. 248) argued that simple dichotomies such as state versus market, regulation versus deregulation, monopoly versus competition, and public versus private obscure as much as they illuminate:

> Competition has, paradoxically, often served to strengthen monopolies. State and market interpenetrate more than ever before. In modern industrialized countries the boundaries of traditional categories have eroded beyond repair; states are massively implicated in all areas of the economy. . . . Within state bureaucracies market systems spring up, while market sectors create their own quasi-state organizations. . . . In both broadcasting and telecommunications global competition between transnational corporations is closer to medieval jousting for territorial control than the classic vision of atomistic markets.

I am not intending to deny the significance of private ownership for the increase of productivity or to object to the processes of depublicization of the economic sphere as essential for the (re)constitution of civil society. However, I strongly disagree with the belief that changes in the ownership of the means of production in general and of the media in particular can radically transform former socialist economies and democratize societies without other important structural changes initiated and supported by the state and civil society itself. As the monthly *Direct Line* published by the International Federation of Journalists critically observed, the newly developing democracies have inspired enthusiasm for trade unionism among journalists, but "hopes of a rapid move towards press freedom have given way to unease among many journalists about the commitment of their leaders to building new media structures which will protect independent journalism. Little action has been taken in any of the new democracies to limit the advance of the Western-based media monopolies which are beginning to take major stakes in the written press" (*Mass Media* 1990a, p. 1). And Sparks (1991b, p. 14) noteworthily added, "Moves towards the extension of the market can easily be combined with increased government intervention and censorship. The peoples in East Europe rightly demand democracy. The unfettered market will deny most people both a voice in the media and the information they need to exercise rational political choice."

The criticism of private commercial interests as being the most (or even the only) suitable medium for democratization of communications is certainly not new, and it is directly related to the concept of public service and the need to revise it (e.g., Williams 1976; Keane 1991). In Armand Mattelart's perspective, commercialization and privatization appear as the guiding principles of pluralization of society only in the absence of a reexamination of the concept of plurality itself: "The plurality of the groups making up civil society and the diversity of their interests *demolishes* a strictly juridico-political and, more often than not, formal conception of pluralism as the doctrinaire foundation of the public service" (Mattelart and Piemme 1984, p. 221; italics added).

It is true that the awareness of the importance of market competition, commodity production, and exchange among private individuals was an essential element in the modernization of the classical concept of civil society, but the economy in that time was a *preindustrial economy* based on loosely structured and almost perfect and *transparent* competition among small propertied worker-entrepreneurs. In addition, civil society consisted of a great number of diverse *nonentrepreneurial* (and even antibourgeois) groups and associations that had in common a "fear of despotism," which stimulated—much more than the love of capitalism—a political fight against state despotism (Keane 1988, p. 64). The rhetoric of the privatized economy as the cornerstone of political pluralism and parliamentary democracy simply misses these important accounts of modern civil society.

Although traditionally a (free market) economy was considered the guarantor and the basis of individualism—the key dimension of the autonomy of civil society in relation to the state—contemporary corporate capitalism (re)produces *economic inequalities* to the degree that they prevent a large part of citizens from participation in, and control of, "democratic" decisions. Indeed, by the second half of the nineteenth century, the press had begun to be dominated by chain-owning proprietors. This was the result of an escalation in publishing costs, which "did not just affect individual access to the public sphere: it debarred access for large sections of the community" (Curran 1991, p. 41). It shifted citizens away from participation in decisionmaking and control, which became increasingly governed by a bureaucratic organizational imperative and technocratic knowledge, and strengthened their consumer function. As a consequence, *"political* choice was limited to the prescriptions formulated by business and *politicized* in its advertising" (Ewen 1977, p. 91). Oligopolistic tendencies and forces tended to prevail over those of a "spontaneous" and "free" market and disqualified the traditionally political realms of government and civil society. "The crystallization of groups into firms, associations and corporations, and subsequent mergers, takeovers and syndications points towards the development of a network of mutual dependencies and recognitions which makes the fluidity of the civil society as it was originally conceived quite problematic" (Giner, 1985, p. 259).

The consequence of this process is a steady *erosion of civil society*. As Chantal Mouffe (1988, p. 97) concluded, "Democracy is thus emptied of all of its substance." In a seminal work on the restructuring of the public, Habermas (1969) saw this process of "refeudalization" of the public as the key feature of advanced capitalist societies, where civil society has been *derationalized* and *commodified*. It has been intruded on by state control and manipulation and by commodity relations—specifically through the distortion of communication in the form of political marketing and advertising—so that civil society has turned into a "counterfactual" ideal.

The traditional line of separation between "associations of *equals*" in the economic sphere and civil society and "associations of *unequals*" in the political sphere and the state (Bobbio 1989, p. 6) has become problematic because of the growing discrepancy between formal equality and actual inequality in the economic sphere. The boundaries between the state and civil society are "mediated by the bargaining, jostling and shifting compromises of 'public' officials and state machinery and private, 'non-state' agencies" (Keane 1991, p. 107). Equality of citizens in its broadest sense as the fundamental democratic (political-ethical) value pertinent to civil society is becoming subordinated to a certain form of individual liberty—*economic liberty and private property*. At this point, it is worth recalling Gramsci's (1971) idea of "moving" civil society (in contrast to Karl Marx) from the sphere of the "material base" to the "superstructure," thus stressing civil society's distinctiveness from both political power in the strict sense or "direct domination" ("political society" or the state) and economic power.

The role of the marketplace has been changed similarly to that of political parties. According to Bobbio (1989, p. 25), political parties must be placed among subjects of economic, social, ideological, and religious conflicts constitutive of civil society. At the same time, modern political parties also belong to authoritative institutions. This major change in the position of political parties is indicated by special legal and constitutional provisions defining the role and rights of political parties. They are totally integrated neither in the state nor in civil society but rather constitute a "political society" that mediates between the state and civil society. The contemporary state largely became a "party-state"; parliament became a site where the representatives of political parties, rather than of citizens, met to validate claims of their own political party in terms of generalized interests. The phenomenon of the party-state was particularly significant for the socialist state, which institutionally achieved stability and uniformity by suppressing the plurality of political parties. However, a similar process of domination of political parties and their specific interests in parliament must be regarded as an essential element in the ongoing transformations of the capitalist state, although it does not suppress differentiation to such a degree as the socialist state did.

Apart from political parties, the contemporary state is differentiated internally into other semisovereign organizations, such as trade unions and large enterprises (Bobbio 1989, p. 16). Powerful and traditionally autocratic economic actors (e.g., large enterprises, especially transnational corporations) may be considered to have a "mediating role" similar to that of political parties, provided that attempts to extend democratic procedures and control to these actors will be successful. If not, powerful economic actors will continue to act in the sphere of "invisible power"; and this is precisely what often happens. Corporate influence on the economy, the state, and the media remains almost untouched: Neither the state nor the media are able to challenge it. As Bagdikian (1983, p. 238) put it, corporate power prefers "private greed to public civilization" and uses the media and government to ridicule "governmental functions that serve ordinary people, while demanding that government further enrich private fortunes." Precisely because of this, it is even more important for the projects for democratization of society to imply both a revitalization of democratic institutions of the state and an extension of principles of democratic association to the economy (Arato and Cohen 1984, p. 273).

Although the role of political parties and powerful economic actors has significantly changed during the last century, thus making the borderline between the state and civil society less transparent, the principal function of mass communication remains, at least theoretically, unchanged. The mass media operate simultaneously in the realms of the state (politics) *and* economy (within or without civil society) and mediate between them. Or, according to Gouldner (1976, p. 123), they "stand *between* the public, on the one side, and, on the other, the official managers of institutions, organizations, movements, or the society's hegemonic elites," thus making the relations of the media "to political parties here and elsewhere, the relations to the business world and to the numerous groups and interests who influence and who are influenced by the public" (Weber 1976, p. 99) the real site of the problem. If the mass media by definition link the two opposing spheres and simultaneously perform political and economic functions, there is no rationality for the media to be totally subsumed under either of them.

The problem with market liberalism, which insists that market competition of the media is the most important precondition of their freedom, is precisely in such an invalid subsumption. Market liberalism assumes that the basic right to private property—because *everyone* has this right—guarantees both freedom of the media (their independence from the state) and freedom of citizens (free choice among different media and contents). In fact, this is clearly an ideal type of "free market," which in practice does not exist given the processes of capital concentration and centralization. As a consequence, the "free" media market is largely oligopolized, and "free" choice is severely limited by constrained supply. According to Downing (1984, p. 6), "Commercial media conventionally portray themselves as virtual slaves to 'the market'—as providing people with exactly what they want! They quietly gloss over the power of major advertisers and corporations to define *poor* people's media wants as irrelevant, compared to those of the more affluent sectors of the market. . . . Only the extraordinarily gullible believe in the democratic passions of commercial media executives."

On the consumer side, the expansion of commercialized media "pluralism" is limited because "the audience pie is not getting bigger," which implies that "seekers of slices of it have to wrest them from each other, making the chase for viewers almost a zero-sum game" (Blumler 1991, p. 5). Even for producers, the free market does not ensure free access to the "deregulated" marketplace because of the levels of investment required to enter the market, rising program production costs, and/or already existing oligopolies (particularly resulting from syndicatable entertainment programming). In Jay Blumler's words (1991, p. 9), the "gathering momentum" of organizational concentration and conglomeration in mass communications tends to limit the opportunities of independent producers to offer profitably something different from mainstream supply and fosters standardization of program supply across the entire media (particularly television) industry. At the same time, it jeopardizes media pluralism because it creates a risk that the main channels of access to the public may eventually be controlled by a small number of strategically placed and minimally accountable gatekeepers. This process is already taking place in the former socialist countries. In the CSFR, for example, many student cable radio stations went off the air as a result of the invasion of Western-dominated commercial stations, and the student stations did not even apply for FM broadcast licenses because they did not have any chance to survive.

Evolution toward an oligopolistic media structure is paralleled by two opposing tendencies (Servaes 1991, p. 15). On the one hand, an obvious tendency toward diversification, fragmentation, and individualization is developing in the *hardware* (video, cable, satellites, computer technology, etc.) and *software* (special programs, such as news, sports, movies, entertainment) sectors resulting in specific and distinguishable products supplied to specific target audiences. On the other hand, in terms of quality and contents most of these products are standardized, aimed at (and actually producing) a collective, rather than an individual, choice and increased uniformity and conformity on the consumer side. A recent German study provided accounts of the consequences brought about by the shift from a public television monopoly to a dual (public and private) broadcasting system: "Certain politicians' expectations that more stations would offer an increased variety of political perspectives have probably been disappointed: the audience interested in political information and current affairs continues to choose the public channels, though in somewhat reduced numbers. The decline of political viewing on public television has not been compensated by the private stations; instead the audience drifts away from political to entertainment content" (Holtz-Bacha 1991, p. 231).

Latin American experiences show that the competition between public and private corporations leads to a "self-commercialization" of the public media. Specifically, the emerging privatization reduces the amount of in-house (particularly cultural and educational) programming and increases the amount of imported programs. "Although the private sector could sometimes serve as a guarantee against government control and manipulation under dictatorial or authoritarian regimes, it had neither the public accountability nor the mechanisms to enforce these freedoms for others, especially for the disadvantaged. The abandonment of communication rights to the exclusive criteria and responsibility of the private sector could leave important sectors of society *unprotected and open to exploitation*" (Fox 1988, p. 33; italics added).

But the failure of market liberalism to perceive all these severe restrictions on the democratic potency of private media are not a matter of principle. Market liberals' *fundamental failure,* however, is the inability to distinguish and then comprehend the contradiction *between the economic sphere* (representing either a part of civil society or an autonomous subsystem as conceptualized by Gramsci) *and the political sphere* of the state, "between the economic and the political at the level of their value systems and of the social relations which those value systems require and support" (Garnham 1990, p. 110). If two incompatible economic and political sets or systems of values and relations exist, and the media mediate between them, why should the media be subjected to the laws of economy rather than polity? The media are political institutions par excellence, not just commercial enterprises. By forcing *political communication* to channel itself via *commercial media,* the advocates of market liberalism transform public communication into the politics of consumerism, and citizens are made into consumers.

There is no doubt that the need for the political independence of the media is still great and perhaps greater than in the past. As Garnham (1990, p. 110) argued, it is also possible that the "pursuit of political freedom may override the search for economic efficiency." However, this is only one side of the contradiction between the two spheres. The other is that "the extent of possible political freedom is constrained by the level of material productivity" (Garnham 1990, p. 110). Advertisers who seek increasing amounts of time and space for their commercials in the media "strive for congenial programming environments, and deliberately fashion messages that are unobtrusive and difficult to avoid" (Blumler 1991, p. 12).

Opportunities for citizens to act independently presuppose direct participation in the regulation and control of those organizations and institutions that directly affect citizens' lives and, primarily, the existence of community services, self-managed (nationally, socially, and cooperatively owned) enterprises, and public institutions in addition to private enterprises. To create *equal* opportunities for citizens, the unequal distribution of all kinds of private-property–based resources (material and mental) in the economy (productive property) should be fundamentally changed to obtain at least the minimum quantity of resources necessary for the protection and exercise of citizens' individual and collective rights. "Without clear restrictions on private ownership, a necessary condition of democracy cannot be met" (Held 1989, p. 294). Marx's (1974) famous remark that the first freedom of the press is that of not being reduced to business can be rephrased nowadays: The right to democracy cannot be reduced to the freedom to maximize profit, because this would imply a decline of the right to democracy.

The contradiction between the economic sphere of civil society and the political sphere of the state is fully developed in Western capitalist societies. As a number of studies report, the contents of privately owned television stations (still) diverge significantly from those of public corporations in terms of structure and values. However, public broadcasters do not strengthen their distinctive image of serious public affairs journalism, cultural programming, and educational programming vis-à-vis commercial stations. On the contrary, they largely yield to the competitive pressures of commercial stations and include more fiction and other "denationalized" lightweight entertainment programs. As an NBC executive in the United States pointed out, "A network cannot bow to higher standards if its competitors all round adopt lower ones. It becomes a greyer issue when it's all around you, and you're the last person crying 'Wait a minute'" (Blumler 1991, p. 9).

In the former socialist countries in East-Central Europe, this contradiction is partly "softened" by the absence of a truly developed market economy and the continuing domination of the state over the economy. At the same time, however, this contradiction is strengthened by the low level of investment in domestic programming. Rising production costs lead to an increase in less expensive imported commercial programs transmitted by "public" television stations. Thus, the contradiction between the state and civil society in the media sphere is not just a question of (formal) ownership and control; it is much more a question of values and ideologies dominating the global market.

Even if civil society is colonized by the state, which is still the case in the republics of the former Soviet Union, international commercial forces are becoming decisive. Apart from this, even there clear indigenous differences exist between those media regulated by the political values of the state and those regulated by the values of civil society, although the latter are not related to economic efficiency. According to a recent analysis of the media in Byelarus

(Manaev and Jefimova, 1991), the "official" media present the relationship between the opposing spheres (the state versus civil society) primarily as differences between the "pro*perestroika*" (democratic) and "anti*perestroika*" (conservative) tendencies *within* the same organizations and groups, which suggests that no tensions exist between the state and civil society. In contrast, the "unofficial" media interpret the same relationship as a confrontation *among* different social actors (government, parties, associations, social movements). Whereas the former present the differences as largely solvable, the latter see no solution other than open confrontation. These examples clearly indicate the importance of recognizing analytically the contradiction between the two spheres and their importance for de- or reregulation of the media.

4 The Mobilization of the State and the Control of Media Organizations

The ideal of civil society and the media autonomous from the state did not lose its viability as a fundamental condition of democracy in spite of often invisible market and state forces penetrating both the media and civil society. In the previous chapter I tried to show why (re)privatization of the means of production and particularly of the media is paradoxical in terms of their democratization. However, while postsocialist theorists argue for a "pure" market economy, they largely neglect the role of state institutions. In practice, however, national state institutions are not only indispensable given the socialist and broader cultural heritage and the lack of a genuine market economy; they also tend to reappropriate the power that limits the autonomy of both the economy and civil society. To a certain degree, democratic reforms in East-Central Europe were certainly successful, mainly for having introduced parliamentary political democracy and party pluralism. But even if parliamentary democracy is formally established, it is not in terms of fundamental procedural rules resulting from the ideals of *toleration* (against any form of fanaticism and revenge) and *nonviolence* (Bobbio 1987, pp. 41–42) that in the West represent the base for a culture of tolerance and permissiveness. In contrast to the mature democratic countries, which passed through a lengthy period of "protodemocracy" (Dahl 1991, p. 14), the newly emerging democracies in East-Central Europe are lacking in any democratic political culture. It is not surprising, then, that political institutions in these countries are extremely fragile and often seem to be a replay of paternalistic politics aimed at the reconstruction of a version of the party-state. This can be best exemplified by the growing role of the state in services, state- and/or party-supported nationalisms, the lack of political opposition, intolerance of criticism (e.g., of nationalism or privatization) or arguments for a different social system, and, particularly, the absence of any consensual model of democracy. As Held (1989, p. 194) suggested, "The social prerequisites of a functioning polyarchy—consensus on the rules of procedure; consensus on the range of policy options; consensus on the legitimate scope of political activity—are the most profound obstacles to all forms of oppressive rule. *The greater the extent of consensus, the securer the democracy*" (italics added).

Although civil society was the most important revolutionary moment, revolutionary changes reintegrated it with the state. The newly emerging political parties (re)presented in parliament their own, rather than citizens', interests and "political will." Limited participation among large segments of citizenry points to the fact that new political regimes are losing legitimacy. In Hungary, for example, voter turnout averaged 48 percent nationwide in the 1990 parliamentary elections, and local elections had to be repeated because of low turnout. In Poland, only 40 percent of the electorate voted in the 1991 parliamentary elections.

In capitalist democracies, the control of state institutions by economic interest groups is often considered dangerous because of the development of bureaucratic interests and structures within the realm of the state. In East Europe, however, the danger of the (re)development of a bureaucratic party-state structure stems from the nonexistence of powerful interest groups in the sphere of the economy. Paradoxically, this trend is reinforced by the fact that the state apparatus largely consists of former socialist public officers and civil servants (with the exception of the command positions), who are primarily a special interest group (interested in their own careers) rather than representatives of the interests of the former ruling class. Generally, power is still contested by a limited number of groups in society and shared by an even smaller number of groups. It is not surprising, then, that the media are easily controlled by the state, particularly where no genuine competition exists at all—in broadcasting.

The Persisting Tradition of the Paternalistic State

The ability of the state (or any other power actor) to maintain *control* over the social system and its environment to prevent its own internal disintegration is inseparably related to communication and information processing. In fact, the growing complexity of the world gives rise to a permanent crisis of control. A policy tending to restore whatever limited control over its "own" system aims at separating the system from its environment by maintaining boundaries that are often deliberately exaggerated by the power structure (Kivikuru 1990, p. 2). As Jacques Semelin (1991, p. 17) argued for East Europe, "On the one hand, these countries need and want Western aid, but on the other, they cannot allow their 'audiovisual space' to be invaded and *controlled* by foreign companies, Western or otherwise" (italics added).

The reason for such a defense policy "is always a 'conservative' one: the unwanted pieces of information are believed to be negative and painful, i.e., to threaten the stability of the *present* internal information structure" (Geyer 1980, p. 53). Although there are normally different ways to reduce system complexity and to maintain control, forms of social, political, or economic control (e.g., through language, customs, norms of behavior, economic policy, and, of course, the media) often *favor system* (group, nation, class) *identity* against the identity of individuals and thus against intrasystem differences. This is typically the case with peripheral societies.

However, a *total* control implying the elimination of any uncertainty is simply not possible. It is limited by a constant tendency toward the change, differentiation, and evolution inherent in any system. Contrary to peripheral systems that largely tend to achieve a state of *independence* or even closure (autarky), core systems aim at shaping and transforming their environment into an output environment (one that does not influence the system, but is strongly influenced by it) so that they can influence ever-larger groups of people and societies. These systems also aim at increasing the permeability of their boundaries so that more inputs and outputs can pass through them, which increases both integration and differentiation within the system. Apparently, the former policy is that of territory-based identity, and the latter is that of an interdependence-based identity and aimed at globalization and universalization. The problem is, however, that choosing between one or the other type of strategy is associated, among other things, with available material resources.

A striving for system identity generally tends to appear more frequently on the periphery and in small, less populous, and less (economically) developed societies than in the core or metropolis and more populated societies (nations). On the power dimension, a periphery always implies a state of underdevelopment (e.g., economic, political, cultural), inferiority (e.g., cultural, racial, linguistic), and low self-esteem and generally an inability to control others' activities. Peripheries represent an input environment where a one-way "external" influence is exerted by the core on the periphery, which lacks the ability to constrain the power exerted on it or to adapt to external challenges. The peripheral environment can be constituted from the personal to the global level; a typical input environment (as opposed to the output environment) is represented by the exposure to the mass media that is characteristic for both national (exposure of individuals and groups to "national media") and global scenes (exposure of nations and cultures to the "global media"). It is meaningful, then, to distinguish between an internal and an external periphery:

1. An *internal periphery* represents powerless, marginal, and underprivileged groups or subsystems suppressed by the center, which is represented by the state (versus civil society), "national interests" (versus "local" interests), the economy (versus culture), and so forth.

2. An *external periphery* represents whole societies (states) pushed into a peripheral position globally (e.g., the "Third World").

The role of the state in the processes of internal and external peripheralization is contradictory: In the former case, the state represents a power actor tending toward integration (even centralization and uniformity) within society, whereas in the latter case, the state represents a tendency toward (international) differentiation since it acts as the guarantor of "national" freedom and individuality. To a certain degree, the two processes correspond in the sense that "the stronger the state and therefore less limited internally, the stronger it is and less limited externally. . . . The more a state succeeds in binding its own subjects, the more it succeeds in becoming independent of other states" (Bobbio 1989, pp. 97–98). Analytically, the two roles can be clearly separated; politically, this is much more difficult to do. In fact, this was the main controversy in the longlasting debates on the new world information and communication order: Whereas the West "internationalized" internal peripheralization and conceptually reduced the role of the state to that of coercion (e.g., as an obstacle to freedom of the press), the South "internalized" external peripheralization as the state would be the guarantor of freedom both externally (national sovereignty) and internally (equality of citizens).

One of the central questions here is whether contemporary global changes transform the relationship between the state and individuals in civil society and, if so, how these changes (may) occur in different political and cultural settings. In the Western industrialized societies, the development of the public sphere at the national level is challenged by the development of transnational, private, high-cost, proprietary information and communication networks and services (Garnham 1990, p. 114). To avoid the danger of "dysfunctional ignorance" of citizens, a tendency exists toward *internationalization of the public sphere*, which supports (and is supported by) the revival of the "national" public sphere and parallels new trends in the "world economy": "If by communicative democracy we understand in part the ability of every group or social force to seek to affect policy-making on matters of importance to them by means of reaching the policy-makers with information and opinions on those matters, then this now increasingly involves introducing those messages into international communication" (Jakubowicz 1993a, p. 48).

In the developed part of the world, globalization, which is largely based on informatization, reduces (at least relatively), rather than expands, the state power because of the growing "ungovernability" of modern complex societies, shifting internal boundaries between the state and civil society, and the growing interdependence of states on the global level. The powerfulness of the state is apparently counterbalanced, or reduced, both nationally and internationally by an increasing complexity of social systems and their environment: More and more internal and external information is needed for the same relative level of control in/over society. Because more control is in principle available to all, according to Mulgan (1991, p. 5), "the relative impacts of this on the balance between different social classes, professions or institutions are inherently hard to predict."

At the same time, the new information sector in society adds new functions to government, and thus the apparatus of government and its power to control expand because of the same process of informatization. More, and more detailed, information is available to governments and state institutions, which enables them to perform effectively their tasks but also to interfere with the political and social freedoms of individual citizens. As Webster and Robins (1989, p. 327) argued, the function of social management and administration and the function of surveillance and control are closely related and mutually reinforcing functions of information technologies. In principle, the more efficient and professional the state becomes, the more the freedom of individuals is threatened. The old question of the democratic system—"Who guards the guards?"—can now be reformulated as, "Who controls the controllers?" (Bobbio 1987, p. 34).

Indeed, global economic and communication restructuring implies a *redefinition*, rather than a suppression of the role of the state. Although the capitalist economy has since its beginnings been a world economy constructed by "integrating a geographically vast set of production processes" (Wallerstein 1990, p. 35) *in opposition* to predominantly national political pressures (the state), its globalization does not lead to the withdrawal of the state, just as privatization in underdeveloped East-Central-Europe did not do so. On the contrary, "in Britain, the effect of privatising monopoly utilities may well have the result of creating a situation of *more detailed and more explicit interventionism* through the publicly-appointed regulatory authorities" (Vickers and Wright 1988, p. 28; italics added). State institutions are less and less limited to political-administrative institutions and more and more involved in all kind of relationships traditionally understood as belonging to civil society. The economy is clearly a sphere where a clear-cut borderline between the state and civil society is becoming less and less feasible because in the recent history of the Western developed countries, in the socialist countries, and in the less developed countries, the state has become part of everything in the economy (Martinelli and Smelser 1990, p. 43). As summarized by Mulgan (1991, p. 137):

> In the past, the control of communications networks was primarily determined by considerations of security, nation-building or social equity. By the late 1980s and early 1990s the needs of the economy for productivity growth and competitiveness far outweighed other considerations. Paradoxically deregulations coincided with an ever more active role for governments and state agencies in creating what they believed to be the best climate for the communications economy. What was happening was not the end of state control (although there was a clear erosion of the powers of the national state) but rather a change in its forms, a change that can best be understood as one from control within a closed system to control within an open one.

The expansion of the state into all spheres of social life—as employer, regulator, educator, manager of public services, producer and consumer of (particularly military) products, entrepreneur, and investor—and the great semipublic coalition between the state and capital change the traditional relationships between the state and civil society. What the consequences are of the expansion of the information sector at the level of individual knowledge and consciousness is another question. The expanding economic role of the state has become even more critical with the globalization of the economy. On the one hand, this development weakens the contemporary state and its control over the "national economy" (except in autocratic states). On the other hand, this process of "peripheralization" of nation-states activates their involvement in, and responsibility for, national economies to protect them from international economic forces. In both cases, however, decisions are largely "depoliticized," removed from political (public) control and given to experts in either corporate organizations or the state, and citizens lose their ability to participate in political processes.

In fact, more effective, sophisticated, and professionalized control supports bureaucratic domination by the state and multinational corporations in the form of political leadership, with significant business participation resulting in a kind of "subterranean government" over civil society. The intangibility of the private sphere of civil society is eroded, as is the public character of political power, its openness to the public. Since a clear distinction between the private (economy) and the public (polity) does not exist, the distinction between the state and civil society is eroded as well. The penetration of the state into every sphere of social life means, at best, "an erosion of what was once considered an inviolable sphere; at worst, it blurs the essential distinction between the public and the private, and between the state and civil society" (Giner 1985, p. 260).

The state has taken over a number of cultural and ideological functions relating to economic life that were traditionally attached to individuals, communities, and associations in the cultural sphere (religion, ideology, education). Administrative penetration into the life worlds of individuals increases their dependence on "public" administrative agencies and undermines previously existing forms of "private" associations. As Alberto Martinelli and Neil Smelser (1990, p. 43) maintained, "These cultural-ideological roles of the state and other agencies are an important component in economically relevant matters such as generating and sustaining labour motivation, defining priorities between economic and other societal goals, and securing the legitimacy of competing economic interest groups and classes."

The plurality of these "interest groups and classes," the distribution of power among them, and their autonomy from the state represent the hallmark of classical conceptions of democracy as a form of political participation. From this particular perspective, a reexamination of traditional thoughts about the state and civil society is certainly needed given fundamental technological, economic, and political changes. For example, the relation between the state and the media cannot be reduced to a simple disengagement of the state in the name of a liberal philosophy of market-based pluralism. Even contemporary practice in West Europe (e.g., France) falsifies such a naive managerial ideology (Miege and Salaun 1989).

Although present developments in West Europe could be a useful guide to future outcomes in East-Central Europe, no simple "analytic transplantation" is possible. There is no doubt that the merger of economic and political activities in the hands of the former socialist state produced a totalitarian system suppressing differentiation, individuality, and freedom (and thus civil society) and blocking the system's own development. Did the democratic changes after the velvet revolutions "revolutionize" these relations? The answer is hardly affirmative. The system of state socialism was overthrown overnight, but it has not been replaced by effective parliamentary democracy or a market economy. Rather, a kind of postsocialist system has been established that is still determined more by the old structural relations than by the new ones. Whereas the former restrictions on plurality of interests and opinions and freedom of the press were aimed at class-ideological homogenization, the new ones were introduced in the name of sovereignty and independence. Similarly, the introduction of a multiparty political system did not challenge the traditional concept of the party-state as *the* embodiment of freedom. As Marc Plattner (1991, p. 39) observed, "The strongest argument in favour of authoritarianism today is its alleged ability to dismantle a socialist economy." Consequently, the control of the media by parliaments (i.e., political parties) is regarded as a "natural" and the highest "democratic" form of the regulation of the communication sphere.

New elites often tend to monopolize the media. In Russia, as Sergei Muratov (1991, p. 181) observed, both the defenders of independent television and the representatives of the state-run television consider a centralized broadcast leadership unavoidable:

> On more than one occasion even Gosteleradio spoke out against the Minister of Communications' monopoly of information, insisting that the means of electronic communication should be in the hands of program-makers. It goes without saying that Gosteleradio's antimonopoly stance was mostly interested in *replacing one monopoly with another*. But a trace of the *same kind of thinking* comes through even in NIKA-TV President Lutshenko's proposal to entrust all the functions of public television to the employees of his independent television station. (italics added)

In the former socialist countries, the cultural sphere—in contrast to the economy—became during the 1980s relatively much more internationalized (including the media) and less state controlled (with the exception of the media, particularly broadcasting). "While in the age of tolerant repression the depoliticization and Westernization of popular culture proceeded slowly, from the late 1970s on American mass culture flew into these [countries of] Eastern Europe in unprecedented quantity" (Sukosd 1990, p. 54).

Nevertheless, during the entire period the media were largely insulated from both internal and external competition because of a centrally planned economy, the absence of a market economy, and political pluralism. Both political (or ideological) and economic frontiers (limited financial possibilities for importing foreign cultural goods) effectively protected national cultures and the media from "cultural imperialism," which, however, even stimulated some quality TV programming (e.g., in the CSFR). Nevertheless, the former Yugoslav model of media organization, which was based on (the ideology of) "self-management" and in a number of ways was similar to public service broadcasting in West Europe, raised several possibilities for the active participation of citizens, although in practice these possibilities were not generally realized (Splichal 1990a). Similarly, Solidarity in Poland had already declared in 1981 the transformation of society into a "self-governing commonwealth" as the ultimate goal of social and political reforms and the removal of all barriers to communication to be achieved by means of the "socialization of the media" (Jakubowicz 1990, pp. 336, 340). However, as in the West, enthusiasm for a pluralist and democratic society has not been accompanied by a "sufficiently concrete articulation of the means at hand by which the new social movements can secure and sustain freedom of communication and participation in national and supranational discourse" (Calabrese, forthcoming).

In contemporary practice in East-Central Europe, the spirit of these ideas is subverted by the fact that the media lack much of their autonomy and are largely assessed (even discriminated against) according to the general political and ideological division between the new (anticommunist) and the old (procommunist) parties. A rather typical example was the decree issued by Boris Yeltsin immediately after the failed coup d'état in August 1991. The decree banned all newspapers published by the Soviet Communist Party. Although the suspension was a reaction against the restrictions imposed on the majority of the media by the State Committee for the State of Emergency during the anti-Gorbachev coup, Yeltsin's decision violated one of the basic preconditions of democracy—the protection of groups with a different political orientation and those that enjoy less than majority power.

Obviously, the effectual overthrow of the former socialist regimes would not have been possible without latent alternative political elites. Although the former regimes considered the intelligentsia (including *some* journalists) the main potential enemies and were continually trying to suppress their opposition, these regimes did not succeed in subordinating universities, cultural institutions, or even the media to a total state or party control. With the partial exception of Poland, where trade unionism represented the most powerful opposition to the Communist Party during the 1980s, civil movements and criticisms largely originated from the cultural sphere. To a certain degree, the political importance of the cultural sphere in East-Central Europe was not exceptional, as Gouldner (1976, p. 185) would argue: "The university today is the key modern institution for the training of ideologues: it is also that single institution from which most modern ideologues derive their livings. . . . While the political dispositions of the university-based ideologists are quite various, there is little doubt that the modern university is also the largest single site for the production and storage of *anti*establishment ideologists; this means antibourgeois ideologists in Western countries and anticommunist ideologists in the Eastern."

What was unique in the postsocialist countries, however, was intellectuals' massive "invasion" of polity after the decay of the former regimes and "migration" from the domain of civil society to that of the state. Everywhere former university professors, writers, and artists occupied high political offices in the governments and parliaments. In the socialist regimes, intellectuals by and large represented the only opposition to the state or to the party and thus constituted, at least to a limited extent, the autonomy of civil society. During the democratic elections in 1990–1991, however, they joined different (new) political parties contesting for political power. The old power elites were overthrown overnight, but in the process the former civil society was largely destroyed again and reabsorbed by the state. This essentially unchanged structure of power—with a powerful state and a quasi-independent civil society—may be related to two distinct "traditions." On the one hand, Gouldner (1976, p. 291) suggested that "the conflict between the practice of oligarchy and the principles of popular sovereignty is a *universal contradiction of all modern societies, and of revolutionary movements* in which many originated. It is this contradiction between their claim to represent the whole, and the reality of their partisanship, that is the grounding of ideology today in both capitalist and socialist societies" (italics added). On the other hand, the nature of the relationship between the state and civil society is culturally bound. With the exception of Czechoslovakia, both the former and still existing socialist countries did not have any experience with democratic government in their presocialist history. In Russia, for example, civil society "had perished ingloriously at the first onslaught of revolution because it had always been extremely weak" (Giner 1985, p. 258). According to Mihaly Vajda (1988, p. 340), the contradiction between the state and civil society is specifically rooted in common East-Central European traditions: "Historically, these traditions simply mean that these societies have in many ways wrested a measure of independence from political power: that is, have ceased to be purely 'statal societies' on the Eastern model. It is true that their attempts at demanding a share of political decision-making, their efforts at making the state representative, have mostly been unsuccessful. Politics has always been a preserve of the elite, of 'our masters.'"

The new power actors (governments and political parties in power) in the former socialist countries tend to reproduce, at least partly, the old form of hegemony, which is supported by the lack of indigenous economic elites and based on the new but still exclusive (political and nationalist) ideology of political parties not readily allowing adversary power actors and civil society to participate in decisionmaking and to control the activities of the state. The absence of two essential elements—a substantial middle class and a democratic culture—limits the possibility of a quick transition from socialism to Western-type democracy. As in the former socialist period, the ruling elites claim to represent the whole society, but they cannot overcome the reality of their own partisanship. However, they expect citizens to assess elite actions from a perspective entirely different from the one those elites imposed on the former regime. The paradoxical situation of the new political elites is similar to that of Richard Nixon, as described by Sennett (1978, p. 286): "Having all his life sought legitimacy through his rage against the Establishment, when he became supreme as ruler, he suddenly expected the public to judge him in terms completely different from and more realistic than the terms in which he hoped them to judge his political enemies on the way up." The new political classes justify their power on an ethical basis with reference to history—as a necessary consequence of generally accepted anticommunist political doctrine. Their appeals to history and traditions and particularly their reinterpretation of history do not represent a return to the past; rather, they are an endeavor to reinterpret the past to achieve popular support for their goals and future activities. Their claims to legitimacy are both conservative and revolutionary at the same time. Their universalistic reference to the long-lasting history of capitalism in the world as the only rational system reveals the conservative principle of legitimacy. Their reference to the new, postsocialist (in fact, capitalist again) order as a progressive step in the development of their particular country connotes the revolutionary dimension of legitimation.

Although the electorates in East-Central Europe acclaimed the overthrow of the old regimes and made new parliaments and governments legitimate, they are much more critical of the newest developments, particularly of the political and economic ineffectiveness of the new authorities. The reaction of the Polish electorate might be typical: Only 40 percent of voters participated in the 1991 parliamentary elections. After the new elites came to power, their cooperation with the intelligentsia and the media became problematic—a situation similar to that which occurred after the bourgeois revolution, when the alliance between the emerging middle class and the intelligentsia, which had been based on their suppression by the feudal regime, was broken up.

New ruling coalitions in East-Central Europe, which include such diverse political parties as Christian democrats and social democrats, were basically founded as anticommunist coalitions without any significant and transparent differentiation in terms of their political platforms. A number of new anticommunist ideologists were close collaborators of the former regimes. All coalitions were basically patched up for a tactical electoral advantage aimed at overthrowing the former socialist regimes and introducing parliamentary democracy. Nevertheless, after a few months these alliances did not seem as easily discardable as was the case before the elections. In terms of homogeneity and hostility to oppositional parties, the party political alliances in power resemble the former communist parties.[1] They are often organized on the principle of *democratic centralism* introduced by the Communist Party. Different forms of "informal coordination" actually disqualify parliament as a site of decision-making and transform it into an obedient agent of informal ruling political elites. As the president of the parliament of the Republic of Slovenia argued, such an exclusive dichotomy is not accidental: "The socialist system from which the present society emerged is characterized by a total social atomization. No intermediate levels exist between the individual and the top of society. Social structure simply does not exist. And the top is kept by the power in the hands of the Party. Consequently, political struggle until today took place from the positions defined by the former regime: we or you. There is no room for both of them. Until now, we cannot speak of a genuine political pluralism" (Bučar 1991, p. 20). In spite of political changes aimed at parliamentary democracy and political pluralism, the ruling coalitions in East-Central Europe tend to consolidate themselves in the way typical of the previous one-party systems— as ideologically homogeneous (class) alliances. Despotic regimes use external and internal threats as a means to obtain legitimation; if no real threat exists, it must be invented. The "class enemy" invented by the former regimes to justify their dictatorship of the proletariat is now being replaced with new "enemies"— either with communists, the "enemies of the nation," or both.

From a West European perspective, the most striking characteristic of the emerging democracies is the *absence of social democratic parties* and the absence of a powerful (e.g., workers') opposition in general. Even if social democratic parties or other left-wing parties are formally established, they have not much power within the ruling coalitions, which are mainly dominated by Christian democrats or other parties with a similarly conservative orientation. Generally, in postsocialist countries the Left is almost dead. Social democratic and socialist parties have moved close to the center, primarily because traditional socialist systems, particularly in the economy, have been discredited. This move to the center may also be the result of the failure of social democratic parties in West Europe, where social democrats have lost credibility among the electorate in their own country and elsewhere. In general, a parliamentary opposition does exist in the postsocialist countries, but its political significance is marginalized. It is not paradoxical, then, that a powerful opposition exists only in those countries where no radical political changes have yet been introduced, such as in Romania, Albania, and Serbia.

However, the intelligentsia that mobilized popular support for the new middle-class elites and their political aspirations became less loyal to and tolerant of the new political elites after the overthrow of the old socialist regimes. The most typical case is that of Slovenia, where the leading intellectuals, who actually initiated the democratic revolution and represented the intellectual core of the new government, also initiated the split within the ruling coalition because of its growing hegemonic power. As in all former revolutions, both capitalist and socialist, intellectuals became less loyal to their former natural allies after these allies became the hegemonic class. When the governing coalition Democratic Opposition of Slovenia (DEMOS) started to reintroduce the principles of democratic centralism and censor dissent from the majority opinions, the "natural alliance" was suddenly shaken.

Mass Media as the Institutional–Ideological Complex of the State

As before, the governments (the ruling parties) in East-Central Europe seek to legitimize their power by exerting control over the media, particularly television, and affecting their contents. The ruling coalitions exploit their control over the media to build up exclusive power, which provokes strong reactions mainly among oppositional parties and nonpolitical organizations but also within the ruling coalitions. The media are reregulated as an integral part of the "institutional-ideological" complex (Downing 1980) of the ruling political elites and the state. It is not difficult to identify why the postsocialist state does not significantly change the former strategy of control of the media. It is aimed mainly at restricting the processes of external and internal peripheralization of the state.

The earlier case of the Hungarian government wanting to make sure that when a foreign investor buys a newspaper, it should have political views in accord with those of the government points to the problems new governments have with the media. On the one hand, these regimes need external credibility to attract the foreign investments required for internal legitimation. Too critical voices in the media would certainly overshadow a favorable image of a "democratic government" and a "stable political and economic system" and thus would drive away potential investors. On the other hand, the regimes need internal credibility to stabilize their ruling position in society. Reporting on splits in the ruling political parties and alliances and on any kind of "scandals," mistakes, and deficiencies of the new ruling elites would make them more vulnerable and reduce their internal credibility. Since all postsocialist countries are far from being either "stable economies" or "stable political systems," it is understandable that governments support the tendency to eliminate "too critical" voices in the media, either by privatization (which systematically excludes citizens lacking economic resources) or by a direct (political) control of the media.

This strategy is certainly not unique or limited to the former socialist countries. A similar situation exists, for example, in Greece, where the state plays a decisive role in broadcasting and defines the extent of the relative autonomy of the press—quite in contrast to other members of the European Community. Obviously, then, the strong role of the state and its influence on economy and polity cannot be attributed to the absence of a market economy and private ownership. The autonomy of the state from civil society in Greece is much more related to the fact that the implementation of capitalism was not as successful as in West Europe because of cultural and historical specificities. With the persistence of state "patronage politics," even bourgeois parties and interest groups are not autonomously articulated but rather reside exclusively in the framework of the state in a "clientist/personalistic manner."

As in East-Central European countries, the state promotes the interests of particular types of capital rather than the interests of capital as a whole (Papathanassopoulos 1990, p. 388). Greece is considered "semiperipheral," which is again a typical characteristic of the former socialist countries: Internally, it is autonomous and strong (because of the weakness of civil society); at the same time, however, it is exposed to internal structural constraints and pressures and external constraints. Stylianos Papathanassopoulos, for example, suggested that tendencies toward the deregulation of Greek broadcasting are more the outcome of the internationalization of broadcasting (e.g., liberal and mercantilistic EC broadcasting policy) than the result of pressures from domestic forces.

Similar tendencies appear in East-Central Europe, but the absence of strong external and internal pressures makes the state even more powerful. Although the organization of the state and the media has partly changed, these changes do not imply a shift away from centralization. The media are mainly criticized as having been a tool of the "Bolshevik" state, but at the same time they are forced to play the same role as transmitters of a new ideology and to continue being dominated by the *ruling* political interests. Particularly in broadcasting, the public sector is often considered simply state ownership and thus in fact is "privatized" by the political power elite. The state—either the government or parliament—monopolized control over the broadcast media (primarily television) as if it were their "natural owner." Neither media professionals nor recipients are considered to have a legitimate right to participate in managing "public media."

It is true that this "new" media policy is not everywhere successful and that some media and journalists remain closely connected with the former rulers or genuinely independent. It is more important, however, that the media remain as vulnerable to state control as before because they do not have enough autonomy to put effective limits on state interference. Broadcasting, particularly television, is prevalently organized as a political institution (in contrast to the new ideology of privatization and denationalization) because only political interests and issues are considered to be at stake when matters of democracy are discussed. Paternalistic-commercial media systems based on a highly regulated broadcasting sector and an unregulated print sector are developing because new political elites lack commitment to the nonpower and nonprofit goals and interests of citizens.

In the West, the decline of a traditionally politicized party press was inevitable once mass circulation and a genuinely popular press developed; the political role of the press was adapted to the conditions of bourgeois democracy (Sparks 1991c, p. 60). The rise of radio broadcasting after World War I and television after World War II weakened the position of political parties and introduced the tradition of "politically balanced" media, either because of the nationalization of radio (in Europe) or because of its commercialization (in the United States). The separation of the media from the political parties continued with satellite and cable media. As with shifts in the press in the mid-1800s, this transformation led to the steady transfer of control of the media to capitalist entrepreneurs

(Curran 1991, p. 39; 1982, p. 215). Gouldner (1976, p. 124) shed more light on this transformation:

> With the development of the mass media, then, modern society develops a *dual* system of generating accounts of social reality. Inevitably, these reflect on, compete with, and therefore limit one another. The development of the media means the development of a special subsystem, *not* an *independent* system, but, nonetheless, *not* a mere appendage of society's official management. . . . Authoritative accounts from official sources must now compete with media accountings and, even where they do not compete, official accounts must be transmitted *via* these media, thereby developing a measure of dependence upon them and some vulnerability to their standards.

In East-Central Europe, however, professional communicators still play the former role of sociopolitical workers, that is, professional politicians. In practice, a rivalry between professional politicians and professional communicators based on different definitions of their roles, competing claims to the representation of the public, and a "dual system of generating accounts of social reality" exists only exceptionally. Rather, newspapers and broadcast media have close ties with political parties; some newspapers explicitly present their political credo in their coverage and commentaries.

It should be noted, however, that strong partisanship in the press and even the integration of the media and political elites are not peculiar to the former socialist countries. In Italy, for example, "actors in the two systems share values and a single symbolic universe," and a significant horizontal mobility exists between the world of journalism and that of politics (Mancini 1991, p. 139). Nevertheless, national broadcast organizations in East-Central Europe would like to shift away from the former political partiality, but they are considered by the ruling parties as too important and powerful to be left to "professional communicators." It is a common practice for politicians to intervene openly in editorial decisions. The view that political criteria interpreted by politicians, rather than journalists and editors, should guarantee positive support for parliamentary democracy is widely accepted.

Consequently, the rhetoric of democracy is mainly related to the political parties and parliament. "We believe ourselves to be living in a democracy because from time to time we get to vote on candidates for public office," Mander (1978, p. 352) stated in his conclusions to *Four Arguments for the Elimination of Television*. "Yet our vote for congressperson or president means very little in the light of our lack of power over technological inventions that affect the nature of our existence more than any individual leader has ever done. *Without our gaining control over technology, all notions of democracy are a farce*" (italics added). Similarly, the process of democratization in East-Central Europe is considered primarily a question of "Who votes?" rather than "Where does one vote?" (Bobbio 1987, p. 32) and "What/whom can one vote for?" Thus, this process is reduced to the formal right to participate in making political decisions (i.e., in general parliamentary elections). The representative parliamentary system (re)established after political revolutions is seen as the sufficient condition for democracy to flourish. For a genuine democratization, however, the extension of *contexts* in which citizens can freely exercise their right to participate in decisionmaking is of paramount importance. For a democratic system, the question of equal *social* rights is as important as those of *civil* and *political* rights. However, the questions of how to extend forms of democratic control in the domain of the state and society and how to ensure a genuine political equality of citizens are easily condemned by postsocialist theorists as referring to the old dominant ideology (e.g., of socialist self-management), although traditional representative political institutions in Western democracies were eroded and displaced by "tripartism"—negotiations among the state, corporations, and unions from which "ordinary citizens" were simply excluded. From this perspective, democratic changes in East-Central Europe are little more than the first step toward the "ideal of democracy."

Another Magic Key: State-supported Nationalism

One of the most controversial issues brought about by democratization in East-Central Europe is *nationalism,* particularly because it contradicts the idea that the modern electronic media, especially TV, radically reshaped social and cultural relations on a global scale. States are evermore interlocked by international and transnational processes of (often invisible) economic, political, and military cooperation. The spread of information and communication technologies and their global implications considerably changed the traditional concept of sovereignty. The power of transnational corporations and multinational entities is challenging the national sovereignty not only of the large-scale and powerful countries but also of those on world peripheries. A number of authors, such as Barber (1992), believe that the postmodern era is an era of placeless culture(s), where *territory*-based integrity (or similarity) is losing its power and media influence is simultaneously homogenizing and diversifying culture and audiences. People are becoming more culturally uniform, but ethnic groups try simultaneously to differentiate themselves as specific entities. On the one hand, our planet "is falling precipitantly apart"; on the other hand, it is "coming reluctantly together at the very same moment" (Barber 1992, p. 53). However, it seems that this dialectical perspective represents an invalid universalization of the processes typical of (or even present only in) mature societies established in the early period of industrialization. In postsocialist countries, the identity of the population (nation) is clearly defined in terms of a particular physical place "belonging" to a nation-state rather than in terms of "culture" or "cultural uniqueness." In contrast to the "globalization hypothesis," the proclamation of territorial identity is a widespread media policy.

The growing concern about internal and external *state vulnerability* and the need to achieve *national sovereignty* based on *national integration and solidarity* are important reasons for neglecting (or even suppressing) the questions of "internal peripheries" and the plurality of social (status, gender, class, local) identities by national governments. This is a typical situation in postsocialist countries, although it may be found in other societies as well. The state acts as the dominant integrating force, in contrast to civil society representing the opposite processes of differentiation; in fact, national integration and homogenization represent the most salient strategy of integration. To generate power, the state advances internal (intra-system) ethnic (national) homogenization based on non- and anticommunist identity symbols and stresses diversity externally. As Anthony Giddens (1991, p. 369) argued, the nation-state is the dominant carrier of power in modern ages. One of the most important consequences of nationalism in the sense of laying claims on behalf, or in favor, of the nation—or "ethnicity" in contrast to the dominant "national" group—is an increasing centralization of the power of elites representing national interests and acquiring support for the national regime (Tiryakian and Nevitte 1991, p. 283). This becomes important not only in less developed societies but also in developed ones because the powerfulness of the state is increasingly challenged by the state turning to the global market economy and the "informational mode of development" (Castells 1989), which foster internationalism.

Paradoxically but not ironically, the efforts to (re)gain national sovereignty by a number of republics in the postsocialist East European countries—a process opposing those of globalization and the reduction of nation-state power—are a fundamental condition of citizen participation in world politics. Ethnicity is, according to Peter Klinar (1991, p. 1204), an important element of civil society. After all, the right to a specific identity and ethnic/national self-determination belong to the basic and universally recognized democratic rights, although one can hardly imagine how the latter could be universally materialized. The right to self-determination can certainly be considered a "revolutionary right" because, on the one hand, there are thousands of different ethnic groups in the world, but, on the other hand, there are less than two hundred states. Thus, less than 10 percent of the existing states are ethnically/nationally homogeneous. A universal materialization of this right would face enormous practical problems, including wars (as in the case of the former Soviet Union and Yugoslavia). But this is not to say that such materialization is by definition "unrelated to democracy" and a "mania," as Barber (1992, p. 61) claimed, because it may threaten the territorial integrity of former "nation-states" that were, in fact, multinational states with one single dominant nation. Even if the materialization of this right does challenge the territorial integrity of already established states, it is not necessarily related to undemocratization.

East European nationalisms established the conditions necessary for the development of a democratic political and economic system because under the old regimes no pluralist and democratic representation of national and ethnic interests existed. As Michael Walzer (1992, p. 164) argued, "The popular energies mobilized against totalitarian rule, and also the more passive stubbornness and evasiveness that eroded the Stalinist regimes from within, were fueled in good part by 'tribal' loyalties and passions." Under the socialist regimes, ethnic conflicts were pacified to the detriment of democracy. When the communist system was overthrown, nationalism was revived in different forms everywhere. It emerged from linguistic, religious, and regional (particularly economic) differences that had been suppressed by the former dictatorship of the proletariat. However, nationalism was an instrument not only of the opposition in its battle against former regimes but also of the old authorities trying to remain—as in Serbia—in power.

Particularly in some former multinational (federal) states—the CSFR, the Soviet Union, and Yugoslavia—the awakening of ethnic consciousness and the striving for cultural, religious, and/or linguistic identity represented a cornerstone of the democratic restructuring of society. In this sense, East European nationalisms largely embodied resistance against the centralistic socialist state and its discriminatory ideology and polity. It is extremely oversimplified to claim that contemporary nationalism is nothing but "a powerful irony": "Nationalism was once a force of integration and unification, a movement aimed at bringing together disparate clans, tribes, and cultural fragments under new, assimilationist flags. . . . In the 1920s, and again today, it is more often a reactionary and divisive force, pulverizing the very nations it once helped cement together" (Barber 1992, p. 60).

The nationalisms now emerging in East-Central Europe were partly "frozen" under the old socialist regimes and partly formed anew to fill the ideological vacuum of the late 1980s, when the domination of communist ideology was seriously challenged. They were deeply rooted—with some significant exceptions, such as Romanian or Serbian nationalism—in democratic movements of civil society mobilized against the state-party system and its monopolistic economic and political power and aimed at the (re)creation of civil society. Nationalist movements arose in response to excessive centralization and homogenization in all spheres, which enabled the socialist state to control society. Clearly, ethnic "rebellions" significantly contributed to general democratization. However, in more traditionally oriented societies and in countries where civil society was almost nonexistent, ethnic differentiation largely overrode other elements of civil society. Since ethnic elements are constitutive for the state as well, the domination of ethnic elements over other elements in civil society easily impoverishes civil society and strengthens the power of the state. The (potential) merger of the power of nationalism and state power is the basic reason for considering *extreme nationalisms* and *Islamic fundamentalism* the most dangerous challenge to democracy (Dahl 1991), particularly in young democracies that lack a strong democratic culture. This is certainly true for postsocialist countries.

One may speak of nationalism as having an *ambivalent potential:* It is needed both by forces fighting for political, social, economic, or cultural liberation and by those striving for suppression of other nations. The former nationalism is more culturally driven and not dependent on particular physical places, whereas the latter is based on geographic identity or identity of physical place and often strives for physical (re)unification of nation or ethnicity. Different forms of conservative and aggressive nationalism appeared in a number of postsocialist countries. A significant departure from "democratic nationalisms" in East-Central Europe is represented by the oppositional Party of Great Romania, established in May 1991 from the movement associated with the nationalistic weekly *Romania Mare* (The Great Romania) in Bucharest. According to Romanian democrats, behind the scene of this party are influential forces of the former secret police that are also linked with the new regime. On the one hand, Romanian nationalists demand annexation of the Republic of Moldavia, with some eight hundred thousand Romanians annexed to Moldavia by contract between Romania and the Soviet Union in 1940. On the other hand, nationalist conflicts and violent clashes occurred between Romanian extremists and Hungarians and gypsies in Romania. *Romania Mare* openly called for the rehabilitation of Ceauşescu and proposed an interim military government to bring the country out of chaos (*Mass Media* 1991, p. 2). Another nationalist weekly, *Europa,* was publicly accused of disseminating anti-Semitic propaganda. Similar forms of conservative nationalism appeared in Serbia (against Albanians and Hungarians and particularly against Croatians and Muslims), Slovakia (against Hungarians), Bulgaria (against Turks and Macedonians), and in a number of former Soviet republics. Even in the Hungarian nation-state, the emphasis on nationalism and concern for its displaced nationals in Romania, Slovakia, and some republics of the former Yugoslavia are of central political and propagandistic significance.

Earlier I discussed the hypothesis that the more a state succeeds in fettering its "own" subjects, the more it succeeds in becoming independent of other states. The case of nationalism in East-Central Europe is a clear example of this hypothesis. At the beginning, nationalism clearly supported democratic changes, but soon it challenged new democratic institutions. A number of political parties defined their political programs in nationalist and populist terms to attract more members and voters. In addition, nationalism is fed by a deep economic crisis, which tends to strengthen the power in the hands of the state against civil society. Ethnicities in newly emerging democratic republic/states (Serbs in Croatia, Hungarians in Romania, Serbia, and the CSFR, Italians in Slovenia and Croatia, Turks and Macedonians in Bulgaria, Albanians in Serbia, and ethnic minorities in the former Soviet republics) are pressured by the emerging policies of new "majority nations" aiming to achieve national sovereignty. Governments striving for the autonomy and sovereignty of "their nations" on the basis of the right to self-determination often do not extend the same right to ethnic minorities within the boundaries of the emerging state. As Walzer (1992, p. 169) remarked, "It often seems as if the chief motive for national liberation is not to free oneself from minority status in someone else's country but to acquire (and then mistreat) minorities of one's own."

In a way, we may consider these nationalistic trends paradoxical on the eve of the twenty-first century because in the developed world the idea of the centralized, sovereign nation-state capable of governing the territory and population independently of any external authority has largely gone out of fashion (Keane 1991, p. 142). Although the idea—or fiction—of state sovereignty persists, sovereignty itself is becoming severely limited. By contrast, new governments in East-Central Europe are stepping up their domestic activity to gain strength internationally. Internal centralization and "unification of power" are seen as a means of making the state more independent in the international environment. New governments are much more concerned with their own peripheral position within the international community than with the "sovereignty" of civil society, and they try to strengthen the state power, which is certainly not to the advantage of civil society. Thus, the processes of globalization much more negatively affect the sovereignty of civil society than state sovereignty. Nationalization of the media in the sense of both increased state intervention/control and nationalistic editorial policies warrants particular attention. In contrast to the global production of a *"placeless* culture" (Meyrowitz 1986), which is especially the result of the development of satellite television, the media in postsocialist countries are still (or again) primarily aimed at political and cultural, national homogenization.

Some authors clearly point to, and even overestimate, the importance of intensive social communications for the formation of both nations and nationalisms (Alter 1991, p. 224). Despite the internationalization of the communication sphere and because of it, the (national) state still forms the basis for the communication sphere and the formation of national identities. It is often assumed that nationally controlled media policy and general cultural policy that aims at national cultural sovereignty are a necessary and desirable reaction against the threat to the autonomy and integrity of national identity brought about by the globalization of cultural production and consumption, particularly of media products. As Philip Schlesinger (1990, p. 6) stated, "One should not stretch the military analogy too far, but cultural defence may also be illuminated if looked at as the active mobilisation by states against 'invasions' of their communicative space from outside (e.g., by 'cultural imperialism') or 'subversion' from within (e.g., by challenges to received linguistic and cultural orthodoxies). . . . For the media and wider cultural fields are indeed to be conceived of as *battle*fields, as spaces in which contests for various forms of dominance take place."

These two cultural and communication processes—internationalization or globalization, on the one hand, and national control, on the other—may be considered pertinent to two fundamental processes of contemporary capitalist restructuring based on new information and communication technologies (Castells 1989, pp. 29–30): internationalization of the economy and the weighting of the accumulation and domination functions of state intervention. Although media internationalization is mainly seen as a form of global commercialization, we would be naive to neglect its cultural and political consequences.

If there is at least a vague congruence between internationalization of the economy and globalization of culture, the policy of "national (cultural) identity" in (semi)peripheral countries could be considered functionally equivalent to the new forms of engagement of the state in the economy and society, particularly because this policy is often related to nations and states (and particularly nation-states) as the most typical entities that "laud and enforce the ethnic, religious, linguistic, cultural homogeneity" (Bauman 1990, p. 155). The struggle for national cultural control and power represents an important aspect of power maximization (state) policy on peripheries, particularly in relation to the mass media, although it is not limited to peripheries only. On the contrary, nationalism became—and still is—a political force that in the past two centuries influenced European and world history much more than any other idea, including that of freedom, democracy, or communism. Although current trends of informatization and global economic restructuring seem to reduce nationalism's significance, it has not lost its integrative political power. In Western societies, for example, "the market liberal vision of a free market in communications is seen to require a powerful, authoritative state which acts as an overlord of the market. The sinews of a 'free' society, it is claimed, are provided by coherent administrative power, by the bold, decisive action of statesmanlike politicians, and by *governments' willingness to enforce national traditions and the laws of the land—against the internal and external enemies of the state and the market"* (Keane 1991, pp. 112–113; italics added).

The question is, however, whether the decline of political and economic sovereignty and of the power of the state caused by the processes of globalization can be effectively limited by national(ist) homogenization. Nationalism is a typical (or, perhaps, extreme) example of keeping the permeability of system boundaries as minimal as possible to maintain national cohesion and protect the system from "alien"—both external and internal—cultural and political intrusion; it is often connected with different forms of state control over information. According to Liah Greenfeld (1990, p. 549), "Nationalism locates the source of individual identity within a 'people,' which is seen as the central object of loyalty and the basis of collective solidarity. The 'people' is the mass of population whose boundaries and nature are defined in various ways, but which is usually perceived as larger than any concrete community and always as fundamentally homogenous, and only *superficially divided by the lines of status, class, or locality"* (italics added).

State nationalism suppresses localism, regionalism, or any other form of internal differences within the nation, which are often riven by cultural divisions and other, nonterritorial sources for the construction of (cultural) identity (e.g., ethnicity, class, gender, generation, religion). At least because of this hegemonic pressure, the idea of a national sovereignty policy as a necessary reaction against the threat to the national autonomy and identity brought about by processes of globalization and internationalization deserves much more critical consideration and challenge than are usually the case.

Whereas in the nineteenth century national homogenization in West Europe was a form of accelerated globalization (Robertson 1990, p. 20) based on *integration* and *mobility*, the contemporary upgrading of the boundaries of globalization to the world as a whole transformed it into its reverse—counterglobalization. Nationalism in the postindustrial era is essentially *secessionistic:* "On the one hand, the differentiating impact of globalization strengthens or reactivates national identities, communities and projections. . . . On the other hand, the national level of integration complements, conditions and counteracts the global ones" (Arnason 1990, p. 225). A number of (former) republics in (former) multinational East European states are now in a process of transition from a local ethnic unit (i.e., ethnicity in contrast to the dominant group within a state) to nation-states or of an etatization of the nation that blends "the issue of political loyalty and trustworthiness (seen as conditions for granting citizenship rights) with that of cultural conformity" (Bauman 1990, p. 161). In East-Central Europe, the processes of (re)creation of national identity are closely related to the revival of political democracy and its opposite—nationalistic exclusivism. Ullamaija Kivikuru (1990, p. 20), for example, suggested that "it is easy to accept that exaggerated underlining of sense of border leads to assumed superiority and lack of democracy; documentation is easily found in mass communication with strong nationalist components."

The former localism (periphery against the center) is being transformed into a national homogenization that denies those local diversities that are not nation based. This tendency was typical in past eras when national states were formed, although West European national homogenization in the age of transition to industrialism of the nineteenth century was based primarily on economic *integration,* whereas the contemporary national homogenization occurring in East Europe (the former Yugoslavia is certainly the best exemplification) is based on cultural *differentiation* and/or *disintegration* (secession). Institutionally, this tendency is obvious in national government efforts to centralize politics in all spheres, including communications and culture, which clearly indicates that the introduction of a multiparty parliamentary system does not yet guarantee (greater) democracy.

After democratization of political systems, particularly in countries such as the former Yugoslavia, CSFR, and Soviet Union, a number of political groupings use nationalistic policy to maximize power. The general economic ineffectiveness of multinational socialist states is only one, albeit major, aspect of contemporary disintegration processes. In addition, there are significant regional variations and diversities in cultural and economic development,[2] which have led—also because of a general underdevelopment of these countries—to manifest interethnic conflicts and even warfare. The former communist myth of social harmony in a classless society has been replaced by the myth of national harmony and nation-state sovereignty. It is well known that the animosity between various nations in the former Soviet Union, Yugoslavia, and CSFR has always existed, but the question of nations was marginalized by the communist ideology on account of "proletarian internationalism," or else nationalism and chauvinism of the dominant nation were used to preserve "harsh socialism." The anti-Albanian nationalist politics of the Serbian leader Slobodan Milošević, Todor Živkov's anti-Turk chauvinism in Bulgaria, or the oppression of Hungarians by the Ceauşescu regime in Romania are but the most excessive examples of a conservative nationalist strategy to maximize the political power of the socialist state. Thus, democratization allowed the people for the first time to express their ethnic views freely; at the same time, ethnic issues went to the core of the programs of the new political parties as well as the media.

Some authors (cf. Roeder 1991) see a fundamental difference between the "Western experience with peripheral nationalism" and "the rise of ethnopolitics" in East European multinational states. Whereas in the West nationalisms typically appeared among the less advantaged ethnic minorities, in the former Soviet Union and Yugoslavia mobilization for autonomy and independence was strongest among the most developed nations, economically and otherwise. At least two objections can be made to this oversimplified dichotomy. First, this is not a very accurate differentiation; the cases of the Catalans in Spain, the Moldavians in the former Soviet Union, and the Slovaks in the former CSFR clearly falsify it. Likewise, contemporary regional nationalisms in Italy or Germany appear more likely in more, rather than less, developed regions. Second, the *level of economic development* is not a valid measure for identifying and explaining the pattern of nationalism (see, e.g., Connor 1991). Rather, what is more important in nonmarket economies is the *degree of autonomy possessed by regions, republics, or nations in controlling distribution* of the "national" product. In the case of a number of East European nations (or ethnicities), ethnic conflicts are generated by status incongruence between economic/social development and political/military power. In the case of the most developed republics in the former Soviet Union and Yugoslavia, their ability to control the distribution of the national product was severely limited by federal authorities, which were dominated by the largest (though relatively less developed) nations—Russians in the Soviet Union and Serbians in Yugoslavia. Consequently, federal economic policy was based on the interests of less developed regions and on the redistribution of the national product from more developed to less developed republics. Nevertheless, economic support for less developed regions and/or republics did not prevent them from laying claims to more autonomy.

Even if one tries to relate the rise of nationalisms to more subtle economic factors—for example, to those affecting the immigration and emigration of the work force—the result is far from allowing generalization. This clearly indicates that other factors, such as history, culture, language, and religion, do play an important role in the rise of nationalism and that there is no single universal model of it. Religion in particular is becoming a cultural and political force that plays a significant role in nationalist politics, although this is not to argue that religious differences necessarily tend toward separatism and separation. The fall of socialism has been replaced by the growing role of, and divisions among, three dominant religions: Roman Catholicism in Poland, the former CSFR, Hungary, Slovenia, and Croatia; the Orthodox Church in the eastern part of Yugoslavia, Bulgaria, and Romania; and Islam in Bosnia-Herzegovina and a number of southern republics in the former Soviet Union. Nevertheless, it seems that the question of the redistributive consequences of federal economic policy became decisive with the rapid decline of East European economies.

This is definitely not to say that no fundamental difference exists between West and East European nationalisms. One obvious and important difference is in their possible consequences. Different forms of separatist or autonomist nationalism within developed nation-states in West Europe or Canada are quite another case than that of the disintegration of a union or federation composed of well-defined national entities with their own substate systems (as in the former CSFR, USSR, or Yugoslavia). As Rudi Rizman (1991, p. 946) argued, contemporary West European separatist nationalisms among Basques, Catalans, Corsicans, or Bretons, if they were successful in establishing new nation-states, would not challenge the existence of the "old states" (Spain or France). East European nationalisms of stateless nations, however, may result in the decay of the multinational states established after World War I. As the recent cases of Yugoslavia, the Soviet Union, and the CSFR clearly show, this is not only possible but also almost inevitable.

It is important to stress that even the "reactionary national-populism" now growing in East Europe is not aimed at a "rejection of the West," as some authors wrongly believe (e.g., Semelin 1991, p. 18). Rather, it is aimed at strengthening and legitimizing the sovereignty of the (newly emerging) nation-states in reaction to the multinationalism existing there as a function of *predemocratic* or *antidemocratic* politics (Walzer 1992, p. 164). Neither is this new nationalism used as "an ideological weapon to try to protect a market" (Colas 1991, p. 76); apparently secessionistic efforts—for example, in the former Yugoslavia and Soviet Union—resulted in the reduction of the market size and greater vulnerability of the national economy rather than in the extension and protection of the national market. As Klinar (1991, p. 1203) argued, economic interests were even sacrificed to achieve ethnic goals.

Political changes in a number of East European countries are also legitimized by pointing to the need to promote the "entry into Europe" and—among deprivileged nations within the multinational states—to stop national hegemony of the largest nation (e.g., Russian, Czech, or Serbian). This policy is even over-weighed by a naive romanticism related to a supranational "European identity" as a common denominator of all European nations, which will presumably be equally represented in it. Until a few years ago, this was official policy toward the "Yugoslav identity" or "Soviet identity"; but now this policy has been re-jected because of its hegemonic nature. The shift toward "pan-Europeanism" may be considered a kind of "imported nationalism" that attempts to abolish peripheralism (by claiming, for example, that Slovenia, Croatia, or Lithuania was throughout its history "a part of Europe"). Pan-Europeanism is apparently more culturally and, eventually, politically than economically driven, although it is not based on East European political realities. Indeed, the ideology of pan-Europeanism does not cause destruction of any important component of nation-alism; the "European identity" does not prevail over any particular national identity but rather constitutes a component of national identity.

The new myth of the importance of national identity emerging in national republics tends to marginalize the question of the democratic restructuring of the state because of the idea of the national ("our") state. In the former Yugo-slavia, "much of the media has become a key part of the propaganda arsenal of the new governments in their internecine squabbles about the future political structure of the country" (Stone and Marks 1991, p. 26). Obviously, national confrontations seem to be more productive for new agents of power intending to maximize their political power than for the struggle for human rights and freedoms, the independence of civil society from the state, and economic restructuring. Rising nationalism's dangerous potential is best exemplified by nationalist clashes in the former Soviet Union and Yugoslavia caused by the efforts of the politically dominant nations to overpower the smaller ones. As the authors of a recent *Gannet Foundation Report* (Dennis and Heuvel 1990, p. 73) observed, "Strident nationalism and ethnic chauvinism have tarnished Yugosla-via's once progressive press. . . . Ironically, as Communist control over the country deteriorated, and as new non-Communist governments established themselves in Slovenia and Croatia, the quality of journalism deteriorated. Once-respectable publications have turned into forums for bottled-up resent-ment of ethnic groups and nationalistic passions."

At least in the states formerly constituting Yugoslavia and the Soviet Union, media nationalism is strongly supported and actually generated by the national political elites. On the one hand, media nationalism resulted in the establish-ment of independent "republican" media; on the other hand, it often produced a new monopoly at a lower ("republican") level. That the central "national" media, particularly in the former Soviet Union, significantly underreported non-dominant ethnic groups and ethnopolitical issues was an important reason for the center-periphery conflict. Nationalist governments in Moldavia, Estonia, Latvia, and Lithuania separated their radio and television stations from Gosteleradio, which was centrally administered by the federal state. Programs of TV stations controlled by the central government or broadcast from other republics were often considered antigovernment and antinational propaganda. These programs were barely given access to national channels, in contrast to U.S. and West European programs that were habitually (re)transmitted as a part of "national" programs.

However, media decentralization on the national level was often countervailed by a new, lower-level monopoly. In the largely Albanian-populated province of Kosovo in Serbia, for example, all the Albanian-language media were simply closed down by the Serbian government. In the province of Vojvodina in the same republic, where Hungarians represent the largest minority, radio and television programs in Hungarian were strongly reduced. Similarly, the anti-minority communication policies in Bulgaria, Croatia, Romania, and the former CSFR call our attention to the possibility that democratic (r)evolutions may introduce new forms of domination and hegemony.

Nationalist tendencies in the media, including those of pan-Europeanism, are clearly shown structurally as well, particularly in television programming. For example, the proportion of U.S. and West European programs on Slovenian Television has constantly increased during the last few years, while "imports" from the rest of Yugoslavia have decreased. The tendency toward intensive "indigenization" of television programming is even stronger in some other former Yugoslav republics, particularly Serbia and Croatia. Because of the scarcity of material resources, however, which prevent television from increasing its original production and competing with foreign TV programs, "structural nationalism" in the media is manifested mainly in the more frequent recurrence of homemade programs. Even in the more developed republics, the expansion of homemade TV programming is not feasible since it already far exceeds what could be labeled a "European standard" in terms of the amount of programming relative to the size of population.

A few months after democratic political changes, media nationalism in the former Soviet Union and Yugoslavia escalated to a media war where the media were systematically used as tools of propaganda, lying, and mythmaking. The spiral of war continued toward a real civil war, which first appeared in its manifest and brutal form in Yugoslavia, where the federal army invaded the Republic of Slovenia, which unilaterally declared its independence on June 25, 1991. Military clashes escalated to a much larger scale in the Republic of Croatia and in Bosnia-Herzegovina. Similarly, in August 1991 the army-backed three-day coup d'état in the former Soviet Union definitely made clear that the forces working against democratization should not be underestimated. On all these occasions, the media were directly involved as instruments of political power and propaganda, either by state authorities or by oppositional parties. Instead of a swelling of civil society, a plurality of self-managing civil associations, and the democratization of the media sphere, East-Central Europe is facing ethnic clashes and even civil war. This is perhaps the most bizarre exemplification of the growing importance of the nation-state secured by military strength in East-Central Europe, a tragic "civil society paradox."

Nationalistic ideologies also compete *within* the national boundaries of the former socialist countries in East-Central Europe. "Europeanization" and "renationalization" are the dominant foreign policy orientations of the new political parties. According to Laszlo Poti (1992, p. 56), the policy of renationalization in Hungary ranks as the highest priority, although it is more ideological and emotional than rational and historical.

If a pluralistic and democratic political and communication environment is established, competing nationalistic ideologies can stimulate the differentiation and increasing complexity essential for civil society and the support needed to create a new social structure. As Gyorgy Csepeli (1991, p. 338) argued, "It is precisely in this context that the role of diverse mass media in securing a public sphere and developing a civil society becomes a matter of profound importance. However, in the absence of conditions favouring an open and fearless public discourse concerning questions of nationality there is a real danger that the competition between alternative paradigms of national identity will result in exclusion, intolerance and mutual prejudice." Csepeli's study into competing patterns of national identity in postsocialist Hungary that are significantly related to the *religious background* and *sociocultural traditions* of their proponents reveals the danger of (re)creating marginal groups "defined" by specific national ideologies. If (when) only some of them achieve the status of "normality," while others are considered "deviant" or even inimical to the national interests as determined by the ruling elites, then differences may result in oppression of minorities or at least in a new paternalism. The maintenance of a certain level of plurality and diversity of the media is obviously one of the fundamental preconditions for avoiding oppressive conflicts among exclusive national ideologies in East-Central Europe.

5 Postsocialism and the Media: Between Paternalism and Pluralism

When in 1989 and 1990 the old authoritarian structures began to break down with an almost inordinate speed all around East Europe, it was hard to imagine what the "final" results would be of these dramatic changes in which civil society played a prominent role. Several attempts at counterrevolution initiated by the old power structures took place afterward in Romania, Yugoslavia, and the Soviet Union. Nationalist clashes dramatically appeared in a number of former socialist countries that had previously declared nations (and nationalisms) to be one product of capitalism that would disappear in the face of proletarian internationalism. In countries such as Albania and Bulgaria, radical changes are still impeded by the old political powers. Nevertheless, it is evident now that turning back is no longer possible. In a very short period of time, civil society was created in East-Central Europe; almost overnight, it succeeded in inaugurating parliamentary democracy. But at the same time, the processes of political reconstruction and economic restructuring imperiled the existence of this civil society. On the one hand, the establishment of elitist-pluralist systems of party competition tends to lead "to the demobilization of civil society either directly, or indirectly by reducing its influence to the narrowest possible channels." On the other hand, the establishment of a liberal market economy "tends to reduce civil society to economic society" (Arato 1990, p. 25).

Political and economic processes, often contradictory in themselves, in the former socialist countries are commonly and vaguely labeled *postsocialism*. In an analogy with the introductory discussion of different approaches to the concept of civil society as the *nonstate,* we can certainly claim that these processes are tending toward a positive negation of the previous socialist system. It is more important, however, to determine whether they mean more than just the succession of one system after another. They may imply not only the *succession* of socialism (*postsocialism*) but also an *antithesis* to socialism, both to its specific historical form(s) in East-Central Europe and to socialism in principle (*antisocialism*).

In the foregoing chapters, I have challenged the notion that the burial of authoritarian practices in socialist countries coincides with the rise of democratic systems in general and of communication systems in particular. Instead, I have argued that East European societies are caught up in imitating and duplicating West European practices of economy and civil society—for example, the rise of communication systems under private capitalism that suffer from a loss of control by citizens and from an erosion of theoretical structures—rather than in reexamining the possible contributions of a Western model of communication to the specific situations in East-Central Europe. I have also described the fallacies in attempts to construe developments in East European media as radical changes or departures from previous activities under the socialist regimes.

One of the key issues in the debate about the nature of the reconstruction of former socialist countries is whether the societies that issue from the process will be democratic and, if so, what the nature of that democracy will be. In this, the mass media are certainly of vital importance. However, the courage to question the most "sacrosanct" assumptions of the ruling elites—that the processes in East-Central Europe represent a genuine democratization of societies—should be complemented by an effort to synthesize the balance of the experience with implications for the future. This effort is *not* an attempt to write out a scenario of future developments or to prescibe a new institutional model. Either activity would prove fruitless because dynamic changes in/of the postsocialist societies have not long been under way, several essential components of transition are still missing, and the transition is complex and uncertain. Rather, this effort is aimed at answering the question of whether (r)evolutionary political changes may definitely reform the former rigid structures and result in a new system of relationships among the state, marketplace, and civil society. One of the fundamental questions here is whether changes in the political and economic system will produce significant changes in the media. To answer this question, one should be aware of the specific assumptions and limitations of the social transformations occurring in East-Central Europe.

From Anticapitalism to Antisocialism

It may be that (some of) the former socialist countries are well into the process of developing democratic political systems. In all of them, changes in media systems represent an important issue of predominantly political considerations. It is paradoxical, however, that this process is not accompanied by any discussion, let alone implementation, of the "new" media, such as teletext, video, community media, cable, and satellites, or any radical departure—with the exception of the privatization of the press—from the former media structure. It would be an exaggeration to say that democratic revolutions in East-Central Europe resulted in any major breakthrough in terms of media de- and reregulation, quality programming, or new forms of media organization and management. Although it is beyond doubt that limited economic, technical, and staff resources hinder postsocialist countries from media restructuring, there are other impediments to the development of more democratic systems. In several vital points, discussions on the future of the media are divided along party political lines and are related to the division of power among political agents.

One major source of contemporary problems in the postsocialist countries is certainly an "uncritical critique" of the past, which is often considered the only cause of all difficulties culminating *after* the fall of the old system. At the same time, as Rus (1992, p. 8) argued, the present is still believed to be, as it was in the socialist past, merely a transitional period to the future: "The future is all, the present is nothing. Such an attitude toward the future and the present is inherited from the Catholic and Communist perceptions of time. Both consider the present as a kind of state of transition, as the purgatory, from which there is a way to the happy and cheerful future abounding in religious and social utopias."

As with many other criticisms both from the Left and Right, socialism was conceptualized as a critique of the capitalist economy and state apparatuses. What was unique, however, was the belief that both the economy and state could be radically changed by the intervention of "subjective forces" (i.e., an organized workers' movement and its avant-garde, the Communist Party), which could revolutionize production relations and thus society in its totality. But in practice socialism was caught in the trap of the conflicting interests and needs of equality and diversity (freedom). A clear example of that was the idea and practice of "revolutionary propaganda."

Marxism as an ideology (or "scientific utopia"), which was developed within the German Social Democratic Party at the beginning of the twentieth century, in the USSR with (and after) Lenin, and in East-Central Europe, Latin America, and China after World War II, is certainly not a simple "continuation" of Marx's theoretical approach or orthodox Marxism. The development of Marxist thought implies both a transition from a preparadigm to a paradigm period and differentiation into alternative streams. After Marx's death, his theory began to exert a growing intellectual and political influence in Europe and elsewhere. Discussions of Marxist theory soon resulted in major controversies, initially related to Eduard Bernstein's (1961) criticism of Marx's theory from the point of view of the necessity of empirical validation and ethical justification. Debates about Marx's theory took place in many different forms and in many disciplines, including communication science. As a result, his theory was largely extended, developed, and also reinterpreted and revised—not only because of the development of (new) disciplines and theories but also (and perhaps primarily) because of the incorporation of more and more rapid and profound changes in capitalism. To a certain degree, then, it is very difficult to refer to all these developments in terms of a single but universal body of general science. Particularly during the last decades, it became clear that Marxism could be understood only as one among a plurality of social theories (or paradigms). It retained the aura of a radical alternative to any other theory or practice, but it also became more and more an integral part of the modern, highly complex world of the social sciences.

Marxism as a political doctrine devoted a notable concern to the media. In the revolutionary Marxist communication approach dominant in all socialist countries, the press was conceptualized as the "collective propagandist, agitator and organizer," without any critical function. It was considered an instrument of propaganda and thus in fact aimed to control public opinion rather than express it. Although a "theory" of the press and propaganda was far from being the central part of Marxist political doctrine and Marxist scholarship in socialist countries, it introduced some innovations in Marxism in terms of new fields of study (such as communications), but it was not able to meet the challenges and criticisms of alternative paradigms. This theory's principal element was a criticism of *capitalism* and *capitalist media* intended to show the possibility, if not the necessity, of a new social organization (and media practice).

Revolutionary or, according to Lenin, "unmasking" propaganda was considered a communication practice aimed at recognizing and organizing human forces as *societal* forces. In the organization of a workers' movement before and after the revolution, propaganda was considered a basic means of changing human activities. This view failed to recognize, however, that propaganda inevitably remains, regardless of its specific aims, *distorted communication* because its intrinsic aim is the *universalization of particularistic interests*. That is, propaganda is aimed at hegemony in historically given relations rather than the autonomous, free development of human beings apart from the mass conformity ensured by any integrating ideology. Lenin's view did not acknowledge that with propaganda, communication is suppressed and limited by a material and/or mental production and is thus subordinated to existing relations in which the production of needs far exceeds the possibilities for their fulfillment. This approach also failed to see that regardless of the kind of propaganda, it maintains a division between teachers and pupils, between leaders and lead—a relation between *unequals*. Indeed, propaganda has always propagated the *separate* interests of minorities and their movements against other (different) interests. It was believed that the proletariat did not have any separate interests because it could not liberate itself without simultaneously liberating humanity, but revolutionary propaganda failed to recognize that other groups might have separate interests and that apart from general(izable) interests, specific groups created their own specific identities. It neglected to realize that only a virtual abolition of the *interests of domination and hegemony* could lead to a recognition of the coexistence of *specific interests* and their equality in terms of rights and freedoms. This view neglected, finally, the fundamental paradox that propaganda aimed against hegemony necessarily produces a new form of hegemony.

From a radical or revolutionary system interested in changing the dominant production relations at any price, East European socialism soon transformed itself into a conservative system interested in maintaining the status quo at any price. Here the status quo was defined mainly by the privileges of the ruling elites. The "original sin" of socialism was its anticapitalism—that is, that it was only the antithesis of capitalism. It first suppressed the positive heritage of capitalism and afterward its own positive heritage (Rus 1992, p. 21). In fact, Yugoslavia was the only example of the search for stability through economic and political changes introduced with self-management; it developed a distinct form of social organization with less uniformity and collectivity and more individualism and freedom. Hungary after 1968 and Poland in the 1980s introduced only limited changes to decrease the role of the state in the economy and to develop a limited form of market economy. The inability to cope with global changes in the economy and polity led socialism to a state of anarchy combined with administrative repression—best exemplified by political voluntarism and economic ineffectiveness—which finally resulted in chaos and a total disintegration of the socialist system. This situation was common to all socialist countries in the late 1980s when democratic revolutions emerged. Although they certainly mean a significant step forward in terms of democratization, it would be foolish to believe that the new situation will not produce a new set of problems and limitations, that "the end of historical communism (I stress the word 'historical') has put an end to poverty and the thirst for justice" (Bobbio, 1991, p. 5). The failure of "really existing socialism" or state socialism does not mean that the problems that the Marxist (or Leninist) political doctrine intended—but was not able—to solve do not exist anymore. They do on a global scale!

Dialectic of Relations Between the State and Civil Society

Postsocialist political and economic transformations in East-Central Europe mainly represent processes tending toward *differentiation*, whereas the opposite processes of reintegration of society in a new ensemble and new relationships are much less powerful. The decay of the Soviet Union, Yugoslavia, and the CSFR are typical examples of this process, although *ethnic* differentiation and separation may not be a blueprint for new modes of *societal* organization. Nevertheless, they prove that differentiation and even particularism are the crucial commonality of all social systems. Thus, the nationalisms and ethnic conflicts that opened the door to democratization are likely to represent, in the near future at least, a persistent obstacle to genuine democratization in East-Central Europe. The main reason for this is that the postsocialist countries, although experiencing radical changes in political systems through the introduction of *political pluralism,* are lacking in an appropriate development in other dimensions of plurality and differentiation. This also—or perhaps particularly—holds true for ethnic plurality. As Klinar (1991, p. 1209) argued, low levels of functional differentiation and the autonomy of social subsystems in the postsocialist countries will continue to impede the transition from destructive ethnic conflicts to ethnic pluralism, which can be achieved only on the basis of a qualitative shift from collectivities to individuals as civil society actors.

This is not to say that, for example, only highly individualized "media" can guarantee that ownership and control of the media will be less monopolized and more democratic than under the old regimes. Nationalisms cannot be suppressed simply by decentralizing and denationalizing the media. The same holds true for political democracy. Local autonomy that would support greater access to the media, political and cultural institutions, and so on cannot resolve the problem of "transborder flows" of ideas, values, interests, and needs between specific groups and communities, which must create some form of integrative bonds to maintain the coherence of society. However, the preservation of national institutions and the media should not imply the preservation of old (either socialist or capitalist) forms of control and ownership. Not only *postsocialist* but also *postcapitalist* forms should be discussed when a genuine democratization is at stake.

As I argued earlier, throughout East Europe market-led deregulation is usually seen as the magic key to resolve this problem. But even if it was successful in freeing individuals from state intervention (which is questionable), deregulation would produce new forms of integration and regulation. As Keane (1991, p. 153) claimed, "The actual or optimal shape of a market transaction must always be crafted by *political and legal regulations*. It never emerges spontaneously or grows without the benefits of *non-market* support mechanisms provided by other institutions of *civil society* or through *the state* itself" (italics added).

A number of authors maintain that on the eve of the twentieth century civil society is losing its regulatory power and beginning to disintegrate everywhere, either in contrast to the state (cf. Frankel 1987) or together with it. Giner (1985, p. 263), for example, pointed out that "the state itself will come to an end if civil society finally expires." Civil society, at least in its traditional forms, is certainly endangered by contemporary processes of corporatization, etatization, and internationalization of economy and polity. In East-Central Europe, such qualitative transformations are still marginal. Nevertheless, the reconstruction of civil society that took place in the late 1980s is threatened as well.

The newly established political parties are more authoritative institutions than they are a bridge between the state and civil society. The postsocialist state is still largely a party-state; parliament has become a site where the representatives of political parties, rather than of citizens, meet to validate claims of their own political parties in terms of generalized interests. In a sense, revolutionary changes in East-Central Europe represent "revolution" only in terms of revolutionary *means* because they do not (yet) imply a radical transformation of fundamental societal structures. "Such revolution seemed to presuppose only very quick extra-institutional mobilization, the overthrow of crumbling old regimes, and the establishment of entirely new ones. The reconstruction of civil society, for which there was no time, was not needed as the basis of revolutionary mobilization, and the new political parties and governments had other things to worry about than such reconstruction in the future" (Arato 1990, p. 25).

The resurgence of civil society is not possible without the development of a legal state in contrast to the former socialist and largely moralistic state. As I said earlier, it is precisely the moralistic stance of the new anticommunist legislators that endangers democratization because it does not promote equality but tends to "legalize" a special kind of balance and symmetry between the past and the future: Those humiliated by the previous regime ought to be "saved" in the new regime. In addition, the new political elites play a remarkable economic role because the processes of denationalization and privatization enforced by democratically elected parliaments imply both economic and political consequences. The concentration of political and economic power in the hands of the state may certainly impede the resurgence of civil society.

The actual power of the new elites, however, is itself limited by the vulnerability of power structures. Civil society was strongest during the two- or three-year period of the decay of the former system in the late 1980s, when it simultaneously differentiated and politicized itself. But the new political system that has emerged since the overthrow of the socialist regime is not yet stabilized either internally (e.g., in terms of the map of political parties) or externally (in terms of relationships between political and other actors). This instability enables civil society and the media to play an autonomous role, although it also includes the danger of nationalization of the media by the state. Whether an autonomous role of the media will actually be performed, however, is another question. The outcome depends on the nature of the (political) communication the media maintain in society, which in turn depends on specific sociopolitical, economic, and cultural conditions. Even though some features and functions of the mass media seem to be universal, the media may play quite different roles in different settings.

The key to understanding the essence of the dialectical relationship between civil society and the state is not in their specific forms historically established in specific cultural settings but rather in the universally opposing tendencies of *integration and differentiation.* Contradictory tendencies of integration and differentiation are fundamental to any process of development. "Development of the social systems is unlike the physical pattern, which is conceived to be a unidimensional movement toward increased complexity of the structure of the matter. And it is unlike the biological evolution, which reflects a two-dimensional movement toward complexity and order. It is conceived to be at least a three-dimensional phenomenon of *purposeful* transformation in the direction of increased *integration* and *differentiation*" (Gharajedaghi 1983, p. 13).

Beyond doubt, the development transforms and modifies the agents (forms) of the opposing tendencies, but this does not mean their breakdown. Giner's argument that the withering away of civil society means the end of the state misses the important distinction between the *form* (the state, civil society) and the *process* itself: Without the opposing tendencies of integration and differentiation, development itself would come to an end.

What is primarily changing in contemporary processes of globalization in both East and West are the *boundaries* of integrative and differentiative processes. Whereas formerly the upper limit of integration was represented by the nation-state, now the increasing complexity fosters a shift in the upper limits of integration and consequently a limited sovereignty of nation-states. If no differentiative counterprocesses toward individuality and freedom exist, the process will end in "a complex, stateless network of trans-national managing bodies: agencies of large-scale imperative coordination in the fields of demography, ecology, energy, goods distribution, research and development, and regulatory law generally" (Giner 1985, p. 263).

This is precisely what happened in East-Central Europe under the former socialist regimes, though not in the form of a "complex, stateless network" but in the form of an omnipotent state. As Antoni Kaminski (1991, p. 347) argued, the inevitable feature of all systems organized from the top down is that any instance of social integration not mediated by the official power structure is a threat to its existence. Thus, the "inevitable" final result of the "large-scale imperative coordination" of the socialist state system was the destruction of the whole system when it crossed the critical boundary of an "overintegration" and limitation of individuals' freedoms and autonomy. Obviously, regulative devices of market economy "cannot be replaced by administrative planning without potentially jeopardizing the level of differentiation achieved in a modern society" (Habermas 1991, p. 34). The whole system collapsed economically and politically (and even militarily, as in the cases of the former Soviet Union and Yugoslavia). National overintegration in Yugoslavia and the Soviet Union produced violent nationalist reactions. Political overintegration (the merger of the Communist Party and the state) produced massive uprisings and, after revolutions, a massive flourishing of political parties. The suppression of market mechanisms in the economy disintegrated it into chaos. According to Michael Brie (1991 p.72), administrative socialism represented

> a specific variety of modern mass-society in which the "concentration" [*Vermassung*] and "dispersion" [*Parzellierung*] of people in individual and familial living spaces are strikingly opposed. The autonomous creation of one's cultural life is here more complicated than in other modern societies, although a high level of social security insures that very few people drop out of the social process of reproduction, due particularly to the *administrative integration of the people in this process of reproduction*. (italics added)

Recent experiences with the importance of civil society do not mean that now there is no real danger of a painful agony of civil society in both East and West. However, a possible withering away of civil society would imply not only the end of the state but also the end of the whole system suppressing differentiation, autonomy, and individuality. This is the major lesson provided by the tragic history of socialism, which at the very beginning promised to wither away the state but succeeded only in destroying and discrediting itself as an economic, political, and social system. For this particular reason, the issue of the reconstruction of the former socialist countries should be considered one of the central questions of the decade, not simply for Europe but also for the future of the whole world.

One of the main questions we have to address is whether, and how, a "postsocialist" civil society can be constructed to "deregulate" the dependence of the media on the state and/or the market and to maximize freedom of communication. The situation in East-Central Europe differs from that in the West at least in one crucial dimension. Whereas in the West democratic efforts are aimed particularly at decommodification of the media and limitation of the profit-maximizing principle, East-Central Europe is facing only the first consequences of denationalization and privatization. The commercial motives of the media are thus often regarded as mainly limiting state penetration without having any unfavorable consequences. Journalists see media commercialization as an important instrument for achieving their own autonomy from the state, while the question of how the media care for the interests of the citizens is beyond their "professional" interest. The basic problem is the lack of money and capital needed for a practically efficient privatization rather than the danger of an excessive power of capital. This makes very feasible a monopolistic coalition between the state and media professionals (journalists). Although the latter may now play a more important role than in the former system, where a similar coalition existed, both systems have in common the exclusion of a third part—the audiences. The domination of any of these three groups—the state, media professionals, and audiences—or a coalition between two of them against the third one inevitably produces an imbalance of power and a domination of the interests of the minority (in authoritarian systems) or the majority (in paternalistic systems) against the interests of those not participating in the coalition.

The Unknown Goddess of Freedom of the Press

In early writings on freedom of the press, Marx criticized the liberal conception of freedom of the press, which reduced it to, or subsumed it under, freedom of entrepreneurship. At the same time, however, he (1974, p. 68) admitted that "it is no transgression, when a German perceives the unknown goddess of freedom of the press as one of the goddesses he already knows, and accordingly he names her after them, freedom of entrepreneurship or freedom of ownership." This is exactly the case with the contemporary situation in East-Central Europe after decades of a nonmarket economy and state-controlled media and economy. It is largely believed that freedom of ownership and particularly private ownership are the guarantors of democracy and a free press. Privatization is seen as the only instrument that can reduce and possibly abolish state intervention in the media. Private ownership is simply the only "goddess" known and experienced by the majority of people, although to a very limited extent. Although freedom of the press was declared one of the fundamental freedoms (though not of individuals) under the previous regimes, private ownership was banished; now the goddess of private ownership has been resurrected, along with religion itself. Meanwhile, social and economic equality, which was the highest value in socialism, is devaluated by the anticommunist "movements" or even declared to be a negative value. As with socialism, which neglected (in contrast to Marx) the culturally progressive side of capitalist expansion (Garnham 1992, p. 3) and developed essentially as *anticapitalism, anticommunism* now represents a total negation of socialist values, "not only the suppression of Leninism but of Marxism in general," the rejection of contractual and cooperative relations, and the forcing of egoism, competitiveness, and private ownership (Rus 1992, p. 21).

Apparently, the media in East-Central Europe are not yet dominated by commercial corporate speech—mainly because the process of denationalization and privatization of the former state- and party-owned media is far from being completed—but they continue to exist under another form of domination. The actual autonomy of the media is limited by the state, which tries to exhibit and strengthen its sovereignty. In a way, East-Central European media are in a position similar to those in capitalist countries: On the one hand, they are under the persisting pressure of state censorship and control; on the other hand, they are exposed to the "self-contradictory and self-paralysing tendencies of market-based communications media" (Keane 1991, p. 116). Thus, the fundamental question of whether a genuinely democratic communication system can be worked out may be (and should be) addressed to both capitalist (commercial) and postsocialist (paternalistic-commercial) systems.

The fundamental difference between the two systems is that East-Central European societies have never experienced political democracy in any full sense. With the exception of Hungary and, partly, Poland (which has been often split among Austria, Russia, and Prussia) these societies for centuries represented stateless nations, although with different degrees of autonomy: Bulgarians, Romanians, Serbs, and Montenegrins until the fall of the Ottoman Empire following the war between Russia and Turkey; Czechs, Slovaks, Slovenians, and Croatians until the end of World War I and the fall the of the Austro-Hungarian Empire. Both multinational empires were actually destroyed by nationalisms. Like the other two great empires that dominated East Europe, Russia—though independent itself—always represented the "jail of nations." Political democratization, which started in some of these countries after World War I, was blocked by World War II and, after the end of the war, by Soviet occupation (with the exception of Yugoslavia). As Walzer (1992, p. 164) argued, the internationalism of communists, which was aimed against the imperialism of "great empires" and their dynasties, actually owes a great deal precisely to that imperialism.

The absence of any fully developed democratic tradition certainly prevents these countries from establishing an indigenous political democracy compatible with the nature of their own culture(s). The lack of other—mainly economic and technological—resources makes the dependency road even more likely to be followed by East-Central European countries. Thus, Sparks (1991b, p. 13) was right when he said that by "looking at what is entailed in the profitable operation of the press and broadcasting in a developed market economy we can perhaps gain some insight into the future development of the media in the emerging market economies." This does not imply that East European societies will simply follow the path traced by those in the West, given both internal and external (global) limits to growth. However, it does mean that external patterns of growth and "progress" are so powerful that peripheral societies like those in East-Central Europe cannot compete with them successfully. At best these societies react and adapt to change in a rational way, but their autonomy or rationality is limited to certain "degrees of freedom" in implementing others' experiences and plans.

The importance of the differences between the two systems also applies to the "market *or* democracy" dichotomy, which has specific components in the former socialist countries or even a different nature in comparison to the West, partly because democracy in East-Central Europe is (still) less endangered by the dominant commercial principle of profit maximization and partly because civil society seems to dispose of more indigenous power. The question of the kind of counterpower civil society has at its disposal is one of the main problems related to its autonomy from both the state and the economy. In developed market systems, the autonomy of civil society from the economy seems problematic because huge economic power is concentrated in economic organizations and the state, while the "alternative power" (e.g., moral power and information) in the hands of civil society is severely limited. In East-Central Europe, however, the influence of intellectuals based on their "cultural capital" and ethical—rather than political or economic—power (still) compares favorably with that held by political and economic actors. Under socialist regimes, the cultural sphere represented the only possible alternative to the institutional political sphere. Important political initiatives against monopolized political power were taken by intellectuals, mainly writers and social scientists, under the mask of artistic freedom and cultural autonomy.

In a number of former socialist countries, particularly Czechoslovakia, Poland, Hungary, and Slovenia, the intelligentsia entered on new political careers after the overthrow of the former regimes. In some cases, this appeared as "selling off intellectuals" to different political groups and parties. However, different parts of the former political "alternative" capitalized their former political investments to different degrees; civil society did not simply "come into power" without having restructured itself. In Slovenia, for example, "the new political order brought most disenchantment to that part of alternative which firmly stuck to the 'anti-political' aims. The core of this project was the rejection of the 'battle for power' and striving for a radical remaking, by arousing the potentials of 'civil society,' the relationship between the politics and society" (Bernik 1991, p. 18). Although intellectuals actually caused the decay of civil society by establishing political parties and entering political (state) institutions after democratic elections, they may (and already do) help reconstruct civil society either from within or without. In different forms, the early proponents of democratic changes—dissident intellectuals and radical theorists—have been largely dismissed: "Not only the Velvet Revolution but also the 'Velvet Evolution' has brought to its initiators and protagonists, or at least to some of them, 'hard times.'. . . The difference between both cases is that of quantity rather than that of quality: the relatively smooth transition to democracy has enabled at least some of the 'theorists' to adapt to the changing circumstances, whereas the rapid changes have made the coping with new situations much more difficult" (Bernik 1991, p. 19).

The Media for Audiences—or Vice Versa?

Media democratization might be considered a typical case. Before democratic (r)evolutions, fundamental reforms in the institutions of communication were considered by civil movements essential for any process of democratization. Yet after democratic changes, many East-Central European broadcast organizations remained essentially unchanged or even reregulated as typical state institutions by the newly established political elites. A part of the former "antistate" intellectual opposition was marginalized again and requires public "protection" of the media against party and/or state interference.

The ruling coalitions see the media, particularly television and radio, as a corporate "democratic" organ of the new "pluralistic" party-state—that is, these coalitions use the same perspective that the old authorities did.[1] This old authoritarian conception of the total polity practiced for decades by the old socialist regimes may be found in other activities as well—for example, in controlling nominations of chief personnel in educational, cultural, and health institutions or in wooing intellectuals to become party members or prophets.

As before, the idea of public service media is once again and quite often used as a cover for paternal or authoritarian communication systems (Williams 1976, p. 134), where a high concern for people is based on the protective role of the media, in contrast to commercial systems, which are characterized by a very low concern for recipients *as recipients or users* and a high concern for *consumers* whose consumption capacities can be sold to advertisers (see Table 5.1). What is now needed is to create a new kind of public service media that would be based on public funding, not controlled by the state or dominated by com-

TABLE 5.1   Attention to Audiences and the Media in Different Media Systems

System	Concern for Audiences	Concern for the Media
Authoritarian	Low (restrictive)[a]	Low
Paternal	High (protective)[b]	Low
Commercial	Low (consumptive)[c]	High (imperative)[d]
Democratic	High (supportive)[e]	High (supportive)[f]

[a]*Authoritarian* interest in audiences is *restrictive* in the sense that it limits, by means of censorship, the amount and diversity of contents available to audiences.

[b]*Paternal* interest in audiences is *protective* because media controllers aim at protecting audiences against certain kinds of ideas and values that would be damaging to them.

[c]*Commercial* interest in audiences is *consumptive* because it considers them only as (potential) consumers of the advertised goods and services.

[d]*Commercial* concern for the media is *imperative* because technological and professional development of the media is a necessity to survive the market competition.

[e]*Democratic* interest in audiences is *supportive* because it is aimed at advancing competencies (the right to transmit) and opportunities (the right to receive) of audiences to participate in communication processes, including their access to the media.

[f]*Democratic* concern for the media is *supportive,* because it promotes and subsidizes media diversity.

mercial interests, and characterized by high concerns for production *and* recipients as users who are defined and define themselves in terms of *social and collective needs,* in contrast to consumers who are defined in terms of privatized individual desires. Such a new public system certainly cannot be the only system; rather, it should compete with those developed by the state (paternal systems) and the market (commercial systems). But with a communication system civil society would be less vulnerable than it is now because of the portion of *communication power* it would gain and generate.

The main problem is how to limit the control and power held by commercial groups and political institutions to protect and increase, and not to injure, the independence of the media or prevent coalitions between the media and the state or capital, which go to the detriment of "consumers." From a theoretical perspective this would imply the inauguration of an "autonomous, 'self-organized' public" (Vreg 1990, p. 317) and the "radical democratization" of the public media, political competition, and economic competition. The importance of these three components are defined by Krueger (1991, pp. 26–28) in the following way:

1. The *public use of the media* should allow for a symmetrical change among the diverging perspectives of participants and observers. If not, potentially public media degenerate into economic enterprises or propaganda departments of the state or political parties.
2. Institutional autonomization of *political competition* should be counteracted by a recognition of the public media as the fourth, "soft," or symbolic-argumentative power so as to preclude their subordination under one of the three classic powers;

an ever-renewed "federalization" of all four powers to limit their drives toward centralization; and a lowering of the thresholds of citizen participation in democratic political competition.

3. *Economic competition* should be socioculturally regulated through a political separation of powers; a limitation of the costs of bureaucratization caused by the foregoing separation; and an extension of the customary models of codetermination (e.g., by the inclusion of representatives of the public sphere).

Several practical solutions to this problem do exist, although they still lack effectiveness in terms of restructuring the existing communication systems and redistributing social power. There must be, however, no major doubt about the necessity of using buffers to lessen the effect of power concentration and cultural (and ideological) homogenization produced by a market system and private ownership and to maintain a certain level of plurality of the media and public control. A market-based media system has several shortcomings in terms of what a democratic society requires of its media. "If a sufficient diversity of newspapers is essential in a democracy and commercial conditions threaten such essential diversity, then it is up to democratic governments to find ways of subsidising that do not impair a newspaper's independence of governmental influence. The subsidised newspaper must be free to bite the hand that feeds it" (Ardwick 1982, p. 16).

In most West European countries, privatization and deregulation in broadcasting are resulting in processes of diversification of distribution systems and simultaneous concentration of private (partly transnational) ownership. Different forms of backing *media diversity* and professional autonomy of journalists are thus essential for maintaining a minimum level of plurality in terms of different media actors and representation of different interests. The forms of backing diversity may be summarized in four specific "models" (Curran 1991, pp. 48–52).

1. The model of a *centrally controlled market economy,* or, according to Ronald Pohoryles, Philip Schlesinger, and Ulf Wuggenig (1990, p. 222), the *"model of 'bargained' de-regulation,"* limits the number of private competitors in broadcasting and regulates the relation between public and private sectors by centrally determined terms and rules of media competition. Media are differentiated in terms of ownership (publicly owned, privately owned), organization (local, regional, or national media and their associations), and sources of revenue (license fees, advertising, and subscriptions). Privately owned commercial media thus represent only one—though often major—communication sector. This is a typical West European model, with a strong national public broadcast organization and a number of private and semiprivate competitors. The exemplary model is that of the British television system, which is, however, combined with a highly deregulated and consequently centralized private press sector. The model developed in North European countries and in the Netherlands

enforces legal control and support for both broadcasting and print media, which are regulated against overcentralization.

2. The model of a *mandated market economy* is usually exemplified by the Dutch broadcasting system, where airtime and the use of publicly owned production facilities are allocated to different (from commercial to political) groups on the basis of the size of their membership as defined by the sale of their program guides. In contrast to the first (holistic) model, the model of a mandated market economy actually represents only specific and selective measures to support "internal plurality" within the media under public control. In this respect, the model is fragmentary—as is the model of a regulated market economy.

3. The common rationale of a variety of *regulated market economy* models is to limit the flaws of the commercial media system by a number of safeguards, mainly different forms of press subsidies. General or nonselective subsidy measures are known in almost all European countries, whereas a direct or selective assistance to particular types of media is experienced in only a few of them. *General subsidies* usually include:

- Reduced postal and fiscal rates
- Reduced telephone, telegram, and telex charges
- Reimbursement of the price of paper
- Loans at low (less than commercial) interest rates for technical investments and subsidies for rationalizations and innovations

Selective measures to support the plurality of the media, particularly press competition, comprise strategies such as:

- Cross-subsidies within the media industry based on value-added tax on advertising revenue
- Special public subsidies such as "low-coverage newspapers" (Sweden)
- Subsidies to newspapers participating in joint distribution schemes
- Special facilities for journalistic cooperatives (as in Italy)
- Special funds for endangered newspapers
- Special funds for cultural broadcast productions
- Funds for high-risk and expensive journalistic projects (as in the Netherlands)
- Investment in the education of journalists
- Legal limitations to media association with large conglomerates outside information and publishing
- Measures against concentration of ownership

Swedish and Austrian experiences show that a general system of subsidies based on the trickle-down principle may even *accentuate the unfavorable effects of market mechanisms,* favor the powerful media, and accelerate the concentration process rather than hinder the operations of the market. A selective system, in contrast, weakens market mechanisms, favors disadvantaged newspapers, and can reverse a negative course of structural development (Swedish Institute 1984, p. 3). It is not surprising, then, that many entrepreneurs strongly oppose the system of selective subsidies because it keeps alive competitors that would otherwise release a significant portion of readership for the profitable operation of more powerful media. It is more surprising, however, that these forms of regulation of market-driven media are largely neglected in East European discussions about privatization and commercialization of the press.

4. Different types of subsidies and/or limitations are aimed primarily at the reduction of unfavorable, sometimes unexpected consequences of market-driven media. Nevertheless, these subsidies may themselves produce some unfavorable and undesired consequences, a kind of "sclerosis" impeding any innovations, as Francois-Xavier Hutin (1991) noted regarding the contemporary situation in France. Like the first model, the fourth model of a *regulated mixed economy composed of public, civic, and market sectors* largely departs from these "corrective approaches" because it is aimed at the formation of a specific system with a different mode of organization. Unlike the former models, however, this model is more a prescription for a possible media system than a description of how it functions in practice. This model combines *socialization* of former state-owned media (i.e., subjecting them to social control and orienting their goals toward a public service model), *privatization* and *commercialization* of some areas of the media system, and the establishment of a new *civic* sector consisting of flexibly organized professional, interest, and citizens' groups (Jakubowicz 1992). Although several examples exist of how the power of the state, the market, and professionals can be balanced and effectively limited, no such practical solutions have been found to bring forward the interests of recipients.

This model includes different forms of regulation of commercial media systems experienced in West Europe and adds an important new element—that of the civic sector, which ought to be autonomous from both the state and market. The model is clearly compatible with the trichotomy "the state—the market—civil society" since it represents a positive negation of both purely state-owned and market-driven media: The civic sector is a systemic alternative in the sense of a subsystem to public and market sectors (subsystems). In this context, "the realistic question to ask is not whether there will be forms of public intervention in the future, but rather what form they could and should take, and how collective freedoms can be reconciled with those of individuals and minorities" (Mulgan 1991, p. 259).

What exactly should (or could) be the nature of such a system is certainly beyond the scope of this chapter, as is the question of whether democratic revolutions in East-Central Europe may and will continue. Mulgan (1991, p. 260) believed that three types of "regulation and public control seem likely to survive in most conceivable societies": (1) traditional contents regulation of the core mass media, (2) infrastructure policies to ensure universal access to the basic communication networks and their connectivity, and (3) policies and laws regulating common standards and providing free public services. If there is much doubt about institutional forms of future public regulation, it is clear, however, that the marketplace alone, or in combination with political (party) pluralism, does not guarantee *equality in freedom;* rather, it is only a terrain for different possible policies and coalitions based on different ideologies. Asle Rolland and Helge Ostbye (1986, p. 122) argued that different media systems are "established, maintained and eventually abolished by decisions made in the political system, and only indirectly by actions taken in the market." And it is also clear that as long as the new media policy in East-Central Europe is based on *anti*communism rather than on *post*socialism, the idea of *non*market- and *non*state-driven media will be marginalized even more than in capitalist societies.

"Italianization" of the Media in Postsocialism?

Different measures supporting equal opportunities of citizens, rather than the media (professional journalists), to make public their own truth should be regarded primarily as a means to achieve a just and free society. Contrary to the principle of maximization of equality as the aim of socialist society, the optimal degree of equality should be determined by justice and freedom, which implies that equality leading either to injustice or to restraint is delegitimized. As Rus (1992, p. 10) argued, to preserve integrity postsocialism (in contrast to anticommunism) should accept equality as a precious value. That is, equality is not a terminal value or a final aim but a *means* to maintain small cultural differences among subpopulations and thus genuine communications among individuals, small social differences among subpopulations and thus national integrity, and a healthy society, which will result from continual efforts to prevent marginal groups from spreading.

From this perspective, and in contrast to stable Western democracies, disintegration of the political state could be countered, perhaps paradoxically in terms of traditional conceptions, by societal reintegration stemming from civil society—from educational, scientific, and cultural institutions; churches; communications media; professional organizations; and interest groups. As I argued earlier, the specific importance of civil society in the postsocialist countries is based on the fact that political (r)evolutions and the inauguration of parliamentary democracy resulted from "intellectual opposition" developed within civil society. Autonomous groups of civil society succeeded in destroying and delegitimizing the former one-party political system in the late 1980s, but the new system is still in the process of formation. The moral power of civil society seems to be strong enough to reintegrate society beyond political institutions, following the patterns of previous transformations initiated by civil society, especially by defining the "key issues" to be discussed and institutionally resolved. Certainly, the formation of a new system also depends on the behavior of other actors affecting the system state.

However, the democratic role of civil society should not be absolutized because it can also suppress the differentiation of democratic institutions and lead to the "over-unification of society and a form of political polarization without ways of resolving it" (Arato 1990, p. 31). The importance of political parties and political pluralism cannot be ignored in the process of democratization. Apparently, one of the key questions is whether new political parties in the postsocialist countries will be able to overcome the old practice of the omnipotent Communist Party, which tried to control every bit of the political and economic system and of the life world of individuals. As in West Europe, new political parties in East-Central Europe both compete for political (and also economic) power and cooperate so that they can participate in the power structure. It seems that many of them still prefer *dogmatic* anticommunist models of institutionalized democracy, which induce elitism and even charismatic power similar to the former socialist party-state model. Yeltsin in Russia, Wałensa in Poland, Milošević in Serbia, and Tudjman in Croatia exemplify the growing importance of charismatic/autocratic power in the period of transition, when the old dictatorial rule (the dictatorship of the proletariat) and the principle of democratic centralism have not yet been replaced by the of rules of democratic government. "Charismatic power . . . is the product of the great crises of the past, whereas legal and traditional power represent the long intervening periods of relative calm between. Charismatic power flares up in those brief and intense periods which come between an end and a beginning, between decadence and regeneration, between the death agony of the old order and the birth pangs of the new" (Bobbio 1987, p. 155).

In a number of postsocialist countries, the issue of elitism refers to the mass media, which are at the crossroads between state ownership and the free market media system now seen as the optimal model, at least for the press. The tendency to exclude broader societal interests and those of marginal groups with limited or no financial resources, cultural homogenization, and concentration of ownership—a tendency strengthened by a market-driven system—is largely neglected. The media are prevalently seen as the battleground of party elites tending to maximize their political power and change the political map. Not surprisingly, broadcasting is still organized in accordance with the former collectivist ideology and the dominant role of the party-state because radio and television are considered the most appropriate means of getting public support for new political leaders.

The traditional paternalistic or even authoritarian model of broadcasting favors the interests of elites in power and enables them to transmit their ideas, attitudes, and instructions to the people. Alternative ideas, those held either by parliamentary oppositional parties or by nonparliamentary parties and civil movements, are considered irrelevant and easily excluded or at best are seen and evaluated as remnants of the old system and/or a kind of insurrection against the new democratic government. As formerly, such attitudes and relationships between the ruling elites and the media are not legal but *ethical*. This is particularly the case in those former socialist countries where democratic changes (e.g., party pluralism and free parliamentary elections) have been formally introduced but the former political elites have retained political power, which is justified in terms of a specific class ethics and owes a great deal precisely to the media they had under control.

However, a similar position is taken by new anticommunist ideologies and political groupings in power, which try to use the same means as the former regimes did to achieve different ends in terms of the desired future. If one compares Serbia, where the former Communist Party (now Socialist Party) is still in power, and Croatia, with the straight anticommunist government of the HDZ, one would hardly find any difference in terms of media regulation. In both countries, which obviously do not share common ideals and objectives, the media are subjected to a similar form of political control and even censorship. One should only compare news programs of Croatian and Serbian television stations to see how extremely biased is their reporting whenever it is related to "national interests" (e.g., the war in Croatia).

It is clear that democratic changes in the former socialist countries are still at a relatively early stage, which entails a great deal of confusion about the final course(s) these changes may take. There are four related processes on which the future of the media in East-Central Europe mainly depends:

- The development of parliamentary democracy
- The development of a market economy
- The resurgence of civil society
- The improvement of communication technologies

All four processes have to overcome considerable impediments inherited from the socialist as well as nonsocialist past: political voluntarism and exclusivism, a devastated economy, and technological backwardness. We would run into severe difficulties and contradictions if we were to conceive of these processes as simple dichotomies: democracy versus a market economy, nationalism versus democracy, technological development versus regulation, or civil society versus the state. At least in some dimensions, *all* these processes will continue, but although the new opportunities will probably (we hope) outweigh the detriments, serious difficulties and drawbacks will nevertheless be generated in the postsocialist future.

In a recent analysis of the Italian public sphere, Mancini (1991, p. 139) identified four fundamental characteristics that differentiate the media in Italy from a number of West European democracies, particularly in the Anglo-Saxon countries:

1. The media are under strong state control, either directly as in the case of state-owned television or indirectly as in the case of various forms of state-owned and/or economically supported press.

2. The degree of mass media partisanship is strong; "the political parties have always been involved in editorial choices and the structure of mass media."
3. Equally strong is the degree of integration of the media and political elites; for example, there is a strong professional mobility between the worlds of politics and journalism.
4. There is no consolidated and shared professional ethic among media professionals.

These four characteristics of the Italian system (and some other South European systems) are surprisingly close to the present situation in East-Central Europe. As in Italy, these characteristics are also related to the fact that the postsocialist political systems represent a kind of *coalitional complex* consisting of a large number of parliamentary parties or single "great coalitions" (as, for example, in the CSFR), that have been established to fill the political space after the withdrawal of the communists. This is not to say, however, that the Italian system may serve as the blueprint for future developments in East-Central Europe. The fundamental difference is in the fact that the coalitional complexity of the Italian political system is a *stable* one,[2] whereas in East-Central Europe that complexity is a *transitional* one. Of no less importance is the fact that, in contrast to Italy, the media landscape in East-Central Europe is much less differentiated, which is the result of the transitional nature of the ruling political coalitions and general economic crisis.

In terms of the stabilization of East European political systems, an important question concerns the relative importance of the former communist parties and their (oppositional) allies in the future. Whereas in Italy no clash exists between the two major opposing parties, the governing Christian democrats and the opposing (former) communists, in East-Central Europe the former communists are largely marginalized politically and are excluded from an active parliamentary life (with the exception of those countries where only formal democratization took place). Similarly, social democratic parties have only a minor political importance, regardless of whether they participate in the ruling conservative coalitions or represent a part of the parliamentary opposition. If this relationship stabilizes and no authentic and powerful alternative (or opposition) to the ruling elites appears, the danger of remonopolization of political power and paternalistic control over the media will be considerable. Even more, according to Gyorgy Csepeli and Antal Orkeny (1992, p. 2), if no strong social democratic movement emerges, the present conflicting realities may result in national socialism or populism.

Another important question concerns the nature of political communication. In Italy the media are aimed at horizontal *intermediation* and *negotiation* between parliamentary majority and opposition and then among the factions of government coalitions (Mancini 1991, p. 142). In contrast to North and West Europe, the Italian media are not depoliticized, and they are not separated from the political parties. On the contrary, although control of the media is partly transferred to capitalist entrepreneurs, the reality produced by the media *does not* compete with that of political parties and the state. Although such a "symbiosis" also exists in the former socialist countries, they fundamentally differ from Italy in terms of the nature of political communication. The postsocialist media do not perform the function of intermediation among political actors. Rather, they are (still) dominated by the ideology of "verticality," providing audiences with information they (should) need. This function is similar to the once official roles of media education and propaganda.

Beyond doubt, no single model of future developments in East-Central Europe can be developed on the basis of a short transitional period. The shift toward Western type(s) of political democracy certainly influenced the media, as did the installation of some principles of the marketplace, but in a number of important dimensions the media remained essentially unchanged. This undoubtedly applies to the reinstitutionalization of the state-owned broadcast media. In all countries, the connection between the media and polity remains very close and similar to that experienced during socialism. The effects of media commercialization and privatization are still limited by the severe economic problems all East-Central European countries have and by the paternalistic actions performed by governments.

My skepticism about existing institutional logic and practical arrangements is mainly related to the absence of a complex and truly democratic philosophy and a coherent policy for the media that would incorporate both different media and the different functions they may serve for individuals and society. It is not possible to foresee how different actors will behave in the future, particularly because they are still generally cautious about supporting both public media and radical denationalization. Such inconsistency and hesitancy seem to be common characteristics of media policies throughout East-Central Europe. As in Western Europe, "it is not that the specific actors involved are not usually clear and hardheaded about what they want to gain or defend in their own interest, but there is much unclarity about what is really on offer or what is to be feared" (McQuail, Siune, and Tunstall 1986, p. 197). In contrast to Western Europe, however, where media policymaking is strongly influenced by considerations of the economic and technological challenges presented by new media, East-Central European policies are typically framed in party-political terms, and the media (particularly broadcasting) are largely used for political benefits rather than for commercial value. But both parts of Europe are similar in that they neglect the social and cultural importance of the media.

Nevertheless, I am not as pessimistic as Zeleny (1991, p. 3), who assessed the situation in the CSFR a year after the velvet revolution as "a twilight, not only in terms of economy, but in terms of polity and society as well: it is long night before us. Dilettantism, mediocrity, vulgarity and stubbornness—this is the worst which happened to us after 45 years of regression." In contrast to this view, I have more positive expectations. The development of new media systems in East-Central Europe can bring new opportunities for media democratization and valuable experiences for all those countries that still have to initiate democratic processes.

Notes

Chapter Two

1. A number of laws in West European countries include the same kind of provisions for the protection of the state, the head of the state, the democratic system, the constitutional basis of the state, territorial integrity, national defense, public order, and so on. Legal restrictions of freedom of expression are justified by Article 10, Paragraph 2, of the European Convention on Human Rights. However, contrary to the former socialist regimes in East Europe, these restrictions are more clearly defined and selectively used.

2. As Fisher (1982, p. 23) pointed out, the difference between opposing views on the locus of human rights and the source of sovereignty—located either in the nation (state) or in the individual—is clearly reflected in media laws. Whereas in democratic societies "every citizen" or "everyone" or "any person" is declared to have the right to freedom of expression and other rights and freedoms, the subject of these rights in the former socialist countries was society, not the individual. According to Shanor (1983, p. 327), freedom of the press in the "Communist world" was what the governments agreed to grant to citizens "in order to achieve certain ends": "Freedom of the press, of assembly, and of expression are not rights that citizens enjoy but limited privileges that the regimes sometimes permit to further their own goals."

3. The phenomenon of abrogating fundamental civil liberties in the name of "national security" is not restricted to the newly emerging democracies in East-Central Europe. Government actions in the interest of national security (to protect a country from its enemies or potential enemies) were taken during the Falklands War in the United Kindgom and during the Persian Gulf War in the United States. But military priorities and the tendency to award to the security organs of the state an ultimate authority to define what national security is can place democratic structures under extreme pressure, particularly in a period of economic decline. Thompson (1984, p. 78) listed a number of such cases in the United Kingdom and concluded that "ironically, as the post-Stalinist Communist states are beginning to construct some fragile infrastructure of Whiggish legal forms these same forms are being eroded in the 'free West'." And the irony continues: Civil rights are now threatened in a number of former socialist countries. In the Republic of Croatia, for example, ultimate power is concealed within the National Council appointed by the president and subject to no parliamentary accountability.

4. The 1972 report of the Twentieth Century Fund Task Force in the United States, for example, dealt with press subpoenas issued by public prosecutors in efforts to compel journalists to disclose information obtained from confidential sources; government's interference in the editorial affairs of radio and television stations, including the threat of withholding the license that has to be renewed every three years; police impersonation of journalists; and heavy-handed treatment of the radical or "underground" press by law enforcement officials.

5. The following countries were included in the study: Australia, Austria, Brazil, Bulgaria, Canada, Colombia, Finland, West Germany, Ghana, India, Japan, Malaysia, Mexico, Nigeria, Norway, Peru, Poland, Slovenia, Spain, Tanzania, the United Kingdom, and the United States. In these twenty-two countries, 1,855 first-year students of journalism were interviewed.

Chapter Three

1. A recent comparative study into different approaches to the West and East European media systems in transition clearly points to the fact that, for example, East European scholars tend to define "transitions" primarily in political terms, whereas West European scholars are more concerned with the changes in media contents, genre structure, and audience behavior or with the separation of broadcasting from production functions and its consequences on programming (Luthar and Kropivnik 1991).

2. The economic and communications infrastructure in East-Central Europe is substantially less developed than in West Europe. For example, main telephone line penetration does not exceed fifteen lines per hundred inhabitants (fourteen in the former CSFR, thirteen in the former Soviet Union and Yugoslavia, nine in Hungary, eight in Poland), compared to forty-three in the European Community. While telex services are relatively well developed, digital telephone networks, mobile telephony, electronic mail, videotex, data communications networks, and ISDN facilities are practically absent, with the rare exceptions of some urban areas in some countries (e.g., data networks, message handling systems, videotex systems, and mobile telephony in the former Yugoslavia). In addition, the gap existing in the levels of telecommunications investments between East and West Europe gives little prospects for modernization of the infrastructure to levels similar to those in West Europe.

Chapter Four

1. Mencinger (1991, p. 25), one of the leading economists in Slovenia and the first minister in the new Slovenian government who had to retire from his post (as vice president) because of his "antiorthodox" views on the subject of privatization, provides an excellent account of this situation: "I was 'black' in the 'red' times; in the 'black' ones I am 'red.' I did not change my views, I hear mass as often as before, but nevertheless I became very quickly a 'leftist' where I was once a 'rightist.' I do not object. But I do not understand why I am scolded for being a Bolshevik by those 'anticommunists' who dedicated their scientific work (as a joke?) to the memory of Mr. Kardelj [the late leading Slovenian Communist ideologist] in the 'leaden Communist times,' wrote silly texts on social ownership and associated labor, as Party secretaries dismissed 'unsuitable' people, wrote membership applications to the Party, took large slices of social pie as directors in 'associated labor,' or, if I am personal, advised me in a 'friendly' way on 'appropriate' behavior, asked me 'anxiously,' why I dared to say something, and the most malicious even, why I didn't dare to say even more. . . . I hope that their present anticommunism, on which they build their careers, does not speak of similar future times."

2. For example, the Republic of Slovenia, which is the most developed part of the former Yugoslavia with only 2 million inhabitants, has increased the number of its people employed to 50.3 percent, while in Kosovo it is still less than 25 percent. But in addition to economic and demographic diversities, the relations between nations and republics in Yugoslavia were further complicated by enormous cultural differences. More than ten languages are spoken in different parts of the country, two alphabets (Cyrillic and Latin) are used, and three religions (Roman Catholicism, Serbian Orthodox Church, and Islam). Since one-fourth of the nations live outside of their respective republic (particularly Serbs in the Republic of Croatia), the relations between republics are even more complicated. Finally, after the democratic elections in 1990, Yugoslavia was split into two (or even more) different political systems—from the Western-type parliamentary democracy in the Republic of Slovenia to the essentially unchanged socialist political system in the Republics of Serbia and Montenegro. Similar differences and contradictions can be easily found in the former Soviet Union or CSFR as well as in Poland (German minority) and Romania (Hungarian minority).

Chapter Five

1. A recent case in point was the political manipulation of the national radio station and its listeners in Slovenia. As was the case in the past, the station organized a two-week contest in December 1991 for the most and the least popular personalities in Slovenia during that year. Listeners were invited to call in or write to the station to nominate their personalities and to include a short justification with the nomination. A few days before the end of the contest, when it became obvious that the prime minister and the president of the Christian Democratic Party was going to become the least popular personality and the president of the Presidency (the former leader of the Communist Party) the most popular, conservatives organized the collection of votes for the prime minister. In the last three days of the contest, hundreds of nominations arrived for the prime minister as the most popular personality and for the president as the least popular personality. At the end, the prime minister appeared as both the most and the least popular personality in Slovenia in 1991, followed in both positions by the president of the Presidency. According to a public opinion poll conducted by the Slovenian daily *Delo* a few days later, the president of the Presidency was chosen by 62.2 percent of respondents as the most popular Slovenian (with no negative votes), and the prime minister was chosen by 40.5 percent of respondents as the least popular (the prime minister received only 3.9 percent of favorable votes).

2. Recent political developments and corruption affairs in 1993 in Italy that resulted in the decay of the traditionally dominant political parties (Christian Democrats and Socialists); the rise of new, less ideologically determined political parties (e.g., the Northern League); and governmental crisis actually falsify the thesis of the stability of the Italian political system. However, the destabilization of the Italian political system even increases the similarity of the new East-Central European political systems to the Italian one and makes the concept of "italianization" of the media in postsocialism even more persuasive.

References

Alter, Peter. 1991. "Kaj je nacionalizem?" In *Študije o etnonacionalizmu*, edited by R. Rizman, pp. 221–237. Ljubljana: Krt.

Andrén, Gunnar. 1993. "A Concept of Freedom of Expression for Super-Industrialized Societies." In *Communication and Democracy*, edited by S. Splichal and J. Wasko, pp. 55–68. Norwood, N.J.: Ablex.

Androunas, Elena. 1991. "The Struggle for Control over Soviet Television." *Journal of Comunication* 41, 2: 185–200.

Arato, Andrew. 1990. "Revolution, Civil Society and Democracy." *Praxis International* 10, 1–2: 24–38.

Arato, Andrew, and Jean Cohen. 1984. "Social Movements, Civil Society, and the Problem of Sovereignty." *Praxis International* 4, 3: 266–283.

Ardwick, John Beavan. 1982. "Economic and Financial Aspects of the Daily Newspapers." In *Economic and Financial Aspects of the Mass Media*, pp. 13–42. Mass Media Files, No. 3. Strasbourg: Council of Europe.

Arnason, Johann P. 1990. "Nationalism, Globalization and Modernity." *Theory, Culture and Society* 7, 2–3: 207–236.

Bagdikian, Ben H. 1983. *The Media Monopoly*. Boston: Beacon Press.

Bajt, Aleksander. 1991. "Zdaj bi pa že bil čas, da se kaj stori za gospodarstvo." *Naši razgledi* 40, 16: 453–455.

Baker, Simon. 1991. "Satcom Impacts on Eastern Europe." *Transnational Data and Communications Report* 14, 3: 18–19.

Barber, Benjamin R. 1992. "Jihad vs. McWorld." *Atlantic Monthly*, March: 53–63.

Bauman, Zygmunt. 1990. "Modernity and Ambivalence." *Theory, Culture and Society* 7, 2–3: 143–170.

Becker, Jörg. 1992. "Das Verhältnis von zensierter zu kommerzialisierter Oeffentlichkeit im osteuropäischen Systemwandel." Unpublished manuscript.

Belič, Dragan. 1991. "Oficir uvježbava medij." *Slobodna Dalmacija* (Split), April 25, p. 22.

Benhart, František. 1991. "Skupinskost kot fenomen." *Delo* (Ljubljana), April 19, p. 7.

Beniger, James R. 1986. *The Control Revolution: Technological and Economic Origins of the Information Society*. Cambridge, Mass.: Harvard University Press.

Bernik, Ivan. 1991. "The Role of Intellectuals in the Slovenian 'Velvet Evolution' from Authoritarianism to Democracy." Paper presented at the symposium Intellectuals of the European Small States or Boundary-Culture Countries, University of Joensuu, Finland, September.

Bernstein, Eduard. 1961 [1899]. *Evolutionary Socialism*. New York: Shocken Books.

Bertalanffy, Ludwig von. 1971. *General System Theory*. Harmondsworth: Penguin Books.

Bibič, Adolf. 1990. *Civilno društvo i politički pluralizam*. Zagreb: Cekade.

Blackburn, Robin. 1991. "Fin de Siecle: Socialism After the Crash." In *After the Fall: The Failure of Communism and the Future of Socialism,* edited by R. Blackburn, pp. 173–249. London: Verso.

Blumler, Jay G. 1991. "Broadcasting Policy in a Changing Information Environment." *Bulletin of Institute of Journalism and Communication Studies* (University of Tokyo) 43: 1–13.

Bobbio, Norberto. 1987. *The Future of Democracy: A Defence of the Rules of the Game.* Cambridge: Polity Press.

―――――. 1989. *Democracy and Dictatorship: The Nature and Limits of State Power.* Cambridge: Polity Press.

―――――. 1991. "The Upturned Utopia." In *After the Fall: The Failure of Communism and the Future of Socialism,* edited by R. Blackburn, pp. 3–5. London: Verso.

Brie, Michael. 1991. "The General Crisis of Administrative Centralized Socialism: A Sketch Towards a Theory of Reproduction." *Praxis International* 11, 1: 65–77.

Bučar, France. 1991. "Novi politični zemljevid Slovenije." *Delo,* October 5, p. 20.

Calabrese, Andrew. [Forthcoming]. "Free Speech in America: Social Movements in an Information Society." In *Information Society and Civil Society,* edited by S. Splichal, A. Calabrese, and C. Sparks. Lafayette, Ind.: Purdue University Press.

Castells, Manuel. 1989. *The Informational City.* Oxford: Basic Blackwell.

Cerroni, Umberto. 1983. *Tehnika in svoboda.* Ljubljana: Komunist.

Chereskin, Dimitry, and Mikhail Tsalenko. 1989. "Informatization and Restructuring of Soviet Society." In *Information Processing,* edited by G. X. Ritter, pp. 1083–1087. Amsterdam: Elsevier Science.

Cohen, G. A. 1978. *Karl Marx's Theory of History. A Defence.* Princeton: Princeton University Press.

Colas, Dominique. 1991. "Nationalism, Culture and the New Information Technologies in Europe." *KEIO Communication Review* 12: 75–90.

Connor, Walker. 1991. "Ekonomski ali etno-nacionalizem." In *Študije o etnonacionalizmu,* edited by R. Rizman, pp. 297–317. Ljubljana: Krt.

Csepeli, Gyorgy. 1991. "Competing Patterns of National Identity in Post-Communist Hungary." *Media, Culture and Society* 13, 3: 325–339.

Csepeli, Gyorgy, and Antal Orkeny. 1992. "From the Old Communist Parties to the New Social-Democratic Parties." Paper presented at the conference Attori sociali e progettazione del mutamento nell'est europeo. Gorizia, Italy, January.

Cui, Zhiuyan. 1991. "Market Incompleteness, Innovation, and Reform: Commentary on Adam Przeworski's Article." *Politics and Society* 19, 1: 59–69.

Curran, James. 1982. "Communications, Power and Social Order." In *Culture, Society and the Media,* edited by M. Gurevitch, T. Bennett, J. Curran, and J. Woollacott, pp. 202–235. London: Methuen.

―――――. 1991. "Rethinking the Media as a Public Sphere." In *Communication and Citizenship,* edited by P. Dahlgreen and C. Sparks, pp. 27–57. London: Routledge.

Curran, James, Michael Gurevich, and Janet Woollacott. 1982. "The Study of the Media: Theoretical Approaches." In *Culture, Society and the Media,* edited by M. Gurevitch, T. Bennett, J. Curran, and J. Woollacott, pp. 11–29. London: Methuen.

Dahl, Robert A. 1991. "Transitions to Democracy." In *Democracy and Political Transformation: Theories and East-Central European Realities,* edited by G. Szoboszlai, pp. 9–20. Budapest: Hungarian Political Science Association.

Datapro. 1990. *Eastern European Telecommunications*. Delran, N.J.: Datapro.

Delo. 1990. "Javnost o medijih," July 28, p. 1.

————. 1991. "Neuspel poskus udara na madžarske medije," September 11, p. 20.

Dennis, Everette E., and Jon Vanden Heuvel. 1990. *Emerging Voices: East European Media in Transition*. New York: Gannett Center for Media Studies.

Deutsch, Karl W. 1963. *The Nerves of Government*. New York: Free Press.

Downing, John. 1980. *The Media Machine*. London: Pluto Press.

————. 1984. *Radical Media: The Political Experience of Alternative Communication*. Boston: South End Press.

EESTR. 1990. "CIA Anticipates Economic Decline in Eastern Europe." *Eastern European and Soviet Telecom Report* 1, 2: 4.

Economic Reform Today. 1991. (Fall): 25.

Ewen, Stuart. 1977. *Captains of Consciousness: Advertising and the Social Roots of the Consumer Culture*. New York: McGraw-Hill.

Fedorowicz, Hania. 1990. "Civil Society as a Communication Project." In *Democratization and the Media: An East-West Dialogue*, edited by S. Splichal, J. Hochheimer, and K. Jakubowicz, pp. 73–87. Ljubljana: Communication and Culture Colloquia.

Ferguson, Marjorie. 1992. "The Mythology About Globalization." *European Journal of Communication*, 7, 1: 69–93.

Fisher, Desmond. 1982. *The Right to Communicate: A Status Report*. Paris: UNESCO.

Fox, Elizabeth. 1988. "Media Policies in Latin America: An Overview." In *Media and Politics in Latin America: The Struggle for Democracy*, edited by E. Fox, pp. 6–35. London: Sage.

Frankel, Boris. 1987. *The Post-Industrial Utopians*. Cambridge: Polity Press.

Freeman, Christopher. 1987. "The Case of Technological Determinism." In *Information Technology: Social Issues*, edited by R. Finnegan, G. Salaman, and K. Thompson, pp. 5–18. Sevenoaks: Hodder and Stoughton.

Gallagher, Margaret. 1982. "Negotiation of Control in Media Organizations and Occupations." In *Culture, Society and the Media*, edited by M. Gurevitch, T. Bennett, J. Curran, and J. Woollacott, pp. 151–173. London: Methuen.

Garnham, Nicholas. 1985. "Telecommunications Policy in the United Kingdom." *Media, Culture and Society* 7, 1: 7–29.

————. 1990. *Capitalism and Communication: Global Culture and the Economics of Information*. London: Sage.

————. 1992. "Media Internationalisation and Cultural Identities." Paper presented at Giornate Fiorentine della communicazione, Florence, Italy, April 9–11.

Geyer, Felix R. 1980. *Alienation Theories: A General System Approach*. Oxford: Pergamon Press.

Gharajedaghi, Jamshid. 1983. "Social Dynamics: Dichotomy or Dialectic." *Human Systems Management* 4, 1: 7–17.

Giddens, Anthony. 1991. "Nacionalna država, narod, nacionalizem." In *Študije o etnonacionalizmu*, edited by R. Rizman. pp. 365–370. Ljubljana: Krt.

Gill, Colin. 1985. *Work, Unemployment and the New Technology*. Cambridge: Polity Press.

Giner, Salvador. 1985. "The Withering Away of Civil Society?" *Praxis International* 5, 3: 247–267.

Goban-Klas, Tomasz. 1990. "Making Media Policy in Poland." *Journal of Communication* 40, 1: 50–54.

Gouldner, Alvin W. 1976. *The Dialectic of Ideology and Technology: The Origins, Grammar, and Future of Ideology.* New York: Seabury Press.

Gramsci, Antonio. 1971 [1930]. *Selections from the Prison Notebooks of Antonio Gramsci.* London: Lawrence and Wishart.

Greenfeld, Liah. 1990. "The Formation of the Russian National Identity: The Role of Status Insecurity and Ressentiment." *Comparative Studies in Society and History* 32, 3: 549—591.

Habermas, Jürgen. 1969. *Javno mnenje* (Strukturwandel der Oeffentlichkeit). Belgrade: Kultura.

———. 1982. *Theorie des kommunikativen Handelns.* Vol. 2. Frankfurt: Suhrkamp.

———. 1991. "What Does Socialism Mean Today?" In *After the Fall: The Failure of Communism and the Future of Socialism,* edited by R. Blackburn, pp. 25–46. London: Verso.

Hallin, Daniel C. 1992. "The Passing of the 'High Modernism' of American Journalism." *Journal of Communication* 42, 3: 14–25.

Havlik, Peter. 1989. *Information and Related Technologies and Their Impact on East-West Relations.* Vienna: Vienna Institute for Comparative Economic Studies.

Hegel, Georg W. F. 1981 [1821]. *Grundlinien der Philosophie des Rechts.* Berlin: Akademie Verlag.

Held, David. 1989. *Models of Democracy.* Cambridge: Polity Press.

Held, David, and John Keane. 1984. "Socialism and the Limits of State Action." In *The Future of the Left,* edited by J. Curran, pp. 170–181. Cambridge: Polity Press.

Hennigham, J. P. 1984. "Comparisons Between Three Versions of the Professional Orientation Index." *Journalism Quarterly* 61: 302–309.

Hepworth, Mark, and Kevin Robins. 1988. "Whose Information Society? A View from the Periphery." *Media, Culture and Society* 10, 3: 323–343.

Holtz-Bacha, Christina. 1991. "From Public Monopoly to a Dual Broadcasting System in Germany." *European Journal of Communication* 6, 2: 223–233.

Hummel, Roman. 1990. "A Summary of the Media Situation in Austria." *Innovation* 3, 2: 309–320.

Hutin, Francois-Xavier. 1991. Discussion at the Fifth Colloquium on Communication and Culture, Media Systems in Transition, Piran, Slovenia, September 7–12.

IOJ. 1991. "Berlin Struggle of the Giants." *IOJ Newsletter* 11, June, p. 4.

Jakubowicz, Karol. 1990. "'Solidarity' and Media Reform in Poland." *European Journal of Communication* 5, 3: 333–353.

———. 1992. "From Party Propaganda to Corporate Speech? Polish Journalism in Search of a New Identity." *Journal of Communication* 42, 3: 64–73.

———. 1993a "Stuck in a Groove: Why the 60's Approach to Communication Democratization Will No Longer Do?" In *Communication and Democracy,* edited by S. Splichal and J. Wasko, pp. 33–54. Norwood, N.J.: Ablex.

———. 1993b. "The Five-Year Plan or the Long Story of the Polish Broadcasting Act." In *Broadcasting in Transition. The Changing Legal Framework in the Eastern Part of Europe,* edited by W. Kleinwächter, pp. 3–11. Leipzig: Netcom Papers.

Kaminski, Antoni Z. 1991. "Res Publica, Res Privata." *International Political Science Review* 12, 4: 337–351.

Karch, John J. 1983. "News and Its Uses in the Communist World." In *Comparative Mass Media Systems*, edited by L. J. Martin and A. G. Chaudhary, pp. 111–132. New York: Longman.

Keane, John. 1988. *Civil Society and the State: New European Perspectives*, edited by J. Keane. London: Verso.

———. 1991. *The Media and Democracy*. Cambridge: Polity Press.

Kivikuru, Ullamaija. 1990. "Locality in Mass Communication: An Irreplaceable Quality or a Relic from the Past?" Paper presented at the Seventeenth IAMCR Conference, Bled, Slovenia, August 26–30.

Kleinwächter, Wolfgang. 1992. "Old Problems in a New Environment: Broadcasting Legislation in Eastern Europe and the Republics of the Former Soviet Union." Paper presented at the Eighteenth IAMCR Conference, Guaruja, Sao Paulo, Brazil, August 16–20.

Klinar, Peter. 1991. "Slovenija in jugoslovanski etnični konflikti." *Teorija in praksa* 28, 10–11: 1201–1211.

Kovats, Ildiko, and Gordon Whiting. 1992. "Evolution and Revolution in the Hungarian Mass Media." Budapest: Unpublished manuscript.

Kozminski, Andrzej K. 1990. "Market and State in Centrally Planned Economies." *Current Sociology* 38, 2–3: 133–155.

Krstulovič, Z. 1991. "Ministar kao higijeničar." *Slobodna Dalmacija* April 25, p. 12.

Krueger, Hans-Peter. 1991. "Radical Democratization." *Praxis International* 11, 1: 18–36.

Kudriavtzev, Guennadi G., and L. E. Varakin. 1990. "The Economic Aspects of Telephone Network Development." *Telecommunication Journal* 57, 2: 105–116.

Kumar, Krishan. 1978. *Prophecy and Progress: The Sociology of Industrial and Postindustrial Society*. Harmondsworth: Penguin Books.

Lazarsfeld, Paul. 1972. *Qualitative Analysis: Historical and Critical Essays*. Boston: Allyn and Bacon.

Lee, Jae-Kyoung. 1991. "Press Freedom and National Development: Toward a Reconceptualization." *Gazette* 48, 3: 149–163.

Lenin, Vladimir I. 1949 [1917]. *Država in revolucija*. Ljubljana: Cankarjeva Založba.

Letica, Slaven. 1992. "Hadezeova dalmatinska akcija." *Globus* (Zagreb), 96 (October 9): 36.

Luthar, Breda, and Samo Kropivnik. 1991. "Transitions in Media Systems Studies: Differences in Approaches." Paper presented at the Fifth Colloquium on Communication and Culture, Media Systems in Transition, Piran, Slovenia, September 7–12.

Lyon, David. 1988. *The Information Society: Issues and Illusions*. Cambridge: Polity Press.

Maloča, Mladen. 1991. "Privatizacija demokracije." *Danas* 10, 495: 9.

Manaev, Oleg. 1992. "Mass Media in the Political and Economic System of Transitional Society." Paper presented at the Eighteenth IAMCR Conference, Guaruja, Sao Paulo, Brazil, August 16–21.

Manaev, Oleg, and Nadejda Jefimova. 1991. "Mass Communication in Modern Political Context of Soviet Society: From Totalitarianism to Democracy." Paper presented at the Fifth Colloquium on Communication and Culture, Media Systems in Transition, Piran, Slovenia, September 7–12.

Mancini, Paolo. 1991. "The Public Sphere and the Use of News in a 'Coalition' System of Government." In *Communication and Citizenship,* edited by P. Dahlgreen and C. Sparks, pp. 137–156. London: Routledge.

Mander, Jerry. 1978. *Four Arguments for the Elimination of Television.* New York: Quill.

Martinelli, Alberto, and Neil J. Smelser. 1990. "Economic Sociology: Historical Threads and Analytic Issues." *Current Sociology* 38, 2–3: 1–49.

Marx, Karl. 1971 [1847]. *Beda filozofije.* Ljubljana: Cankarjeva Založba.

———. 1974 [1842]. *Die Verhandlungen des 6. Rheinischen Landtags.* In *Marx-Engels-Werke,* Vol. 1, pp. 28–77. Berlin: Dietz Verlag.

Marz, Lutz. 1991. "Illusions and Visions: Models of and in Modern Societies." *Praxis International* 11, 1: 37–50.

Mass Media in the World. 1990a. Special issue on Central and Eastern Europe, No. 2. Prague: International Journalism Institute.

———. 1990b. Special issue on Central and Eastern Europe, No. 3. Prague: International Journalism Institute.

———. 1991. Special issue on Romania, No. 4. Prague: International Journalism Institute.

Mattelart, Armand, and Jean-Marie Piemme. 1984. "Twenty-three Guidelines for a Political Debate on Communication in Europe." In *The Critical Communications Review. Vol 2: Changing Patterns of Communications Control,* edited by V. Mosco and J. Wasko, pp. 211–223. Norwood, N.J.: Ablex.

McQuail, Denis, and the Euromedia Research Group. 1990. "Caging the Beast: Constructing a Framework for the Analysis of Media Change in Western Europe." *European Journal of Communication* 5, 3: 313–331.

McQuail Denis, Karen Siune, and Jeremy Tunstall. 1986. "A New Media Order in Europe—Actuality or Illusion?" In *New Media Politics: Comparative Perspectives in Western Europe,* edited by D. McQuail and K. Siune, pp. 197–208. London: Sage.

Meech, Peter. 1990. "The British Media: Structures in Transition." *Innovation* 3, 2: 227–251.

Mencinger, Jože. 1991a. "Pismo slovenskemu parlamentu." *Delo* (Sobotna priloga), August 24, p. 23.

———. 1991b. "Vlada, bobni, harmonike, zastave." *Delo,* October 19, p. 25.

Meyrowitz, J. 1986. *No Sense of Place: The Impact of Electronic Media on Social Behavior.* New York: Oxford University Press.

Midttun, Atle. 1990. "Government-Industry Relations and Liberalization in Complex Structured Markets." Paper presented at the Twelfth World Congress of Sociology, Madrid, Spain, July 9–13.

Miege, Bernard, and Jean-Michel Salaun. 1989. "France: A Mixed System. Renovation of an Old Concept." *Media, Culture and Society* 11, 1: 55–66.

Mills, Rilla D. 1983. "Mass Media as Vehicles of Education, Persuasion, and Opinion Making in the Communist World." In *Comparative Mass Media Systems,* edited by L. J. Martin and A. G. Chaudhary, pp. 167–186. New York: Longman.

Morishima, Michio. 1990. "Ideology and Economic Activity." *Current Sociology* 38, 2–3: 51–77.

Mouffe, Chantal. 1988. "Hegemony and New Political Subjects: Toward a New Concept of Democracy." In *Marxism and the Interpretation of Culture,* edited by C. Nelson and L. Grossberg, pp. 89–101. Urbana: University of Illinois Press.

Mulgan, Geoffrey J. 1991. *Communication and Control: Networks and the New Economies of Communication.* Cambridge: Polity Press.

Muraro, Heriberto. 1988. "Dictatorship and Transition to Democracy: Argentina 1973–86." In *Media and Politics in Latin America: The Struggle for Democracy,* edited by E. Fox, p. 117–124. London: Sage.

Muratov, Sergei A. 1991. "Soviet Television and the Structure of Broadcasting Authority." *Journal of Communication* 41, 2: 172–184.

Murdock, Graham, and Peter Golding. 1977. "Capitalism, Communication and Class Relations." In *Mass Communication and Society,* edited by J. Curran, pp. 12–43. London: Edward Arnold.

Mytton, Graham. 1991. "1990–91: A Year of Challenge for Public Service Broadcasting in Europe." Paper presented at the Annual Meeting of the Helsinki, Finland, May 12–17.

Nain, Zahorom. 1991. "Politics, Economics and the Media in Malaysia." *Media Development* 38, 3: 39–42.

Naisbitt, John. 1984. *Megatrends. The New Directions Transforming Our Lives.* London: Macdonald.

Novinar. 1991. "Kanal A." November: p. 4.

Paletz, David L., and Robert M. Entman. 1981. *Media, Power, Politics.* New York: Free Press.

Papathanassopoulos, Stylianos. 1990. "Broadcasting, Politics and the State in Socialist Greece." *Media, Culture and Society* 12, 3: 387–397.

Park, Robert E. 1972 [1904]. *The Crowd and the Public and Other Essays.* Chicago: University of Chicago Press.

Plattner, Marc F. 1991. "The Democratic Moment." *Journal of Democracy* 2, 4: 34–46.

Pohoryles, Ronald J., Philip Schlesinger, and Ulf Wuggenig. 1990. "Europe and the Media: Changing Structures in a Changing Context." *Innovation* 3, 2: 219–225.

Pool, Ithiel de Sola. 1983. *Technologies of Freedom.* Cambridge, Mass.: Belknap Press.

Poti, Laszlo. 1992. "The Aspirations and Dilemmas of the Hungarian Foreign Policy vis-a-vis the Yugoslav Crisis." In *Nastajanje slovenske državnosti,* edited by D. Fink-Hafner and B. Strmčnik, pp. 55–62. Ljubljana: Slovensko Politološko Društvo.

Przeworski, Adam. 1991a. "Could We Feed Everyone? The Irrationality of Capitalism and the Infeasibility of Socialism." *Politics and Society* 19, 1: 1–38.

———. 1991b. "Political Dynamics of Economic Reforms: East and South." In *Democracy and Political Transformation: Theories and East-Central European Realities,* edited by G. Szoboszlai, p. 21–74. Budapest: Hungarian Political Science Association.

Raboy, Mark. 1989. "East-West Dialogue on Media and Democratization." *Democratic Communique* 8, 3: 7–8.

Richeri, Giuseppe. 1990. "The Fininvest Group, Its International Strategy and Its Activities Towards Eastern European Countries." Paper presented at the Second International Conference, Europe Speaks to Europe, Moscow, Russia, December 17–21.

Rizman, Rudi. 1991. "Teoretske strategije v študijah etno-nacionalizma." *Teorija in praksa* 28, 8–9: 939–954.

Robertson, Roland. 1990. "Mapping the Global Condition: Globalization as the Central Concept." *Theory, Culture and Society* 7, 2–3: 15–30.

Robinson, Gertrude J. 1991. "German Media Unification: Promise and Performance."

Paper presented at the Fifth Colloquium on Communication and Culture, Media Systems in Transition, Piran, Slovenia, September 7–12.

Roeder, Philip G. 1991. "Soviet Federalism and Ethnic Mobilization." *World Politics* 43, 2: 196–232.

Rolland, Asle, and Helge Ostbye. 1986. "Breaking the Broadcasting Monopoly." In *New Media Politics: Comparative Perspectives in Western Europe,* edited by D. McQuail and K. Siune, pp. 115–129. London: Sage.

Rosanvallon, Pierre. 1988. "The Decline of Social Visibility." In *Civil Society and the State: New European Perspectives,* edited by J. Keane, p. 199–220. London: Verso.

Rowland, Willard D., Jr., and Michael Tracey. 1990. "Worldwide Challenges to Public Service Broadcasting." *Journal of Communication* 40, 2: 8–27.

Rus, Veljko. 1991. "Demosov socialni in ženiring." *Naši razgledi* 40, 18: 509–510.

———. 1992. *Med antikomunizmom in postsocializmom.* Ljubljana: FDV.

Sawisz, Anna. 1990. "Back from Monopoly to Normal: Changes in Mass Media in Poland." *Innovation* 3, 2: 385–402.

Schlesinger, Philip. 1990. "Media, the Political Order and National Identity: A Perspective from Scotland." Paper presented at the international symposium Public Communication, Cultural Identity and Cross-Cultural Relations, Barcelona, Spain, November.

Semelin, Jacques. 1991. "Reshaping East-West Communications Flows." *Transnational Data and Communications Report* 14, 3: 17–18.

Sennett, Richard. 1978. *The Fall of the Public Man.* New York: Vintage Books.

Sepstrup, Preben. 1989. "Implications of Current Developments in West European Broadcasting." *Media, Culture and Society* 11, 1: 29–54.

Servaes, Jan. 1991. "Europe 1992: The Challenge." Paper presented at the Fifth Colloquium on Communication and Culture, Media Systems in Transition, Piran, Slovenia, September 7–12.

Shanor, Donald R. 1983. "Press Freedom in the Communist World." In *Comparative Mass Media Systems,* edited by L. J. Martin and A. G. Chaudhary, pp. 321–340. New York: Longman.

Shlapentokh, Vladimir. 1990. "Public Opinion in Gorbachev's USSR: Consensus and Polarization." *Media, Culture and Society* 12, 2: 153–174.

Simonds, A. P. 1989. "Ideological Domination and the Political Information Market." *Theory and Society* 18, 2: 181–211.

Slack, Jennifer Daryl. 1984. *Communication Technologies and Society: Conceptions of Causality and the Politics of Technological Intervention.* Norwood, N.J.: Ablex.

Sparks, Colin. 1991a. "The British Media System." Paper presented at the Fifth Colloquium on Communication and Culture," Media Systems in Transition, Piran, Slovenia, September 7–12.

———. 1991b. "From State to Market: What Eastern Europe Inherits from the West." *Media Development* 38, 3: 11–15.

———. 1991c. "Goodbye, Hildy Johnson: The Vanishing 'Serious Press.'" In *Communication and Citizenship,* edited by P. Dahlgreen and C. Sparks, pp. 58–74. London: Routledge.

———. 1991d. "The Mass Media Market in Eastern Europe." *Transnational Data and Communications Report* 14, 3: 20.

————. [Forthcoming]. "Civil Society and Information Society as the Guarantors of Progress." In *Information Society and Civil Society,* edited by S. Splichal, A. Calabrese, and C. Sparks. Lafayette, Ind.: Purdue University Press.

Sparks, Colin, and Slavko Splichal. 1990. "Journalism Education and the Role of the Media as Fourth Estate." Paper presented at the Seventeenth IAMCR Conference, Bled, Slovenia, August 26–30.

Splichal, Slavko. 1981a. *Množično komuniciranje med svobodo in odtujitvijo.* Maribor: Obzorja.

————. 1981b. "Od javnog do slobodnog mnjenja: O kategorijama gradjanskog društva u 'revolucionarnoj' komunikologiji." *Naše teme* 25, 10: 1609–1616.

————. 1986. "Razvoj novinarskega študija in komunikologije." *Teorija in praksa* 23, 12: 1413–1422.

————. 1990a. "Self-Management and the Media." In *Studies in Communications.* Vol. 4: *Censorship and Libel: The Chilling Effect,* edited by T. McCormack, pp. 1–20. Greenwich: Jai Press.

————. 1990b. "Transplantation of Information Economy to Eastern Europe: A Telecom Dream or a Nightmare?" Paper presented at the Second Conference, Europe Speaks to Europe, Moscow, Russia, December 17–21.

————. 1991. "Spremembe komunikacijskih potreb in pravic v slovenski demokratizaciji." *Teorija in praksa* 28, 5–6: 491–504.

Splichal, Slavko, and Colin Sparks. 1990. "Democratization of the Media from Two Perspectives: Political and Professional Orientations Among Journalism Students in 22 Countries." In *Democratization and the Media: An East-West Dialogue,* edited by S. Splichal, J. Hochheimer, and K. Jakubowicz, pp. 149–172. Ljubljana: Communication and Culture Colloquia.

————. [Forthcoming]. *Journalists for the 21st Century: Tendencies of Professionalization Among First-year Journalism Students in 22 Countries.* Norwood, N.J.: Ablex.

Stone, Marvin L., and Leonard Marks. 1991. *Impediments to the Development of Free Media in Eastern Europe.* Washington, D.C.: International Media Fund.

Streckfuss, Richard. 1990. "Objectivity in Journalism: A Search and a Reassessment." *Journalism Quarterly* 67: 973–983.

Sukosd, Miklos. 1990. "From Propaganda to 'Oeffentlichkeit' in Eastern Europe: Four Models of Public Space Under State Socialism." *Praxis International* 10, 1–2: 39–63.

Swedish Institute. 1984. *Mass Media in Sweden.* Stockholm: Swedish Institute.

Szekfu, Andras, and Emoke Valko. 1990. "Film, Television and Video Industries in Hungary: An Overview." Paper presented at the Seventeenth IAMCR Conference, Bled, Slovenia, August 26–30.

Szucs, Jeno. 1988. "Three Historical Regions in Europe." In *Civil Society and the State: New European Perspectives,* edited by J. Keane, pp. 291–332. London: Verso.

Tamas, Paul. 1990. "International Media Capital and Conflicts of the Changing National Media Systems: The Hungarian Case." Paper presented at the Second International Conference, Europe Speaks to Europe, Moscow, Russia, December 17–21.

Telecommunications Update. 1990. "MTV Sets Sights on Eastern Europe" 15, 2–3: .

Terestyeni, Tamas. 1990. "Changing Media Policies in Hungary." *Innovation* 3, 2: 403–417.

Thompson, E. P. 1984. "Comment: Response to A. Arato and J. Cohen, 'Social Movements, Civil Society and the Problem of Sovereignty.'" *Praxis International* 5, 1: 75–85.

Tiryakian, Edward A., and Neil Nevitte. 1991. "Nacionalizem in modernost." In *Študije o etnonacionalizmu,* edited by R. Rizman, pp. 267–295. Ljubljana: Krt.

Traber, Michael. 1993. "Changes of Communication Needs and Rights in Social Revolutions." In *Communication and Democracy,* edited by S. Splichal and J. Wasko, p. 19–32. Norwood, N.J.: Ablex.

Twentieth Century Fund Task Force. 1972. *Press Freedoms Under Pressure.* New York: Twentieth Century Fund.

Vajda, Mihaly. 1988. "East-Central European Perspectives." In *Civil Society and the State: New European Perspectives,* edited by J. Keane, pp. 333–360. London: Verso.

Vasle, Vinko. 1991. "Na Hrvaškem si s pogromi proti medijem delajo medvedjo uslugo." *Delo,* August 15, p. 3.

Vickers, John, and Vincent Wright. 1988. "The Politics of Industrial Privatisation in Western Europe: An Overview." *West European Politics* 11, 4: 1–30.

Vogel, Milan. 1991. "Računajte z mojo preteklostjo." *Naši razgledi,* April 19, pp. 238–239.

Vreg, France. 1990. *Demokratično komuniciranje.* Maribor: Obzorja.

Walker, Gerald M., and WBN Correspondents. 1991. "Broadcasting in Eastern Europe: The Hurricanes of Change." *World Broadcast News,* May 1991: 32–46.

Wallerstein, Immanuel. 1990. "Culture as Ideological Battleground of the Modern World-System." *Theory, Culture and Society* 7, 2–3: 31–56.

Walzer, Michael. 1992. "The New Tribalism." *Dissent,* Spring: 164–171.

Weber, Max. 1976 [1924]. "Toward a Sociology of the Press." *Journal of Communication* 26, 3: 96–101.

Webster, Frank, and Kevin Robins. 1989. "Plan and Control: Towards a Cultural History of the Information Society." *Theory and Society* 18, 3: 323–352.

Williams, Raymond. 1976. *Communications.* 3d ed. Harmondsworth: Penguin Books.

Willnat, Lars. 1991. "The East German Press During the Political Transformation of East Germany." *Gazette* 48, 3: 193–208.

Windahl, Swen, and Karl Erik Rosengren. 1978. "Newsmen's Professionalization: Some Methodological Problems." *Journalism Quarterly* 55: 466–473.

Young, T. R. 1982. "The Structure of Democratic Communications: Interaction and Information in Public Life." *The Red Feather Institute Papers* (Livermore), No. 87. Red Feather, Colo.: The Red Feather Institute.

Zeleny, Milan. 1991. "Soumrak československeho hospodarstvi." *Tvorba* 36–37: 3–6.

About the Book and Author

Media Beyond Socialism treats the changing relationships among media, state, economy, and civil society in the current period of transition in East Europe from socialism to the establishment of Western-type democracies. Analyzing the relevance of mass communication and particularly of the media in the democratization process, the book addresses such issues as the problems of civil society, the principles of power and profit maximization in the communication sphere, the role the media have played in the "velvet revolution," and concerns surrounding East Europe's new "information age."

First offering a fundamental theoretical discussion, Splichal goes on to share empirical data documenting the changes in the East-Central European print and broadcast media in terms of ownership, political control, the role of the media, and journalism practices as well as paradoxes stemming from the economic and political restructuring of the former socialist societies. He closely examines the claim that the media have taken a radical departure from their previous activities in East-Central Europe and challenges the notion that authoritarian control of the media has been buried in the transition to democracy. Indeed, Splichal asserts that the media are in the process of mimicking the Western design and are often placed under the control of paternalism, commercialism, and nationalism.

Slavko Splichal is professor of communication science and sociology of information processes at the University of Ljubljana, Slovenia.

Index